M000287915

# The Disruptive Impact of FinTech on Retirement Systems

# The Disruptive Impact of FinTech on Retirement Systems

EDITED BY

Julie Agnew and
Olivia S. Mitchell

OXFORD
UNIVERSITY PRESS

# OXFORD
UNIVERSITY PRESS

Great Clarendon Street, Oxford, OX2 6DP,
United Kingdom

Oxford University Press is a department of the University of Oxford.
It furthers the University's objective of excellence in research, scholarship,
and education by publishing worldwide. Oxford is a registered trade mark of
Oxford University Press in the UK and in certain other countries

© Pension Research Council,
The Wharton School, University of Pennsylvania 2019

The moral rights of the authors have been asserted

First Edition published in 2019

Impression: 1

All rights reserved. No part of this publication may be reproduced, stored in
a retrieval system, or transmitted, in any form or by any means, without the
prior permission in writing of Oxford University Press, or as expressly permitted
by law, by licence or under terms agreed with the appropriate reprographics
rights organization. Enquiries concerning reproduction outside the scope of the
above should be sent to the Rights Department, Oxford University Press, at the
address above

You must not circulate this work in any other form
and you must impose this same condition on any acquirer

Published in the United States of America by Oxford University Press
198 Madison Avenue, New York, NY 10016, United States of America

British Library Cataloguing in Publication Data
Data available

Library of Congress Control Number: 2019941415

ISBN 978-0-19-884555-3

Printed and bound in Great Britain by
Clays Ltd, Elcograf S.p.A.

Links to third party websites are provided by Oxford in good faith and
for information only. Oxford disclaims any responsibility for the materials
contained in any third party website referenced in this work.

# Preface

Many people need help planning for retirement, saving, investing, and decumulating their assets, yet financial advice is often complex, potentially conflicted, and too expensive. The advent of computerized financial advice offers huge promise to make accessible a more coherent approach to financial management, one that takes into account not only clients' financial assets, but also human capital, home values, and retirement pensions. Robo-advisors, or automated on-line services that use computer algorithms to provide financial advice and manage customers' investment portfolios, have the potential to transform retirement systems and peoples' approach to retirement planning. This book offers cutting-edge research and recommendations regarding the impact of financial technology, or FinTech, to disrupt retirement planning and retirement system design. The volume will also interest policymakers, researchers, and employers seeking to design better retirement plan offerings.

In preparing this book, many people and institutions played key roles. Co-editor Julie Agnew was deeply engaged in editing and revising the chapters. We are grateful to our Advisory Board and Members of the Pension Research Council for their intellectual and research support. Additional support was received from the Pension Research Council, the Boettner Center for Pensions and Retirement Research, and the Ralph H. Blanchard Memorial Endowment at the Wharton School of the University of Pennsylvania. We also offer deep gratitude to Oxford University Press which publishes our series on global retirement security. The manuscript was expertly prepared and carefully edited by Lauren Sukovich and Lauren Colby.

Our work at the Pension Research Council and the Boettner Center for Pensions and Retirement Security of the Wharton School of the University of Pennsylvania has focused on aspects of pensions and retirement well-being over 60 years. This volume contributes to our mission, which is to generate research on and engage debate around policy for global pensions and retirement security.

Olivia S. Mitchell
Executive Director, Pension Research Council
Director, Boettner Center for Pensions and Retirement Research
The Wharton School, University of Pennsylvania

# Contents

## Part III.  New Roles and Responsibilities for Plan Sponsors and Regulators

# List of Figures

# List of Tables

# Notes on Contributors

**Julie Agnew** is the Richard C. Kraemer Professor of Business at the College of William and Mary's Mason School of Business. Her research and consulting activities focus on behavioral finance and its relationship to financial decisions made by individuals in their retirement plans. She is also TIAA Institute Fellow, serves on the Advisory Board of the Wharton School's Pension Research Council, a Research Associate for the Center for Retirement Research at Boston College, and a board member of C&F Bank. Previously she served as an elected member of the Defined Contribution Plans Advisory Committee (DCPAC) for the Virginia Retirement System. Dr. Agnew earned a B.A. degree in Economics and a minor in Mathematics from the College of William and Mary, and she received a Ph.D. in Finance from Boston College.

**Yomna Aly** is a Master's student in Computer Science at the University of Toronto under the supervision of Dr. Cosmin Munteanu in the Technologies for Ageing Gracefully lab (TAGlab). Her main research interests are at the intersection of psychology and computer science, applied to human–computer interaction. She is developing an information-sharing platform named MyCare to allow instant collaboration between family caregivers and seniors through crowd sourcing on health matters.

**Benett Axtell** is a Ph.D. student working with Dr. Cosmin Munteanu at the Technologies for Ageing Gracefully lab (TAGlab) at the University of Toronto. Her research interests focus on the design of new speech interactions for older adults, among others. Her current work investigates the digital management of family picture collections and their memories.

**Tom Baker** is the William Maul Measey Professor of Law and Health Sciences at the University of Pennsylvania. His research covers insurance law, risk, responsibility, and health insurance exchanges using methods and perspectives drawn from economics, sociology, psychology, and history. He is the Reporter for the American Law Institute's Restatement of the Law, and he co-directs the Health Insurance Exchange Research Group of Penn's Leonard Davis Institute of Health Economics. He received the Robert B. McKay award, a lifetime scholarly achievement award given by the Tort Trial and Insurance Practice Section of the American Bar Association. He earned his Bachelor's and J.D. from Harvard University.

Julianne Callaway is Strategic Research Actuary for RGA's Global Research and Data Analytics team, where she oversees research development. She also was part of RGAx, the wholly owned innovation incubator subsidiary of Reinsurance Group of America, Incorporated, where she developed economic models for business concepts and market intelligence. Previously she was a Senior Actuarial Analyst at Towers Watson, responsible for loss reserving, establishing funding amounts for self-insurance funds, developing predictive models, and developing methods to estimate asbestos liabilities for corporations and insurers. She began her actuarial career at American Family Insurance. She received the Bachelor of Science and Master of Arts (M.A.) degrees, both in economics, from the University of Missouri—Columbia.

Peter Chandler is the Financial Industry Regulatory Authority's Director of Investor Education, where he develops investor education campaigns, tools, and resources, including FINRA's Investor Alerts. He previously worked at the National Association of Securities Dealers and the NASDAQ Stock Market, where he was NASDAQ's Director of University and Investor Programs. He earned his B.A. in English and Philosophy from the University of Wisconsin, Madison, and a Masters in Marketing from The Johns Hopkins University.

Benedict Dellaert is a Professor of Marketing and Director of the Department of Business Economics at the Erasmus School of Economics, Erasmus University Rotterdam, The Netherlands. His research focuses on consumer decision-making and consumer-firm interaction, and he works with financial services firms on projects to support consumer decision making with online (risk) communication and personalized recommendations. He is concurrently a research theme coordinator at the Network for Studies on Pensions, Aging and Retirement (NETSPAR), a fellow of the Erasmus Research Institute of Management (ERIM), and a research fellow at the Tinbergen Institute; he is also a visiting professor at the UCL School of Management, London, UK. Previously he held positions at the University of Sydney, Tilburg University, and Maastricht University. He earned his Ph.D. from Eindhoven University of Technology.

Stephen L. Deschenes is a senior product development manager of investment services at American Funds, part of Capital Group, where he previously was a senior business manager of defined contribution. He also served as the general manager for the retirement income solutions division at Sun Life Financial; chief marketing officer for retirement income at MassMutual Financial Group; and product development and marketing lead for defined contribution at Fidelity Investments. He founded the online financial advice site mPower (now part of Morningstar) which pioneered investment advice in 401 (k) plan administration. He earned his bachelor's degree in Psychology and Social Relations from Harvard University.

**Jill E. Fisch** is Saul A. Fox Professor of Business Law and co-director of the Institute for Law and Economics at the University of Pennsylvania Law School, where she writes on corporate law, corporate governance, and securities regulation. She has received recognition including the Penn LLM Prize for Excellence in Teaching, and the Robert A. Gorman Award for Excellence in Teaching. Previously she was the T. J. Maloney Professor of Business Law at Fordham Law School and Founding Director of the Fordham Corporate Law Center. She also has practiced law as a trial attorney with the United States Department of Justice, Criminal Division, and as an associate at the law firm of Cleary, Gottlieb, Steen & Hamilton. She earned her B.A. from Cornell University and her J.D. from Yale Law School.

**P. Brett Hammond** is Research Leader at the American Funds for Capital Group. Previously he directed applied index and modeling research teams at MSCI; served as Chief Investment Strategist at TIAA-CREF; was on the senior management team at The National Academies (The National Research Council); and an Adjunct Professor at The Wharton School. His expertise includes target-date funds, inflation-linked bonds, and individual financial advice, and he served as Board member for the Q Group. He earned his BS in economics and political science at the University of California at Santa Cruz and his Ph.D. from the Massachusetts Institute of Technology.

**Allison Itami** is a principal at The Groom Law Group where she collaborates with providers in the IRA and employer plan industry including multinational financial institutions, national and regional broker-dealers, banks, record-keepers, and insurance companies, as well as state and municipal governmental units. She has also worked with employers to draft, maintain, or terminate tax qualified retirement savings plans, and she assists plan fiduciaries with compliance processes from drafting policies to assisting with internal or Department of Labor audits. She earned her B.S. from Cornell University and her J.D. from the University of Minnesota Law School.

**Jennifer Klass** is partner at Morgan Lewis where she is a regulatory counseling lawyer with a broad background in investment management regulation and a practice in investment advisory matters, including investment adviser registration and interpretive guidance, disclosure and internal controls, regulatory examinations, and enforcement actions. She previously was vice president and associate general counsel at Goldman, Sachs & Co. She earned her Bachelor's degree at Lehigh University and her J.D. from Widener School of Law.

**Robert Klitzman** is Professor of Clinical Psychiatry in the College of Physicians and Surgeons and the Joseph Mailman School of Public Health, and Director of the Masters of Bioethics Program, at Columbia University. He writes about ethical issues in medicine and public health. He has received awards and fellowships from the Guggenheim Foundation, the Russell Sage Foundation, the Aaron Diamond Foundation, the Robert Wood Johnson Foundation, the Rockefeller Foundation and the Commonwealth Fund. He is a gubernatorial appointee to the NY State Stem Cell Commission, and a member of the Research Ethics Advisory Panel of the US Department of Defense. He earned his B.A. from Princeton University and his M.D. from Yale University.

**Marion Labouré** is a Visiting Scholar in the Department of Economics at Harvard University. Previously, she worked at Barclays and at the European Commission on pensions, public finance, investment banking, and central banking. She also taught economics and finance at Sciences Po Paris, University Paris-Dauphine, Yale, and Harvard. She earned her Ph.D. in Economics from the Ecole Normale Superieure, as well as three masters degrees in Economics, Government, and Management from the London School of Economics and Paris Dauphine University.

**David N. Levine** is a principal at Groom Law Group, Chartered, where he advises plan sponsors, advisors, and other service providers on employee benefits matters from health and welfare, to retirement and executive compensation matters. He is also a member of the Executive Committee of the Defined Contribution Institutional Investment Association. Previously he served as Chair of the IRS Advisory Committee on Tax Exempt and Government Entities. He is recognized in the Chambers USA guide for Employee Benefits & Executive Compensation. He earned his J.D. from the University of Pennsylvania Law School and his B.A. from Johns Hopkins University.

**Amna Liaqat** is a student studying information at the University of Toronto. She works with Dr. Cosmin Munteanu at the Technologies for Ageing Gracefully lab (TAGlab) at the University of Toronto.

**Olivia S. Mitchell** is the International Foundation of Employee Benefit Plans Professor, as well as Professor of Insurance/Risk Management and Business Economics/Policy; Executive Director of the Pension Research Council; and Director of the Boettner Center on Pensions and Retirement Research; all at the Wharton School of the University of Pennsylvania. Concurrently Dr. Mitchell serves as a Research Associate at the NBER; Independent Director on the Wells Fargo Fund Boards; Co-Investigator for the Health and Retirement Study at the University of Michigan; Member of the Executive Board for the Michigan Retirement Research Center; and Senior

Scholar at the Singapore Management University. She also advises the Centre for Pensions and Superannuation UNSW and is Faculty Affiliate of the Wharton Public Policy Initiative. She earned her M.A. and Ph.D. degrees in Economics from the University of Wisconsin-Madison, and her B.A. in Economics from Harvard University.

**Gary Mottola** is the Research Director of the FINRA Investor Education Foundation and a social psychologist with extensive research experience in the financial services industry. At FINRA he oversees and conducts research projects on Americans' financial capability, protecting investors from financial fraud, and improving financial disclosure statements. He was a Visiting Scholar at The Wharton School and is an Adjunct Professor of Statistics at Villanova University. He earned his B.A. from the University at Albany, his M.A. from Brooklyn College, and his Ph.D. from the University of Delaware.

**Cosmin Munteanu** is an Assistant Professor at the Institute for Communication, Culture, Information, and Technology at the University of Toronto Mississauga, and Co-Director of the Technologies for Ageing Gracefully lab at University of Toronto. His research focuses on human-computer interactions, automatic speech recognition, natural user interfaces, mobile computing, ethics, and assistive technologies. He designs and evaluates systems to improve humans' access to and interaction with information-rich media and technologies through natural language; he explores speech and natural language interaction for mobile devices, mixed reality systems, learning technologies for marginalized users, usable privacy and cyber-safety, assistive technologies for older adults, and ethics in human-computer interaction research. He earned his engineering diploma and M.A.S. from the University Politehnica Timisoara in Computer and Software Engineering, and his M.Sc. and Ph.D. in Computer Science from the University of Toronto.

**Eric Perelman** is an associate with Morgan, Lewis & Bockius LLP's Investment Management practice, where he advises hedge funds, private equity funds, venture capital funds, large financial institutions, and other market participants on securities regulatory matters including structure and operations, regulatory guidance and interpretation, investment adviser compliance and controls, internal and regulatory investigations, and enforcement actions and examinations by the SEC. He also counsels clients on mergers, acquisitions, and joint ventures involving asset managers and investment advisers. Eric previously served as a law clerk with the Divisions of Enforcement and Investment Management at the US Securities and Exchange Commission. He earned his J.D. at the George Washington University Law School.

**Thomas Philippon** is Professor of Finance at New York University's Stern School of Business, where he researches topics in finance and macroeconomics including financial distress, systemic risk, government interventions during financial crises, asset markets and corporate investment. Recently his work has focused on the evolution of the financial system and on the Eurozone crisis. He was elected Global Economic Fellow by the Kiel Institute for the World Economy; he was also named one of the 'top 25 economists under 45' by the IMF; he won the Bernácer Prize for Best European Economist under 40; the Michael Brennan & BlackRock Award; the Prize for Best Young French Economist, and the Brattle Prize for the best paper in Corporate Finance. He graduated from Ecole Polytechnique and earned his Ph.D. in Economics from MIT.

**Steven Polansky** is Senior Director in FINRA's Office of Regulatory Programs where he leads cross-firm reviews; prior to that worked in FINRA's International Department, where he was responsible for analyzing international regulatory developments and FINRA's relationships with financial regulators in Europe and Asia as well as international financial institutions. In addition, he focused on risk-based supervision (including associated training), prudential oversight and market surveillance. Previously he worked at PricewaterhouseCoopers and staffed the Committee on Foreign Relations in the United States Senate. He earned his MBA in finance from The Wharton School at the University of Pennsylvania, his MPA from the Kennedy School of Government at Harvard University, and his bachelor's degree in history from Colgate University.

**Hiba Rafih** is a User Experience Designer at the University of Toronto. Previously, she was a Master's student at the University of Toronto's Faculty of Information specializing in User Experience Design. She is a research assistant at the Technologies for Aging Gracefully Lab examining the relationship between older adults, social isolation, and attitudes towards technology adoption. She earned her Bachelor's in Digital Enterprise Management at the University of Toronto.

**Tim Rouse** is Executive Director of the Society of Professional Asset-Managers and Record Keepers (SPARK) Institute, where manages an inter-industry professional association servicing mutual fund companies, banks, insurance companies, investment advisers, third-party administration, recordkeepers and benefit consulting firms in the retirement plan industry. Members represent most of the major service providers in the retirement plan industry and serve more than 95 percent of the US defined contribution plan participants. He earned his B.S. in Finance from Villanova University.

**Ben Taylor** is a senior vice president and defined contribution (DC) consultant in Callan's Fund Sponsor Consulting group. Previously, Taylor was a DC Specialist at R.V. Kuhns & Associates. He also taught economics at

Harvard University, where he received an award for excellence in teaching. He is president of NAGDCA's Industry Committee and on the NAGDCA Board, serves as vice chair of the SPARK Data Security Oversight Board, and has provided expert testimony to the ERISA Advisory Council. Taylor earned his B.A. from Reed College, Master's of International Political Economy and Development from Fordham University, and Master's of Public Policy from Harvard University's Kennedy School of Government.

**John A. Turner** is Director of the Pension Policy Center. Previously he was Deputy Director of pension policy research at the US Department of Labor; researcher at the Social Security Administration; and worked at the International Labour Office in Geneva, Switzerland. He was a founding member of the European Network for Research on Supplementary Pensions, and he received research awards from the Journal of Risk and Insurance, the Society of Actuaries, the International Actuarial Association, the Department of Labor, and AARP. He earned his Ph.D. in Economics from the University of Chicago.

# Chapter 1

# How FinTech is Reshaping the Retirement Planning Process

*Julie Agnew and Olivia S. Mitchell*

It is indisputable that technology transforms human behavior. Consider how the internet has reshaped work practices, and how mobile phones have changed the ways in which we communicate, purchase goods, save, and bank. Moreover, new technologies focused on financial applications, commonly referred to as FinTech, promise a similar revolution in the retirement planning processes. Robo-advisors and mobile savings apps are a few harbingers of innovations to come. Yet these changes bring with them new ethical and regulatory considerations, design challenges related to promoting adoption by an older population less trusting of technology, and concerns over data security and privacy. This volume takes stock of the disruptive impact of financial technology on retirement planning, saving, investment, and decumulation; and it also highlights issues that regulators, plan sponsors, academics, and policymakers must consider as retirement practices evolve at a rapid pace.

## FinTech and the Retirement Marketplace

The enormous market potential for FinTech retirement products is drawing the attention of a multitude of new entrepreneurs in the online marketplace. There are several compelling reasons why. First, the targeted population holds considerable wealth. While consumers age 50+ represent only 35 per cent of the US population, this group controls over half of investible assets (AARP 2017). Second, this market is also largely untapped. The many complex financial challenges facing this ageing group will require many new solutions, and technological innovations are well suited to provide the answers. Third, this generation is not particularly financially literate, which makes it difficult for them to undertake retirement planning efforts (Lusardi and Mitchell 2007). Interestingly, startups may be in a better position to address these concerns relative to existing financial institutions, though this will largely depend on how the regulatory system evolves around new entrants.

Arguably, robo-advisors are the most well-known of the FinTech innovations, which refer to automated online services that use computer algorithms to provide financial advice and manage customers' investment portfolios. These products are increasingly targeting the retirement marketplace.[1] The advent of a computerized approach to financial advice offers huge promise to provide people access to data they need to make smart retirement plans at very low cost. Currently, robo-advisor algorithms advise people on how much to save, when to claim Social Security, which Medicare plan to buy, and, most importantly, how to manage smart payouts during the decumulation phase of life. Nonetheless, none of the robos available today handle all of these things in one simple system. In view of people's documented low levels of financial literacy and evidence that advice from human advisors is sometimes conflicted, these systems are positioned to fill a substantial gap in advisory services.

Against this backdrop, there has been an upsurge in interest in robo-advisors. At the same time, however, regulations are in flux, competition is increasing, and some recent robo-advisor platform failures raise concerns about the viability of current business models (D'Acunto et al. 2017). To highlight the important role that robo-advisors are already playing in the FinTech revolution, this volume offers several chapters on this topic to provide the reader with a comprehensive overview of the history, issues, and possible future directions of these services. Key questions we address are: How do these systems fit within the current regulatory structure? What are their fiduciary requirements? Will robo-advisors democratize retirement savings by helping ensure that more people will plan for retirement, and plan ahead for decumulation activity once they have entered retirement?

To address several of these issues, Fisch et al. (2019) provides a useful overview of the marketplace for robo-advice, tracing the development of the sector and the services provided. The authors also compare the services, quality, and costs of advice offered by robo-advisors with those provided by human advisors, along with the potential for conflicts of interest. After analyzing the regulatory concerns that arise, the authors conclude that it may be easier to oversee the algorithms used by robo-advisors, compared to the communications of human advisors. The discussion closes with a look at emerging trends, including the move to human–robo hybrids; a transition to more product and service diversification; more vertical integration; and the growing use of robo-advisors by human advisors.

Klass and Perelman (2019) note that digital investment advisory programs account for managed assets in excess of $200 billion globally, and they emphasize that financial advice is fiduciary advice. This is an important regulatory consideration. In the US context, this means that they must act in good faith, to disclose material facts, and to employ 'reasonable care' to avoid misleading clients. They review the duties of loyalty and of care required by investment law, along with the principles-based regulatory regime followed by the US Securities and Exchange Commission overseeing the industry. The authors conclude that, while robo-advisors compete with traditional advisors, the services they offer are still governed by the traditional advisory framework and its regulatory structure.

## FinTech and Retirement Security

Callaway's (2019) interesting chapter explores how initiatives in the life insurance industry may contribute to disruption in the retirement space. She points out that Insuretech investments are already influencing platforms for insurance underwriting, claims payments, and online quoting and application. These changes are informed by new data sources including insurance application histories, prescription drug histories, driving histories, and financial credit records. Such information can also inform retirement planning efforts, including better information on morbidity and mortality projections.

Additional ethical, regulatory and medical considerations stemming from the use of 'big data' in insurance are topics addressed by Klitzman (2019). While at first it may appear that this discussion moves away from the book's main theme, the fact that insurance plays such a key role in people's retirement security makes the chapter an essential component of this volume. Mitchell's (2018) research, along with others, demonstrates that health care cost shocks are a major risk facing aging populations. Yet many may be unaware that even with some insurance, healthcare costs can still be expensive. For example, Fronstin and Vanderhei (2018) have estimated that a US couple aged 65 with both Medicare coverage and median prescription drug expenses would need to save $174,000 merely to have a 50 percent chance of covering their health costs in retirement. They would need to save $296,000 if they wished to boost to 90 percent their probability of having enough financial resources to pay retiree medical expenses alone. (Moreover, this excludes the cost of nursing home care, which can run upwards of $70,000 annually.) Furthermore, lack of health insurance coverage can also impact low-income adults' out of pocket expenditures, thereby imposing a substantial financial burden on this vulnerable group (Kwon et al. 2018). As a result, this chapter provides valuable insight into how an individual's financial security at retirement may be affected by describing how new advances in computing and genomic testing may influence the demand for and pricing of an individual's insurance in the future.

The impact of genetic information on pricing in the insurance market depends on how the information can be used. Klitzman (2019) outlines several key regulatory options from which policymakers might chose. As the author notes, one path might be to prohibit all insurers from using any genetic information; alternatively, insurers could be allowed free access to all genetic information. An intermediate and more realistic path, he suggests, would allow insurers access to genetic information only about certain 'pre-defined, well-characterized, highly-penetrant' genes that would help prediction models do a better job. Still a different alternative could make available some modest level of insurance to all, and insurers could require genetic test results from those seeking to buy additional coverage. More generally, as digitalization and access to personal information spreads, the important question is how risk pooling can evolve to offer more efficient ways to share risk, allow for personalization, and provide protection against the key shocks confronting older persons. Among these are health, inflation, investment, and longevity surprises during the retirement period.

Finally, the regulatory issues that Klitzman (2019) raises also have implications for new insurance products. For instance, Mitchell (2018) reviews products to manage these shocks and highlights the potential for hybrids that engage both the insurance and financial markets. One such product is a 'life care annuity,' addressing both longevity risk and healthcare surprises (Brown and Warshawsky 2013). The market for hybrid annuities consistent with this approach is growing fast: Korn (2018) notes that sales of annuities with long-term care riders (annuity LTC combos) are now surpassing sales of simple LTC contracts. Total sales for such LTC combos amounted to $480 million in 2017, more than double the $228 million in sales recorded for standalone LTC contracts. It is likely, of course, that such products will encounter the same type of regulatory debate surrounding the use of genetic information as those discussed in the context of insurance in this chapter. For this reason, readers will find invaluable the chapter's descriptions of the advances in technology and genetics, as well as future possible changes in related regulation.

The rise of digital data also gives rise to concerns about privacy and cybersecurity. Rouse et al. (2019) (Chapter 6 in this volume) reviews efforts by regulators, plan sponsors, and other financial players to focus more time and resources on the security of participant information held by service providers. After reviewing the legal and regulatory history of prudent protections in the US, the authors outline best practice regarding cybersecurity in the context of the FinTech advice arena. They note that it will be essential to conduct due diligence while avoiding disclosures that could benefit malicious actors.

Research by Munteanu et al. (2019) shows that older persons often avoid online activity due to lack of digital confidence and concerns about fraud, leading to digital marginalization. Yet many seniors will need to avail themselves of potentially very helpful and lower-cost robo financial services in the future, giving rise to the question of how to encourage their comfort with such services. The authors propose and implement a theory of mental models, offering new insights into how to encourage older persons to effectively, and correctly, use online services.


## FinTech and Decumulation during Retirement

Polansky et al. (2019) focused on whether robo-advisors can move from their traditional focus on accumulation, to help seniors manage decumulation of their assets in retirement. The authors note that investors can be encouraged toward more sensible investment and payout approaches, and steered away from overconfidence, loss aversion, mental accounting, framing, and more. In short, robos promise to take the emotion out of decumulation. The authors' interviews with a dozen key market players highlight additional challenges retirees face, including greater uncertainty and the need to make timely and highly consequential decisions, despite their limited or complete lack of experience upon which to draw to make these decisions, and inability to learn from their mistakes. In particular, retirement financial planning necessitates a very broad view of retirees' circumstances, including all relevant assets (e.g., potential social security and pension income) and liabilities (e.g., mortgages), as well as many other quantitative and qualitative factors.

While decumulation is arguably one of the most important, and complex, financial decisions facing older households, Baker and Dellaert (2019) in this volume find that relatively few FinTech firms are informative regarding this phase of the life-cycle. Their review of the marketplace finds that no robo-advisor handles all the key decisions required, including when to claim social security benefits, which Medicare plan to select, how quickly to withdraw and spend assets, and whether (and how much) to annuitize. Moreover, consumers exhibit numerous idiosyncratic behaviors that are not necessarily in line with 'rational' economic behavior, making it even more difficult to develop and deliver financial advice.

Most important to the discussion regarding retiree robo-advice is whether such advice will shape investors' consumption, retirement incomes, and overall well-being, and whether robos will help people do better than people following a more conventional path. Theoretical studies do predict improvements (e.g., Kim et al. 2016), yet there is very little real-world evidence on this point. Deschenes and Hammond (2019) summarize studies indicating that saving and investment results are not necessarily superior for those using financial advisors, though users of robo services may do better, mainly due to lower investment costs. Yet available studies are only short term in nature, and none follows robo customers over an entire business cycle. A related question is whether robo-advice will supplant the need for improved financial literacy. Clearly this is an area ripe for research follow-up.

## A Look to the Future

Taken together, the chapters in this volume explore the nascent and evolving market for robo-technology in retirement planning. The only certainty is that change is coming rapidly, and FinTech will drastically alter how consumers prepare for, and move through, their later years. Recognizing that change is ahead provides stakeholders an opportunity to better shape how the technology will integrate with and potentially improve consumers' lives. We conclude with several important points for market constituents to consider, as participants in the sector's development.

As a first point, the long-term development of the US financial sector has not necessarily lead to efficiency. Philippon (2019) shows that technological change in traditional incumbent financial institutions has not led to cost declines, partly because of the global financial system's complex taxes, subsidies, and rents. Moreover, he views the current system as expensive and risky. By contrast, FinTech startups have the opportunity to build a better system, given their culture of efficient operational design and because they are untethered by existing systems.

Secondly, entrepreneurs in this marketplace will need to avoid overspecialization leading to a fragmented market. Consumers are wary of having to search widely for products that address specific needs, and consumers may have difficulty selecting products when offered too many choices or because of limited time. In addition, many people will benefit from a hybrid approach, rather than utilizing products which solve problems only using technology, intended only for a particular life stage (e.g., the accumulation or decumulation phases), or aimed at specific decisions (e.g., claiming social security or Medicare). More appealing may be hybrid services and software that can encompass many financial decisions, making it easier for consumers to integrate this new technology into their life-cycle planning and decision making. Ideally, households would need to devote less time and effort to learn how to work with the various systems involved, and the technology could limit the time spent re-inputting personal data. FinTech's promise is in creating comprehensive platforms to consolidate people's data and advice platforms.

A third consideration is that comprehensive financial service providers will require more detailed and sensitive information from consumers, as the market consolidates. In turn, this can help refine and improve recommendations and services generated by FinTech products. For instance, robo-advisors cognizant of detailed and comprehensive household data can build better algorithms for financial management. These must take into account a household's financial assets, the partners' human capital and earnings, home value, investments, and pension and Social Security benefits. A well-designed plan would also recommend methods for insuring against health shocks and longevity. With these improvements, of course, there can be increasing danger from storing consolidated and comprehensive private financial information. Accordingly, strong privacy and cybersecurity protections must be top of mind for developers.

A fourth consideration is scalability. FinTech startups have experienced high client acquisition costs, and the history of many robo-advisor firms provides prime examples of the challenges (Kitces 2013). When products are designed to help people of limited means, the cost of engaging these clients can drive ventures under; past robo-advisor causalities include WorthFM, SheCapital, and Hedgeable (Malito 2016; Kitces 2018). These examples demonstrate that, even when robo products are well-designed, they still may not be viable because their survival depends on quickly acquiring a sufficient customer base. This is one reason that FinTech startups have sought out partnerships with large incumbent firms: working together, startups can benefit from the large potential customer base provided by existing financial institutions, while financial institutions can break into areas they otherwise would be excluded from entering.

A fifth observation about the FinTech marketplace is that the industry must consider human behavior when designing products. As Munteanu et al. (2019) point out in their chapter, technological design should be driven by users' needs. Accordingly, startups should consider how the older population interacts with technology and the unique concerns they have, versus Millennials. Furthermore, considerations of culture and gender should help inform developers to create products which can be personalized for subgroups within the older cohort. Treating this population as one homogeneous group ignores important differences within this diverse population (Hodge et al. 2018). The obvious implication is that products may fail to appeal to certain subgroups diminishing the products market potential overall, as well as creating pockets of underserved groups.

A different challenge to the FinTech industry is that purely technological solutions may not work. Several chapters in this volume note that robo-advisors are increasingly moving toward hybrid human/computer approaches, an outcome that is not surprising in light of recent research. For instance, Yeomans et al. (2018) found that humans often do not trust recommendations made by algorithms, even when those recommendations outperform human decision making. While that study did not deal with financial advice, the authors' findings are still relevant in the present context. Specifically, the authors found that trust can be fostered by explaining to clients how the algorithmic recommendations are generated. Clearly, as FinTech entrepreneurs build new advice products for the retirement market, they cannot ignore the importance of carefully testing methods for encouraging acceptance of the products being developed.

Another broad issue highlighted in Baker and Dellaert (2019) and Philippon (2019) is that regulation will play an important role in the how the FinTech market evolves. In the US, industry support from policymakers seems likely but is not certain. A recent US Treasury department report recommended regulatory changes that would aid entry into the startup market (Akolar 2018), among them, the creation of a 'sandbox,' where firms have a simple process to obtain permits to experiment without running foul of US rules. The Office of the Comptroller of the Currency is also accepting startup applications for bank charters, while new sandbox initiatives have been launched by the Consumer Financial Protection Bureau, the State of Arizona, and the Commodity Futures Trading Commission (CFTC 2017). Yet many of the new recommendations require further action from regulators and/or Congress, before they can be implemented. And some states have voiced concern that federal plans may limit states' influence over the FinTech market within their states (Hayashi 2018). For FinTechs in the retirement space to flourish, a cohesive set of regulations will need to be developed and enacted.

In sum, retirement planning is undergoing a revolution as advances in financial technology proceed, though this future will also bring challenges. This volume provides an overview of the market's potential and discusses some of the significant hurdles that must be carefully considered and overcome. By keeping in mind the lessons from this book, entrepreneurs, policymakers, regulators, and academics can help facilitate the thoughtful evolution of this market, ease the introduction of new products and smooth the transition for retirees learning to adapt.

## Note

1. In this volume we generally discuss 'financial advisors' with an 'o' in the spelling. As such, we are referring in broad terms to any broker, financial planner, and/or registered advisor. It is important to note that changing the 'o' to an 'e' changes the context significantly in the US. An 'investment adviser' refers to a particular subset of advisors and is a legal designation used by an individual or a company registered with the US Securities and Exchange Commission (SEC) or a state securities regulator. Robo-advisors in the US can be Registered Investment Advisors (RIAs), who uphold a fiduciary standard and are under the supervision of the SEC. They are also required to adhere to the obligations of the Investment Advisers Act of 1940.

## References

AARP (2017). *Financial Innovation Frontiers*. https://bit.ly/2sYZzhb (accessed February 21, 2019).

Akolar, B. (2018). 'CFPB Launches "Sandbox" for Fintech.' July 19. *WSJ.com*.

Baker, T. and B. Dellaert. (2019). "Behavioral Finance, Decumulation and Robo-Advice." In J. Agnew and O.S. Mitchell (eds.), *The Disruptive Impact of FinTech on Retirement Systems.* Oxford, UK: Oxford University Press, pp. 149–71.

Brown, J., and M. Warshawsky (2013). 'The Life Care Annuity: A New Empirical Examination of an Insurance Innovation That Addresses Problems in the Markets for Life Annuities and Long-Term Care Insurance.' *Journal of Risk and Insurance* 80 (3): 677–703.

Callaway, J. (2019). "Data and FinTech in the Insurance Industry." In J. Agnew and O.S. Mitchell (eds.), *The Disruptive Impact of FinTech on Retirement Systems.* Oxford, UK: Oxford University Press, pp. 61–74.

D'Acunto, F., N. Prabhala, and F. G. Rossi (2017). 'The Promises and Pitfalls of Robo-Advising.' 8th Miami Behavioral Finance Conference 2017. https://ssrn.com/abstract=3122577 (accessed February 21, 2019).

Deschenes, S. L. and B. Hammond (2019). "Matching FinTech Advice to Participant Needs: Lessons and Challenges." In J. Agnew and O. S. Mitchell (eds.), *The Disruptive Impact of FinTech on Retirement Systems.* Oxford, UK: Oxford University Press, pp. 172–89.

Fronstin, P. and J. Van Derhei (2018). 'Savings Medicare Beneficiaries Need for Health Expenses: Some Couples Could Need as Much as $400,000, Up From $370,000 in 2017.' *EBRI Issue Brief.* No. 460, 1–11. https://bit.ly/2zZKZqG (accessed February 21, 2019).

Hayashi, Y. (2018). 'States Spar with Trump Administration Over Fintech Oversight.' August 8. *WSJ.com.*

Hodge, F. D., K. I. Menza, and R. K. Sinha (2018). 'The Effect of Humanizing Robo-Advisors on Investor Judgments.' University of Washington Working Paper. https://doi.org/10.2139/ssrn.3158004 (accessed February 21, 2019).

Kim, H., R. Maurer, and O. S. Mitchell (2016). 'Time is Money: Rational Life Cycle Inertia and the Delegation of Investment Management.' *Journal of Financial Economics* 121(2): 231–448.

Kitces, M. (2018). 'The Latest in Financial Advisor FinTech.' *Nerd's Eye View.* https://bit.ly/2rmDoOn (accessed February 21, 2019).

Kitces, M. (2013). 'The Real Hidden Cost that Has Been Inhibiting Financial Planning for the Masses.' *Nerd's Eye View.* https://bit.ly/2RW3C60 (accessed February 21, 2019).

Klass J., and E. L. Perelman (2019). "The Transformation of Investment Advice." In J. Agnew and O. S. Mitchell (eds.), *The Disruptive Impact of FinTech on Retirement Systems.* Oxford, UK: Oxford University Press, pp. 38–58.

Klitzman, R. "Ethics, Insurance, Pricing, Gsenetics, and Big Data." In J. Agnew and O. S. Mitchell (eds.), *The Disruptive Impact of FinTech on Retirement Systems.* Oxford, UK: Oxford University Press, pp. 75–85.

Kwon, E., S. Park, and T. D. McBride. (2018). 'Health Insurance and Poverty in Trajectories of Out-of-Pocket Expenditure among Low-Income Middle-Aged Adults.' *Health Services Research* 53(6).

Korn, D. J. (2018). 'How Clients Can Use Annuities to Pay for Long Term Care.' *Financial Planning Website.* https://bit.ly/2INtO1j (accessed February 21, 2019).

Lusardi, A. and O. S. Mitchell (2007). 'Baby Boomer Retirement Security: The Roles of Planning, Financial Literacy, and Housing Wealth.' *Journal of Monetary Economics* 54(1): 205–24.

Malito, A. (2016). 'Women-focused Robo-adviser SheCapital Shuts Down.' *Investment-News.com*. https://bit.ly/29VS1Ng (accessed February 21, 2019).

Mitchell, Olivia S. (2018). 'Enhancing Risk Management for an Aging World.' *The Geneva Risk and Insurance Review* 43(2): 115–36.

Munteanu, C., B. Axtell, H. Rafih, A. Liaqat, and Y. Aly (2019). "Designing for Older Adults: Overcoming Barriers toward a Supportive Safe and Healthy Retirement." In J. Agnew and O.S. Mitchell (eds.). *The Disruptive Impact of FinTech on Retirement Systems*. Oxford, UK: Oxford University Press, pp. 104–25.

Philippon, T. (2019). "The FinTech Opportunity." In J. Agnew and O.S. Mitchell (eds.), *The Disruptive Impact of FinTech on Retirement Systems*. Oxford, UK: Oxford University Press, pp. 190–217.

Polansky, S., P. Chandler, and G. Mottola (2019). "Digital Investment Advice and Decumulation." In J. Agnew and O. S. Mitchell (eds.), *The Disruptive Impact of FinTech on Retirement Systems*. Oxford, UK: Oxford University Press, pp. 129–48.

Ramada, M. and A. Harley (2018). '#Insurtech is a Launch Pad to Unimagined Possibilities for Insurers.' Willis Towers Watson. https://bit.ly/2Ekb46T (accessed February 21, 2019).

Rouse, T., D. N. Levine, A. Itami, and B. Taylor (2019). "Benefit Plan Cybersecurity Considerations." In J. Agnew and O. S. Mitchell (eds.), *The Disruptive Impact of FinTech on Retirement Systems*. Oxford, UK: Oxford University Press, pp. 86–103.

Tracy, R. (2018). 'Trump Administration Embraces Fintech Startups.' WSJ.com. July 31.

Turner, J., J. E. Fisch, and M. Labouré (2019). "Emergence of the Robo Financial Advisor." In J. Agnew and O. S. Mitchell (eds.), *The Disruptive Impact of FinTech on Retirement Systems*. Oxford, UK: Oxford University Press, pp. 13–37.

US Commodity Futures Trading Commission. (CFTC, 2017). 'CFTC Launches LabCFTC as Major FinTech Initiative.' May 17. https://bit.ly/2QvRwng (accessed February 21, 2019).

Yeomans, M., A. Shah, S. Mullainathan, and J. Kleinberg (2018). 'Making Sense of Recommendations.' Harvard University Working Paper.

# Part I

# Financial Technology and the Retirement Marketplace

# Chapter 2

# The Emergence of the Robo-Advisor

*Jill E. Fisch, Marion Labouré, and John A. Turner*

In the past ten years, the market for financial advice has changed dramatically with the emergence of robo-advisors, defined as in Chapter 1 as automated online services that use computer algorithms to provide financial advice and manage customers' investment portfolios. This chapter describes the growth of the robo-advisor industry and the services that robo-advisors offer. It compares the services, quality, and cost of advice provided by robo-advisors to those of traditional human financial advisors. It also considers the potential for conflicts of interest to affect the provision of financial advice by both robo- and human advisors.

Susan Axelrod, the Executive Vice President for Regulatory Affairs at the Financial Industry Regulatory Authority (FINRA), has raised several questions concerning robo-advisors, which she equates to digital services or digital investment advice: 'We need to ask ourselves: what role will financial professionals play in tandem with digital services in providing investment advice? To what degree will investors rely primarily on digital investment advice? How well can software know a client? Can the skill, knowledge and service provided by well-trained and ethical financial professionals be incorporated in software? Can that software provide sound personal advice, especially for clients with more complex advice needs?' (Axelrod 2017: n.p). This chapter provides a start at answering these questions.

## Background on Financial Robo-advisors

Many people find investing to be a difficult challenge, marked by complexity on both the demand and supply sides of the market for financial assets. Financial markets have become more complex as more types of investments have become available, particularly in the retail environment. In addition to understanding the growing array of financial products, investors must evaluate risk, the effects of compounding, the tax implications of investment alternatives, and how to stage withdrawals from their investment portfolio over their lifetime.

Some people may face additional challenges in making good investment decisions. Young people may have limited experience with financial markets, and some older people suffer from decreased cognition which makes financial decision-making more difficult (Agarwal et al. 2009). A substantial fraction of the population, both in the United States and elsewhere, lacks basic financial literacy (Lusardi and Mitchell 2014), which can deter people from even trying to save, invest, and plan for retirement. Investors with low financial literacy are particularly likely to make poor financial decisions (Fisch et al. 2016).

**What do robo-advisors do?** Since computers are good at both routine and highly complex tasks, computers can make it easier for clients to manage their investments. Robo-advisors are intended to interact with clients digitally, both to gather client information and to manage the client's investments inexpensively. A client generally creates an account online by responding to a series of questions that may include risk preferences, assets, income, debt, and investment goals. The robo-advisor uses computer algorithms to offer investment selections deemed appropriate in terms of asset allocation and diversification based on the information supplied by the client. These selections most typically include low cost mutual funds and exchange traded funds (ETFs). Robos invest the client's portfolio in accordance with the recommended asset allocation, which can typically be modified by the client. Robos also manage their clients' portfolios on an ongoing basis, providing services that include automatically rebalancing the portfolio periodically to maintain the desired asset allocation, and reinvesting dividends, redemptions, and interest payments. Some robos also harvest tax losses in taxable portfolios (Berger 2015).

Robo-advisors can differ along several dimensions (Berger 2015). Some require clients to transfer their assets to the robo-advisor's custodian, while others allow clients to keep their investments at external brokerage houses. Most robo-advisors offer advice concerning taxable accounts and IRA retirement accounts, although some do not offer advice concerning complex account structures such as SEP-IRA accounts for the self-employed. Some robos manage other specialized accounts such as 529 college savings accounts.

Robos also offer different types of investments: most limit investors to specific ETFs or mutual funds selected by that advisor, while others offer more flexibility, such as allowing customers to invest in individual stocks. Another difference among robo-advisors is the range of advice that they offer. Many robos limit themselves to portfolio management and do not address, for example, retirement planning, estate planning, or insurance issues. In some cases, a robo will only provide advice with respect to the assets that it is managing; in other cases, the advisor, when preparing an investment plan, has the capacity to consider assets not under its management, such as an employer-sponsored 401k plan.

In addition to asset allocation and diversification, robo-advisors generally rebalance clients' portfolios. For example, Wealthfront (2017b) rebalances its customers' portfolios in taxable accounts by reinvesting dividends and new contributions in underweighted asset classes, so that no tax liability is generated by selling assets to rebalance. That firm argues that rebalancing in this way is one of the advantages it offers over many human advisors. It should be noted that robo-advisors are not necessary for rebalancing, since this service is also provided by target date funds, balanced funds, and managed accounts, among others.

Some robo-advisors offer tax loss harvesting which involves selling investments that have lost value to offset the taxes on investments with realized capital gains. Tax loss harvesting is relevant for taxable accounts but not for tax-preferenced accounts such as retirement accounts. In addition, Betterment offers customers real-time tax information through a 'Tax Impact Preview' calculator (Khentov 2014). When clients decide to sell an asset, Betterment calculates the likely tax liability that these sales could generate. This feature can mitigate clients' tendency to sell in response to a market downturn.

One type of robo-advisor that has received little attention to date is online advice programs offered to pension participants through their 401k plans. Firms such as Financial Engines have long operated in this space (Toonkel and Randall 2015). For instance, Reuter and Richardson (2017) investigated the use of online advice by participants in plans where TIAA was the sole record keeper. They reported that about 6.5 percent of participants studied sought asset allocation advice using an online TIAA tool in 2012 and 2013.

Robo-advisory firms tend to describe what they do as providing investors with asset allocations appropriate to their needs and offering financial advice at a lower cost than traditional human advisors. They market their ability to serve clients who previously received no financial advice because they lacked sufficient investible assets. The advantages in terms of cost and access raise the question as to why more assets are not currently managed by robo-advisors. One reason is that any innovation takes time to become widely accepted. Nevertheless, human advisors may still offer services that robos cannot, leading to the emergence of a hybrid model in which some firms pair robo advice with access to a human advisor.

**How are robo-advisors regulated?** The Securities and Exchange Commission (SEC) oversees the enforcement of the federal securities law and, as a result, has the job of protecting US investors in the securities markets (SEC 2017). One way it does so is to regulate the services provided by human and robo-advisors, both of which must register under the Investment Advisers Act of 1940 as Registered Investment Advisers (RIAs). RIAs are subject to the substantive obligations imposed by that statute and have a fiduciary duty to provide advice in the best interest of their clients (Lazaroff 2016).

In addition, if robo-advisors hold customer assets, they must register with the SEC and FINRA as broker-dealers. Currently Betterment holds customers' assets and is a registered broker-dealer, while Wealthfront is not.

The scope of protection afforded by the RIA's fiduciary duty has been the subject of extensive debate. Some commentators argue that the fiduciary concept is weak or vague and operates with a lack of predictability for both advisors and customers (Jordan 2012). The precise requirements imposed by the fiduciary relationship can be modified by contract (Klass and Perelman 2019). In addition, many aspects of the fiduciary obligation may be undermined by disclosure and client consent. Under US law, financial advisors are permitted to have a conflict of interest so long as they disclose the conflict to their clients. Nevertheless, disclosure of conflicts of interest may be ineffective in protecting the interests of clients, both because of clients' actions and because of advisors' actions. In one experiment, Cain et al. (2005) found that people generally did not take into account the biases caused by conflicts of interest as much as they should. Some people may believe that disclosure reveals an advisor to be trustworthy, so disclosure may enhance trust in the advisor. Others may feel that it would be insulting to an advisor to question whether the advisor was acting in their best interests.

One potential advantage of robo-advisors is that the quality of their advice may be easier to review, than it is for human financial advisors. While it would be impossible to monitor all private conversations that financial advisors have with their clients, it is conceptually feasible to evaluate computer models' advice (GAO 2011). This greater transparency may lead robo-advisors to adhere more closely than some human advisors to regulatory requirements.

These regulatory requirements continue to evolve. In 2016, the US Department of Labor (2016) outlined a new Fiduciary Rule seeking to impose a fiduciary duty on all financial professionals, including robo-advisors, who provide advice regarding retirement plan investing (US Dept. of Labor 2016). That rule was subsequently invalidated by a federal court.[1] In 2018, the SEC issued for comment its own proposed fiduciary rule – Regulation Best Interest (SEC 2018).

In 2017, the SEC's Division of Investment Management released regulatory compliance guidance for robo-advisors (SEC 2017). The guidance observed that the unique business model of the robo-advisor raises concerns and emphasized the obligation of robo-advisors to address these concerns. These concerns included the need for adequate disclosure about the robo-advisor and the services it provides, the need to ensure that the robo-advisor is providing suitable advice to its customers, and the need to adopt and implement appropriate compliance programs tailored to the automated nature of the robo's services.

**Evolution of the robo-advisor industry.** The first consumer-facing robo-advisors, Wealthfront and Betterment, began operations in 2008,[2] yet neither company offered financial advice to retail investors until 2010. Wealthfront began as a mutual fund company, KaChing, and it originally used human advisors, not robots, in furtherance of a business model providing high-quality asset management at a lower cost and without the substantial minimum investments required by other professional advisors (Ha 2010). The original objective of Wealthfront's founders, Andy Rachleff and Dan Carroll, was to provide financial advice to the tech community (Taulli 2012). Wealthfront's founders shifted the company's focus when they realized the potential that computer software offered for making invest-ment advice accessible to more people at lower cost (Wealthfront 2017a).

Betterment's co-founder Jon Stein sought to automate the process of selecting and managing investments (Betterment 2017b). The firm offers financial advice at a lower cost than traditional financial advisors, yet the key element of the Betterment strategy is to make investing simple for its clients.

In recent years, additional firms have started to offer robo-advisory ser-vices. A BlackRock (2016) study noted 22 new robo-advisory firms launched in the US in 2014 and 44 in 2015. The first robo-advisors were stand-alone firms, but many existing financial firms including banks, broker-dealers, technology firms, and asset managers, have now entered the market.

Assets managed by robo-advisors have continued to grow, with robos managing $200 billion in assets worldwide in 2017 (Eule 2018). They are likely to continue to grow in the coming years, although estimates of that growth vary considerably, from $0.82 trillion in 2020 of global assets under management (Statista 2017), to $2.2 trillion (Regan 2015) and $8.1 trillion (Kocianski 2016). As of early 2018, the largest US (and worldwide) robo-advisors in terms of assets managed were Vanguard ($101 billion) and Charles Schwab ($27 billion). Betterment had $13 billion in assets under management, and Wealthfront had $10 billion. Other robo-advisors included Rebalance IRA, Acorns, and SigFig, and the market continues to expand, as is outlined in Table 2.1. Notably, although robo-advisors are

TABLE 2.1 Selected top US robo-advisor by assets under management, first quarter 2018

| Robo advisor | $AuM (billion) | Advisory fee as % of AuM (excludes fee for investment in funds) | Minimum assets |
|---|---|---|---|
| Vanguard Personal Advisor Services | $101 | 0.30% | $50,000 |
| Charles Schwab | $27 | 0 (fees for Schwab ETFs) | $5,000 |
| Betterment | $13 | Digital—0.25%/year Premium—0.40%/year | $0 |
| Wealthfront | $10 | 0.25% (free for accounts of $10,000 or less) | $500 |

*Source*: Data from Backend Benchmarking (2018).

growing rapidly, they still control only a small fraction of the $80 trillion of global assets under management (Kelly 2017).

## Who Uses Robo-advisors?

Despite their appeal, only 5 percent of US investors invest with robos, while 55 percent have not heard about them at all (Wells Fargo 2016). Figure 2.1 traces the evidence. Part of the reason for the lack of familiarity with robo-advisors stems from the broader reality that only about one-third of Americans currently seeks financial advice of any sort (Collins 2012). Researchers have documented widespread evidence of low financial literacy in the population (Lusardi and Mitchell 2014) for which financial advice could be an effective substitute (Fisch et al. 2016). Nonetheless, financial advice is not widely used perhaps because consumers view it as too expensive or because they lack sufficient few assets to make it worthwhile to work with a financial advisor.

At the same time, over half of Americans (56%) who hold financial assets outside of pension plans do consult with a financial advisor (FINRA 2016a). The most important reasons people give for using a financial advisor are to improve investment performance and to help avoid losses (FINRA 2016a: 7). Nearly two-thirds also feel it is important to learn about investment opportunities, and over half feel it is important to have access to investments they would not otherwise be able to buy. Most investors who

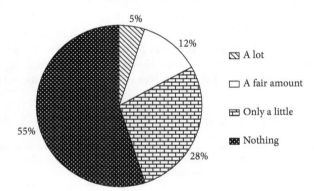

**Figure 2.1** US investors' familiarity with robo-advisors

*Note:* Participants were asked: 'How much have you heard or read about robo-advisors before now? Robo-advisors are digital advisory services that use computer algorithms to select stocks and other investments for people based on the information people provide about their risk tolerance and goals.'

*Source:* Data from Gallup (2016).

use an advisor (80 percent) have a specific person with whom they work. Seventy-three percent have communicated with their advisor by telephone or email at least two to three times in the past year, and 80 per cent have met in person with their advisor (FINRA 2016a). When people must devote time and money to acquire financial knowledge, which can reduce opportunities to invest in one's own job, outsourcing financial management can make sense (Kim et al. 2016).

To date, the evidence shows that younger people, in their 20s and 30s, are more likely to use robo-advisors than are older people. For example, a FINRA (2016a) study found that 38 percent of Americans between 18 and 34 with investments outside a pension had used a robo-advisor, versus 4 percent of those over 55. The average age of Betterment's clients is 36, a number that will rise as young robo users age (Wang and Padley 2017). The age tilt may be due to the fact that the young are often more comfortable with technology than are older individuals (Polyak 2015). Additionally, younger people's smaller asset base makes then less suitable clients for traditional financial advisors (Stein 2016).

## Robos versus Human Advisors

Over 70 percent of US investors currently believe that human advisors are better than robo-advisors, according to a recent Gallup (2016) survey. That is, investors see human advisors as better serving their interests, making good investment recommendations, taking clients' entire financial picture into account, advising clients on risks they are taking, making people feel confident about their investment, and helping clients understand their investments (see Figure 2.2).

Several features of robo-advisors distinguish them from human advisors: **Fees and costs.** Human financial advisors generally charge fees of 1–2 per cent of assets under management, with larger portfolios paying the lower fees in the US (Ludwig 2017). By contrast, robo-advisors typically charge substantially less, with fees ranging from 0 to 50 basis points. Betterment, for example, initially charged 15 basis points for accounts with more than $100,000 and 35 basis points for the smallest accounts, but it has since moved to charging 25 basis points for all accounts (and for accounts that exceed $2 million, fees are capped). For an account of about $50,000, a traditional financial advisor would charge 100 basis points or $500 a year, versus Betterment which charges $125 per year. With $12 billion assets under management at year-end 2017, Betterment's fee structure generated annual revenue of $30 million.

Other comparisons include Wealthfront, which, as of the time this chapter is written, requires a minimum account balance of $500 and charges 25

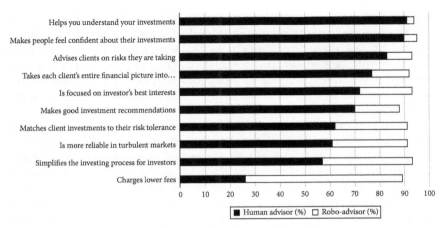

**Figure 2.2** US investors' perceptions of human vs. robo-advice

*Note*: Investors were asked whether each statement applies more to robo-advisors or more to human advisors. Results for the Wells Fargo/Gallup Investor and Retirement Optimism Index survey are based on questions asked May 13–22, 2016, on the Gallup Daily tracking survey, of a random sample of 1,019 US adults having investable assets of $10,000 or more.

*Source*: Robo Advisors Europe (2018).

basis points, while accounts of $10,000 or under are managed for free. T. Rowe Price and Schwab currently charge no fee for their robo-advisors but are compensated via fees on investment products sold to their clients. Ellevest (2018), a robo-advisor that markets to female clients, charges a fee of 25 basis points for its basic digital service and 50 basis points for its premium service.

Robo-advisors can charge lower fees than human advisors because they have the advantage of economies of scale: that is, a single computer algorithm is used to service many clients. By contrast, a human advisor might have 75 or at most 100 clients (Kitces 2017d); if that advisor had one support staff person, this would entail at most 50 clients per employee. Betterment, by contrast, has over 300,000 clients and 200 employees, so its client-to-staff ratio is 1,500 (Kitces 2017d). Over time as robos acquire more clients with more assets, these fees should fall even further, making financial advice accessible to a larger market of people who are unwilling or unable to pay the fees associated with human financial advisors.

Another factor differentiating robo from human advisors is that the former generally use passive index-fund approaches to investing (Lam 2016). By contrast, human advisors tend to recommend higher-fee actively-managed approaches (Kramer 2016). As a result, robo-advisors not only have lower advisory fees, but they also spend less on trades and charge lower investment management fees. For example, Betterment clients pay

9–12 basis points on investments plus 25 bps for an advisory fee (Betterment 2017a). There are, however, robo-advisors that take an active approach to investing which costs more (Napach 2017).

In addition, human advisors may require clients to have minimum investable assets of $100,000 or more (Ludwig 2017), whereas robo-advisors are willing to take customers with much lower balances. Wealthfront, for example, requires a minimum balance of only $500, and Betterment requires no minimum balance. Accordingly, robo-advisors may offer an opportunity to democratize finance and disrupt the wealth management sector through their low-cost, accessible business models (Braunstein and Labouré 2017).

**Convenience of access.** The absence of a human component means that robo-advisors are available to their clients anytime and anywhere, providing a greater level of convenience for clients than previously available. This is particularly appealing to the younger more tech-savvy generation.

## Limitations of Robo-advisors

**Warm body effect.** When comparing robo to human advisors, it can be difficult to measure objectively some of the potential value of working with humans. For instance, human advisors can help their clients overcome limited financial literacy, understand and adjust their levels of risk aversion, and tolerate market volatility. Whether robo-advisors can provide these services to the same degree is unclear but is the subject of on-going research. For instance, Betterment has found that it helps to contact its actively engaged clients during market downturns. By contrast, contacting clients who are not actively engaged may backfire because some do not pay attention to stock market fluctuations (Egan 2017).

There is also evidence that people are more likely to seek investment advice from a person than from a company that provides only online advice. For instance, a recent Retirement Confidence Survey showed that 64 percent of pension participants said they would prefer advice from an independent financial advisor, versus only 28 percent favoring financial advice from an online source (Greenwald et al. 2017).

**Quality of advice.** Several challenges arise when comparing and evaluating the quality of financial advice provided by robos versus human advisors. One has to do with the advisor's recommended asset allocation. Historically, equity investments have outperformed fixed income, particularly during the rise of the robo-advisory industry. Accordingly, an advisor's performance will be heavily influenced by the degree to which that advisor's recommended portfolio has been concentrated in equities over the past decade. For example, FINRA (2016b) compared the advice of seven robo-advisors for a hypothetical 27-year-old, finding that the robos' portfolio allocations to equities varied from 51 to 90 percent.

Market competition may lead robo-advisors to over-concentrate in equities so as to report higher returns and attract more clients, but such a strategy would operate to the detriment of customers in a market downturn. Of course, without additional information on the clients' risk preferences, it is difficult to judge the appropriateness of the portfolio that an advisor recommends. In 2017, the rates of return earned by robo-advisors Betterment (16 percent), Vanguard (16%), Schwab (15 percent) and Personal Capital (14 percent) outperformed the weighted average return of a 60/40 equity/fixed income mix. Robo-advisors' two-year performance for 2016–2017—a period of strong equity market performance—was even better (Eule 2018). Not surprisingly, most advisors that performed better than the benchmark had a higher allocation to equity. For instance, Betterment, Schwab, and Personal Capital had, respectively, 87, 93, and 94 per cent of their portfolios allocated to equity vs. 13, 0, and 2 percent to fixed income in Q1 2018 (see Figure 2.3). It is difficult to evaluate these allocations without more information about the advisors' customers.

These differences in asset allocation can be overcome by evaluating returns on a risk-adjusted basis, but this gives rise to another question: that is, do robo-advisors actually tailor recommended portfolios' risk profiles

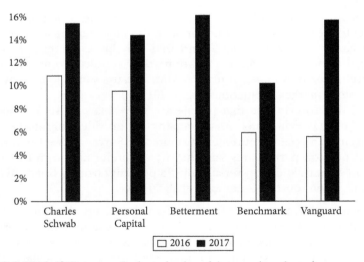

**Figure 2.3** 2016–17 Returns of selected robo-advisors vs. benchmark

*Note:* Benchmark is calculated based on a 60 percent fixed income indices (US 10-Year Bond Yield) and 40 percent Equity (S&P 500) weighted average return.

*Source:* Data from Backend Benchmarking (2018).

appropriately for their customers' needs? Stein (2016) found that robo-advisors gave different advice even when their questionnaires were answered in a standardized way. Rappaport and Turner (2010) found a similar result for online retirement planning software. Of course, asset allocation differences resulting from product differentiation are to be expected, but robo-advisors do not appear to brand themselves based on differences in their approach to investment risk.

Another concern is that standard questionnaires seeking to elicit risk preferences may not be very accurate. Kitces (2017a) has noted that a wealthy person with a capacity for bearing risk but who is deeply risk averse would be placed in a moderately risky portfolio because of his or her wealth, in effect overlooking the client's unwillingness to bear risk. He contends that risk bearing and risk tolerance scores should not be added together, but instead they should be treated as separate constraints. Thus, a person with a high capacity for bearing risk but a low risk tolerance would be put in a low-risk portfolio; and a person with a low capacity for bearing risk but a high-risk tolerance would also be put in a low-risk portfolio.

Robo-advisors' approach to risk aversion can also be compared to target date funds. An advantage robo-advisors have over target date funds is that they help clients pick investments appropriate for their levels of risk tolerance, not just their ages (Fisch and Turner 2018). On the other hand, Porter (2018: n.p.) argued: 'robo-advisers do provide value, but they provide the most value to clients with large taxable accounts and complex goals that are not suited to a simple target date fund. People who are simply saving for retirement or who don't have huge balances in taxable accounts will find that the benefits are offset by the fees.'

**Scope of advice.** Robos differ according to the share of the client's assets over which the robo has purview (Weisser 2016). In some cases, the robo-advisor may know only one of the client's accounts, and it may also not consider the client's spouse's assets. Naturally, similar limitations will be relevant to human financial advisors, but human advisors may be more sensitive to signals that prompt them to inquire about other client assets.

A related issue is the extent to which robo-advisors deal with complexity and variation in their customers' needs. FINRA (2016b: 8) raised the regulatory question: 'What information is necessary to build a customer profile with sufficient information to make a sound investment recommendation?' It concluded that most robo-advisors have between five and eight investor profiles, though some advisors have considerably more. It found that 'client-facing digital advice tools rely on a discrete set of . . . between four and twelve questions, generally falling into five broad categories: personal information, financial information, investment objective, time horizon and risk tolerance' (FINRA 2016b: 9).

Human advisors can offer customers a more personalized approach if they are not limited to standardized formats for gathering customer information. Even when human advisors start with a standard form, face-to-face discussion can enable the advisor to evaluate the intensity of the customer's preferences and to adjust accordingly. How often this happens in practice is unclear. For instance, one Canadian study found that financial advisors tended to ignore differences in risk preferences across their clients and instead recommended the same portfolio for all (Foerster et al. 2017). That study also reported that an advisor's own portfolio was a good predictor of his or her clients' portfolios.

Regulatory requirements are unclear as to the level of personalization required of a broker or financial advisor. Brokers are subject to FINRA's suitability requirement which provides that when making a recommendation, a broker-dealer must use reasonable diligence to obtain and analyze a customer's investment profile. This profile includes, but is not limited to, 'the customer's age, other investments, financial situation and needs, tax status, investment objectives, investment experience, investment time horizon, liquidity needs, risk tolerance, and any other information the customer may disclose to the member or associated person in connection with such recommendation' (FINRA 2016b: 8, quoting FINRA Rule 2111, Suitability). The suitability rule also notes that 'the level of importance of each factor may vary depending on the facts and circumstances of the particular case.' FINRA's rules do not apply, however, to financial advisors that are not broker-dealers and are regulated solely by the SEC.

It is also worth noting that human advisors' ability to tailor their advice to a specific customer may not always be an advantage. Tailored advice is problematic if human advisors are subject to bias based on the customer's age, race, gender, or other observables. A possible advantage of robo-advisors is that they may be less subject to this potential for bias.

Financial advisors help customers deal with complexity in the investing process by providing customers with advice on how to invest their money to meet their financial goals and providing ongoing portfolio management (Glassman 2017). In doing so, advisors face a trade-off between customizing client services and the number of clients they can serve. A financial advisor will generally consider a customer's existing wealth and income, financial goals, risk tolerance, and tax status in developing and implementing an investment strategy. Because of the cost of financial advisors, they tend to focus on clients in the top 20 percent of the income distribution (Kitces 2017d).

Financial advisors can also provide financial planning for a broader range of topics than robo-advisors usually do. For example, some advisors counsel on insurance and estate planning (Kitces 2017b), recommend actively traded mutual funds, and provide access to a broader range of products such as commodities, options, and alternative investments. Thus, they may be better for sophisticated, higher-net worth customers for whom those investments are more likely to be appropriate. Nevertheless, problems have been identified with human financial advice on these topics, such as recommending costly or unnecessary insurance products or recommending that clients rollover assets from a relatively low-fee 401k plan to a higher-fee IRA (Turner and Klein 2014).

There is no firm consensus regarding the effectiveness of financial advisors. Some studies suggest advisors can improve portfolio performance, but other research warns of potential negative consequences related to the relationship. On the downside, advisors may cater to uninformed clients while sometimes recommending unsuitable products (Anagol et al. 2017). In addition, client's behavioral biases and misconceptions are not always effectively addressed by advisors (Bergstresser et al. 2009; Mullainathan et al. 2012) and broker-sold funds tend not to outperform benchmarks (Bergstresser et al. 2009, Chalmers and Reuter 2015). On the upside, clients can improve their portfolio's efficiency by following unbiased computer-generated advice (Bhattacharya et al. 2012), and individuals who have participated in consultations with a financial planner tend to have higher net worth and retirement wealth (Finke 2013).

**Conflicts of interest.** One potential difference between robo-advisors and human advisors is the possibility for conflicts of interest to affect the quality of financial advice. Some human financial advisors have been criticized for providing investment advice and recommending products that generated conflicts of interest (Council of Economic Advisers 2015). Robo-advisors may be less vulnerable to the potential for conflicts of interest to the extent that they are independent and do not sponsor or sell the investments that they recommend. Additionally, robo-advisors tend to charge a flat fee based on assets under management rather than a fee that varies depending on the investment choices made by the client or its advisor. In addition, because robo-advisors compete based on fees, their fees are generally more transparent than for human financial advisors.

These differences depend on the structure and business model of the advisor in question. As Klass and Perelman (2016: 11) explained, '[d]igital advisory offerings are typically comprised of ETFs that, in comparison to mutual funds, offer little room for revenue streams and payment shares that would otherwise create a conflict of interest for investment advisors (e.g., 12b-1 fees, subtransfer agent fees). The absence of such compensation factors means that comparatively fewer conflicts of interest are present even where digital advisors are affiliated with some of the ETFs that they recommend, and independent digital advisors reduce such conflicts even further.'

Similarly, as FINRA (2016b: 6) noted, '[f]irm vs. client conflicts, however, may remain present for both financial professional- and client-facing digital advice tools, for example if a firm offers products or services from an affiliate or receives payments or other benefits from providers of the products or services.' Lam (2016) argued that Schwab Intelligent Portfolios held an unusually large amount in cash at Schwab Bank, allowing the firm to profit from the difference between the rate of return the bank pays and the rate of return it receives on lending. He also noted that Schwab Intelligent Portfolios charged higher expense ratios for its ETFs than did the largest robos, Betterment and Wealthfront.

It is worth noting that robos can also face conflicts of interest. When they offer different levels of service with different fees, they confront a conflict if they recommend the service generating the highest revenues to the firm. In addition, pension rollovers generate a conflict of interest for robos because encouraging rollovers also boosts their fees. The total fees Betterment charges are roughly 35 basis points (25 bps for advisory fee and 10 bps for asset management fee). By comparison, in a study of fees in 401k plans, 10 percent of the 525 plans surveyed had an 'all-in' fee of 28 basis points, while 10 percent had an 'all-in' fee of 138 basis points (Deloitte Consulting 2011). Thus, the fees Betterment charged were lower than the fees of many 401k plans, but most 401k participants are in large plans that tend to charge lower fees.

## Trends in Robo-advisors

This section considers several trends in robo-advisors in the United States. The first is a move to human-robo hybrids; the second is a move to greater product or service diversification in other aspects; and the third is toward vertical integration. These all provide a way for incumbents in the market to compete against the pure robo-advisors, as well as to gain distribution channels. A fourth trend is the use of robo-advisors by human advisors.

**The move to hybrids.** Some financial advisory companies have begun to combine features of robo-advisors and traditional human advisors, creating a type of hybrid. Hybrids charge lower fees than traditional advisors by automating part of the investment process, but they still offer the possibility of talking with a financial advisor.

The stand-alone robo-advisor movement is also slowly declining in relative importance, as robo-advisors are acquired by other financial firms such as custodian and broker-dealer companies. Some of the traditional financial management companies such as Vanguard and Schwab have incorporated robo-advisors into their business model, Schwab being the first to use the hybrid approach. This development, while increasing competition, has also given added credibility to the use of robo-advisors. Vanguard's Personal Advisor Services charged 30 basis points and required an account minimum of $50,000 in 2018. Schwab Intelligent Advisory charged 28 basis points with an account minimum of $25,000 and offers 'unlimited' contact with a Certified Financial Planner 24/7. Schwab Intelligent Advisory combined Schwab Intelligent Portfolios plus the availability of human advisors. It provided comprehensive financial planning services, not just portfolio management, which it implemented with the Schwab robo model (Kitces 2016). Both the Schwab and Vanguard services involved contact with human advisors, so neither was a pure robo-advisor.

In 2017, T. Rowe Price began offering a robo-advisor, ActivePlus Portfolios, reflecting its emphasis on active portfolio management. Advisors could only select T. Rowe Price funds. There was no extra investment management fee. The robo-advisor service was available to clients with at least $50,000 in the portfolios managed by this program (Kitces 2017c). The program only managed IRA money, so presumably there were no tax consequences associated with trading. The fact that it only managed money invested in an IRA with a minimum of $50,000 made the service unavailable to most young people. The program offered a call-in center where participants could talk to advisors, as well as online access to client managers. A website allowed a client to see how the allocation of a portfolio between stocks and fixed income would vary based on the personal information provided (T. Rowe Price 2017). For example, the program recommended that a person aged 25 with medium risk tolerance invest in a portfolio of 88.5 percent stocks and 11.5 percent bonds, while a person with the same risk tolerance who was aged 67 was advised to invest in a portfolio with 58.5 stocks and 41.5 percent fixed income.

Wells Fargo began offering a robo-advisor service in 2017, requiring a minimum investment of $10,000. It was a hybrid service, offering the possibility of speaking to an advisor. It offered seven different portfolios, with a fee of 50 basis points including the expense ratio for the investments and the advice fee (Saacks 2017).

The hybrid business model has spread to the original robo-advisor space. In 2017, Betterment opened a call center and began offering three levels of service. Betterment Digital was the classic robo advice offering with no account minimums, costing 25 basis points (the same fee charged by Wealthfront). Betterment Premium required a $100,000 minimum balance and cost 40 basis points for unlimited access to a 'team of CFP professionals and licensed financial experts' (Benke 2017: n.p). Customers looking for even more hands-on advice could use a dedicated financial advisor assisted by Betterment for Advisors (Neal 2017). These changes were designed to attract wealthier clients than those typically using the basic robo-advisor approach. In 2016 and 2017, about one-third of the assets Betterment managed were owned by investors aged 50 or older, who typically had larger portfolios than did younger investors (Weisser 2016; Kitces 2017d).

**Greater product diversification.** With the growing number of entrants into the robo-advisor market, there has also been a move toward greater product diversification. This is a common pattern in product development as markets mature. It means that robo-advisors need to differentiate themselves with respect to the services they provide instead of competing primarily on fees.

Some robo-advisors offer specialized services to attract a demographic or interest group. For example, because the financial advice industry is supposedly male-oriented in the services it provides, some robo-advisors instead focused on attracting female clients. SheCapital was founded in 2015 to target the specific needs of women investors (Malito 2015), but the firm went out of business after a year because of its inability to attract a sufficient number of clients (Malito 2016). In 2016, Ellevest started as a robo-advisor catering to women. The premise was that because women have longer life expectancies than men, they need to have different portfolios from men the same age (Weisser 2016). Ellevest clientele are well educated—more than 40 percent have a master's degree or doctorate (Ellevest 2017).

True Link focused on older investors and retirees (True Link 2017), while United Income was also oriented toward people near or in retirement. Several robo-advisors, including OpenInvest and Earthfolio, offered investors the opportunity to combine socially responsible investing with a robo platform (Skinner 2017b). The fees of these specialized firms were higher than those of the original robo-advisors.

The original robo-advisors have also expanded the range of products and services that they offer over time. In 2017, Betterment began offering three new options: a fund that took socially responsible investing criteria into account, a low-risk alternative to its standard fund, and a high-risk alternative, which is its Goldman Sachs Smart Beta portfolio. The high-risk fund invests based on factors such as the momentum or the quality of a stock. The same year, Betterment also began offering a program for charitable giving (Betterment 2017c). The client specifies the amount of the desired donation, and Betterment picks the asset that has the most unrealized capital gains to donate to that charity. In this way, the client gets to contribute and deduct the full value of the security, rather than first selling the security, paying tax on the capital gains, and then contributing the after-tax amount.

Robo-advisors are also expanding their operations into a broader range of financial services. For example, Betterment offers Betterment for Business, providing record keeping and asset management services for 401k plans. It also offers Betterment for Advisors, providing asset management services for financial advisors.

**Vertical integration—robo-advisors as distribution channels.** From the perspective of the financial services industry, robo-advisors function as distribution channels for financial products. Some providers of financial products have also purchased or started robo-advisors as a way to distribute their products (Kitces 2017d). Such vertical integration is one way for incumbent financial service providers to compete with the start-up robo-advisors.

Schwab started Schwab Intelligent Portfolios, in which the portfolios primarily consist of its own proprietary products. BlackRock purchased Future-Advisor as a platform to distribute its ETFs. Similarly, Invesco purchased Jemstep to distribute its ETFs. Wisdom Tree invested heavily in AdvisorEngine to distribute its ETFs. Northwestern Mutual purchased LearnVest, and Interactive brokers Online purchased Covestor (Hooper and Andress 2016). By contrast, the CEO of Betterment, Jon Stein, has indicated that he would prefer an IPO for Betterment rather than being bought by a large investment management company because this would preserve its independence relating to its choice of investments (Wang and Padley 2017).

**The use of robo-advisors by human advisors.** A further trend is the use of robo-advisors by human advisors. Human advisors can become more efficient by using robo-advisors to help them advise their clients and manage client investments. For example, Riskalyze only deals with registered financial advisors. Its technology helps advisors determine the risk tolerance of their clients and use that information to construct portfolios that are appropriate for the clients. By analyzing the risk of the prospects' investment holdings, the software allows financial advisors to show prospects whether their investment portfolios have the appropriate amount of risk (Riskalyze 2018). Raymond James Financial announced in 2017 that its 7,100 advisors would have access to a robo-advisor platform that they could use as a tool for advising clients (Skinner 2017a).

## Robo-advisors Internationally

Although robo-advisors began in the United States, the concept has spread to other countries. In Europe, robo-advisors are a relatively new concept. The number of robo advisors in Europe has increased significantly since 2014, and the amount of money robo-advisors manage has also grown rapidly (Table 2.2). Most European robo advisors operate at the national level (rather than internationally) due to legislative and regulatory constraints. However, some such as Quirion operate in several countries. In June 2017, BlackRock took a stake in the Anglo-German digital investment manager Scalable Capital. Robo-advisors now operate in Canada (12), France (17), the United Kingdom (20), Switzerland (12), Germany (31), Italy (5), China (20), Japan (14), Singapore (8), India (19), and Australia (8). By contrast, there are 200 robo-advisors in the United States. However, robo-advisors are rare in South America (3) (Burnmark 2017).

TABLE 2.2 Selected features of European robo-advisors, 2018

| Robo-advisor | Available countries | Advisory fee as % of AuM (does not include fee for investments in funds) | Account minimum | Investment instruments |
|---|---|---|---|---|
| Nutmeg | United Kingdom | 0.75%–0.25% asset management fee on invested money 0.20% fund management fee on invested money (min £100/months for accounts below £5,000) | £500 | ETFs |
| Quirion | Germany Switzerland | 0.48% for asset management fee 0.39% fund management fee on invested money | €10,000 | ETFs |
| Marie Quantier | France | 5% on profits made Trading commissions from interactive brokers apply with a minimum of USD 10 per month | €5,000 | ETFs |
| Ginmon | Germany | 0.39% for asset management fee 10% on profits made 0.37% fund management fee | €5,000 or €1,000 with a reinvestment of €50 per month | ETFs |
| Wealth Horizon | United Kingdom | 0.25% on invested money 0.75% for asset management fee on invested money 0.18% for fund management fee on invested money | £1,000 | ETFs |
| Wealthify | United Kingdom | 0.7% (under £10,000) to 0.5% (over £250,000) for asset management fee on invested money | £250 | ETFs |

*Note*: ETF refers to Exchange Traded Fund.

*Source*: Authors' collection of data from robo-advisor websites (Robo Advisors Europe, 2018).

Although it is difficult to generalize about the European market, robo-advisors there tend to charge higher fees than US robo-advisors, from 40 to 100 basis points (e.g., Nutmeg, Quirion, Marie Quantier). The higher fees may be due to the fact that robo-advisors are a relatively new phenomenon in Europe. In addition, European financial and banking legislation differs across countries, resulting in many different national markets for robo-advisors rather than a single centralized European market. Also, European citizens may tend to be more risk-averse than Americans, resulting in more saving and safer investments (Laidi 2010). These factors may have led European robo-advisors to grow slowly, reducing their ability to benefit from economies of scale.

## Conclusion

Whether robo-advisors will be better generally for investors than human advisors in the long run remains to be seen. Because of their relatively low fees and low minimum account balances, robo-advisors can provide financial advice to people who cannot afford it from traditional financial advisors and for whom many financial advisors would not be willing to provide their services. For this group, robo-advisors are clearly a better option than human financial advisors. A robo-advisor can steer young people who are just starting out away from poor decisions such as inappropriate asset allocations or the selection of overly-costly investments.

In addition, robo-advisors may be less likely to have conflicts of interest related to the products they sell. This, however, may be undercut by the growing trend toward robo-advisors being integrated into traditional full-service banks, brokerages, and asset management firms.

In the future, robo-advisors can be expected to increase the sophistication with which they identify individual differences in risk preference, as well as other aspects of the advice and financial management provided. To assess the relative merits of robo-advisors versus financial advisors fully, more information on and experience with robo-advisors is needed. It is likely that their importance will grow over time as more new cohorts of investors use them and as the asset balances of their current users increase, as they age.

The intangible component of human contact is one service that robo-advisors are unable to provide. The real or perceived value of this human contact appears to be an important difference between robo-advisors and traditional financial advisors, and it likely explains the current trend toward hybrid advisors that involve a robo-advisor working in partnership with a traditional advisor. Such hybrids charge lower fees than traditional advisors, but they still offer the possibility of talking with a financial advisor and may constitute the future of the financial advisory industry.

## Notes

1. Chamber of Commerce v. US Dept. of Labor, 885 F.3d 360 (5th Cir. 2018). Following the ruling, the US Department of Labor (2018) announced that it did not intend to enforce the rule, pending further review.
2. The precursors to robo-advisors such as Mpower and Financial Engines were automated services that employers provided to employees in their defined contribution plans, but these firms offered services directly to retail investors (Deschenes and Hammond 2019).

## References

Agarwal, S., J. Driscoll, X. Gabaix, and D. Laibson (2009). 'The Age of Reason: Financial Decisions over the Lifecycle with Implications for Regulation,' *Brookings Papers on Economic Activity* 2: 51–117.

Anagol, S., S. Cole, and S. Sarkar (2017). 'Understanding the Advice of Commissions-Motivated Agents: Evidence from the Indian Life Insurance Market,' *Review of Economics and* Statistics 99(1–15).

Axelrod, S. F. (2017). 'Remarks at IRI Government, Legal and Regulatory Conference.' June 12: http://www.finra.org/newsroom/speeches/061217-remarks-iri-government-legal-and-regulatory-conference (accessed February 21, 2019).

Backend Benchmarking (2018). 'The Robo Report Second Quarter 2018: Bringing Transparency to Robo Investing.' Edition 8: https://storage.googleapis.com/gcs-wp.theroboreport.com/gZhdpxRTPEhtB8Wj/2Q%202018%20Robo%20Report.pdf (accessed February 21, 2019).

Benke, A. (2017). 'Your Money, Your Way: The Betterment Service Plans,' *Betterment.* January 31: https://www.betterment.com/resources/your-money-your-way-the-betterment-advice-plans/ (accessed February 21, 2019).

Berger, R. (2015). '7 Robo Advisers that Make Investing Effortless,' *Forbes.* February 5: http://www.forbes.com/sites/robertberger/2015/02/05/7-robo-advisors-that-make-investing-effortless/#75eaae1f7e48 (accessed February 21, 2019).

Bergstresser, D., J. Chalmers, and P. Tufano (2009). 'Assessing the Costs and Benefits of Brokers in the Mutual Fund Industry,' *Review of Financial Studies* 22(10): 4129–56.

Betterment (2017a). 'Is Your Old 401(k) Costing You?' *Betterment.* https://www.betterment.com/401k-and-ira-rollover/?gclid=CjwKEAjwja_JBRD8idHpxaz0t3wSJAB4rXW55KvrzvjgmvpQLWhL_4Hzz2De3RXD-tAsyx88We8XiBoC_zzw_wcB (accessed March 25, 2019).

Betterment (2017b). 'The History of Betterment: How We Started a Company That Changed an Industry,' *Betterment.* July 20: https://www.betterment.com/resources/inside-betterment/our-story/the-history-of-betterment/ (accessed February 21, 2019).

Betterment (2017c). 'Introducing Charitable Giving by Betterment,' *Betterment.* November 15: https://www.betterment.com/resources/charitable-stock-donation/ (accessed February 21, 2019).

Bhattacharya, U., A. Hackethal, S. Kaelser, B. Loos, and S. Meyer (2012). 'Is Unbiased Financial Advice to Retail Investors Sufficient? Answers from a Large Field Study,' *Review of Financial Studies* 25(4): 975–1032.

BlackRock (2016). 'Digital Investment Advice: Robo Advisers Come of Age,' *Viewpoint*, September. https://www.blackrock.com/corporate/en-mx/literature/whitepaper/viewpoint-digital-investment-advice-september-2016.pdf (accessed February 21, 2019).

Braunstein, J. and M. Labouré (2017). 'Democratising Finance: The Digital Wealth Management Revolution,' *VoxEU.* November 11: https://voxeu.org/article/digital-wealth-management-revolution (accessed February 21, 2019).

Burnmark (2017). *Digital Wealth,* Burnmark Report April. https://wealthobjects.com/templates/protostar/images/Burnmark-April17.pdf (accessed March 15, 2019).

Cain, D. M., G. Loewenstein, and D. A. Moore (2005). 'The Dirt on Coming Clean: Perverse Effects of Disclosing Conflicts of Interest,' *The Journal of Legal Studies,* 34 (1): 1–25. http://www.journals.uchicago.edu/doi/abs/10.1086/426699 (accessed February 21, 2019).

Chalmers, J. and J. Reuter (2015). 'Is Conflicted Investment Advice Better than No Advice?' NBER Working Paper No. 18158. Cambridge, MA: National Bureau of Economic Research.

Collins, J. M. (2012). 'Financial Advice: A Substitute for Financial Literacy?' *Financial Services Review* 21: 307–22.

Council of Economic Advisers (CEA) (2015). *The Effects of Conflicted Investment Advice on Retirement Savings,* February. Washington, DC: CEA. https://obamawhitehouse.archives.gov/sites/default/files/docs/cea_coi_report_final.pdf(accessed March 25, 2019).

Deloitte Consulting (2011). *Inside the Structure of the Defined Contribution/401(k) Plan Fees: A Study Assessing the Mechanics of the 'All-In' Fee,* Study Conducted for the Investment Company Institute. November. http://www.ici.org/pdf/rpt_11_dc_401k_fee_study.pdf (accessed February 21, 2019).

Egan, D. (2017). 'Our Evidence-Based Approach to Improving Investor Behavior.' October 12. Betterment. https://www.betterment.com/resources/investment-strategy/behavioral-finance-investing-strategy/behavioral-testing/ (accessed February 21, 2019).

Ellevest (2018). 'Simple, Flexible Pricing.' https://www.ellevest.com/pricing (accessed February 21, 2019).

Ellevest (2017). 'We've Rounded Up the Biggest Ellevest Trends,' email to the authors dated September 2.

Eule, A. (2018). 'As Robo-Advisors Cross $200 Billion in Assets, Schwab Leads in Performance,' *Barron's.* Feb. 3. https://www.barrons.com/articles/as-robo-advisors-cross-200-billion-in-assets-schwab-leads-in-performance-1517509393 (accessed February 21, 2019).

Financial Industry Regulatory Authority (FINRA) (2016a). *Investors in the United States: 2016.* December. FINRA Report. Washington, D.C.: FINRA. http://gflec.org/wp-content/uploads/2017/02/NFCS_2015_Inv_Survey_Full_Report.pdf?x28148 (accessed February 21, 2019).

Financial Industry Regulatory Authority (FINRA) (2016b). *Report on Digital Investment Advice,* March. Washington, D.C.: FINRA. https://www.finra.org/sites/default/files/digital-investment-advice-report.pdf (accessed February 21, 2019).

Finke, M. (2013). 'Financial Advice: Does it Make a Difference?' in O.S. Mitchell and K. Smetters, eds., *The Market for Retirement Financial Advice*. Oxford University Press: Oxford, UK, 229–48.

Fisch, J. E., T. Wilkinson-Ryan, and K. Firth (2016). 'The Knowledge Gap in Workplace Retirement Investing and the Role of Professional Advisors,' *Duke Law Review* 66: 633–72. http://dlj.law.duke.edu/article/the-knowledge-gap-in-workplace-retirement-investing-and-the-role-of-professional-advisors-fisch-vol66-iss3/ (accessed February 21, 2019).

Fisch, J. E. and J. A. Turner (2018). 'Making A Complex Investment Problem Less Difficult: Robo Target Date Funds,' *Journal of Retirement* 5(4): 40–5.

Foerster, S., J. T. Linnainmaa, B. T. Melzer, and A. Previtero (2017). 'Retail Financial Advice: Does One Size Fit All?' *Journal of Finance* 72: 1441–82.

Gallup (2016). 'Robo-Advice Still a Novelty for U.S. Investors,' *Gallup*, July 27. http://www.gallup.com/poll/193997/robo-advice-novelty-investors.aspx (accessed February 21, 2019).

Glassman, B. (2017). 'What Does a Financial Advisor Do?' *Forbes*. February 8: https://www.forbes.com/sites/advisor/2017/02/08/what-does-a-financial-advisor-do/#16bc5cb55499 (accessed February 21, 2019).

Greenwald, L., L. Copeland, and J. VanDerhei (2017). *The 2017 Retirement Confidence Survey: Many Workers Lack Retirement Confidence and Feel Stressed about Retirement Preparations, EBRI Issue Brief* No. 431. March 21: https://www.ebri.org/content/the-2017-retirement-confidence-survey-many-workers-lack-retirement-confidence-and-feel-stressed-about-retirement-preparations-3426 (accessed March 25, 2019).

Ha, A. (2010). 'Investing Site KaChing Gets Classier as Wealthfront,' *Venturebeat*, Oct. 19: https://venturebeat.com/2010/10/19/kaching-wealthfront/ (accessed February 21, 2019).

Hooper, T. and M. Andress (2016). 'Robo-Advisory Space Poised for Further Consolidation—Sources,' *Mergermarket*. January 19.

Jordan, R. (2012). 'Thinking Before Rulemaking: Why the SEC Should Think Twice Before Imposing a Uniform Fiduciary Standard on Broker-Dealers and Investment Advisers,' *Louisville Law Review* 50: 491–526.

Kelly, J. (2017). 'Global Assets under Management Hit All-Time High above $80 Trillion,' *Reuters*. October 30: https://www.reuters.com/article/us-global-funds-aum/global-assets-under-management-hit-all-time-high-above-80-trillion-idUSKBN1CZ11B (accessed February 21, 2019).

Khentov, B. (2014). 'Avoid Surprises with Tax Impact Preview,' *Betterment*. October 29: https://www.betterment.com/resources/tax-impact-helps-you-get-the-full-picture/ (accessed February 21, 2019).

Kim, H. K., R. Maurer, and O. S. Mitchell (2016). 'Time is Money: Rational Life Cycle Inertia and the Delegation of Investment Management,' *Journal of Financial Economics* 121(2): 427–47.

Kitces, M. (2016). 'Is Schwab Intelligent Advisory a Threat to Independent Financial Advisors?' *The Nerd's Eye View*. December 22 https://www.youtube.com/watch?v=I8ERYe7JQt0 (accessed February 21, 2019).

Kitces, M. (2017a). 'Adopting a Two-Dimensional Risk-Tolerance Assessment Process,' *The Nerd's Eye View*. January 25. https://bit.ly/2zAKB46 (accessed February 21, 2019).

Kitces, M. (2017b). 'Advisor #Fintech as a Distribution Channel for Insurance and Investment Products,' *The Nerd's Eye View*. December 7. https://bit.ly/2L5uu00 (accessed February 21, 2019).

Kitces, M. (2017c). 'The Latest in Financial Advisor #FinTech (March 2017): Take-aways from the T3 Advisor Tech Conference,' *The Nerd's Eye View*. March 6. https://bit.ly/2uoCZff (accessed February 21, 2019).

Kitces, M. (2017d). 'What Robo Advisers Can Teach Human Advisers About Evidence-Based Behavioral Finance with Dan Egan,' *The Nerd's Eye Vie*. December 19. https://bit.ly/2L4X5FM (accessed February 21, 2019).

Klass, J. L. and E. Perelman (2019). 'The Transformation of Investment Advice: Digital Investment Advisers as Fiduciaries' in J. Agnew and O.S. Mitchell, eds., *The Disruptive Impact of FinTech on Retirement Systems*. Oxford, U.K: Oxford University Press: pp. 38–58.

Klass, J. L. and E. Perelman (2016). *The Evolution of Advice: Digital Investment Advisers as Fiduciaries*. Morgan Lewis. New York, NY: Morgan Lewis. https://www.morganlewis.com/~/media/files/publication/report/im-the-evolution-of-advice-digital-investment-advisers-as-fiduciaries-october-2016.ashx?la=en (accessed February 21, 2019).

Kocianski, S. (2016). 'The Robo Advising Report,' *BusinessInsider*. June 9. https://nordic.businessinsider.com/the-robo-advising-report-market-forecasts-key-growth-drivers-and-how-automated-asset-management-will-change-the-advisory-industry-2016-6/ (accessed March 25, 2019).Kramer, L. (2016). 'Can Robo Advisers Replace Human Financial Advisers?' *Wall Street Journal*. February 28. https://www.wsj.com/articles/can-robo-advisers-replace-human-financial-advisers-1456715553 (accessed February 21, 2019).

Laidi, Z. (2010). *Europe as a Risk Averse Power: A Hypothesis*. Garnet Policy Brief. Princeton, NJ: Princeton University.

Lam, J. W. (2016). 'Robo-Advisers: A Portfolio Management Perspective,' Unpublished Senior Thesis, Yale College, April 4. http://economics.yale.edu/sites/default/files/files/Undergraduate/Nominated%20Senior%20Essays/2015-16/Jonathan_Lam_Senior%20Essay%20Revised.pdf (accessed February 21, 2019).

Lazaroff, P. (2016). 'The Difference between Fiduciary and Suitability Standards.' *Forbes*. April 6. http://www.forbes.com/sites/peterlazaroff/2016/04/06/the-difference-between-fiduciary-and-suitability-standards/#4d42e9a735bf (accessed February 21, 2019).

Ludwig, L. (2017). 'The Rise of the Robo-Advisors—Should You Use One?' *Investor-Junkie*. https://investorjunkie.com/35919/robo-advisors/ (accessed February 21, 2019).

Lusardi, A. and O. S. Mitchell (2014). 'The Economic Importance of Financial Literacy: Theory and Evidence,' *Journal of Economic Literature* 52(1): 5–44. http://www.aeaweb.org/articles.php?doi=10.1257/jel.52.1.5 (accessed February 21, 2019).

Malito, A. (2015). 'Newest Robo-Adviser Targets Female Investors,' *InvestmentNews*. August 27. http://www.investmentnews.com/article/20150827/FREE/150829930/newest-robo-adviser-targets-female-investors (accessed February 21, 2019).

Malito, A. (2016). 'Women-Focused Robo-Adviser SheCapital Shuts Down.' *InvestmentNews*. July 19. http://www.investmentnews.com/article20160719/FREE/

160719922/women-focused-robo-adviser-shecapital-shuts-down (accessed February 21, 2019).

Mullainathan, S., M. Noeth, and A. Schoar (2012). 'The Market for Financial Advice: An Audit Study,' NBER Working Paper 17929. Cambridge, MA: National Bureau of Economic Research.

Napach, B. (2017). 'T. Rowe Price Launches Robo Platform with Only Actively-Managed Funds,' *ThinkAdvisor*. March 16. https://www.thinkadvisor.com/2017/03/16/t-rowe-price-launches-robo-platform-with-only-acti/?slreturn=20180415200353 (accessed February 21, 2019).

Neal, R. (2017). 'Betterment Pivots toward a Human-Robo Hybrid.' Wealthmanagement.com. January 31. http://www.wealthmanagement.com/technology/betterment-pivots-toward-human-robo-hybrid (accessed February 21, 2019).

Polyak, I. (2015). 'Millennials and Robo-Advisers: A Match Made in Heaven?' *CNBC*. June 22. https://www.cnbc.com/2015/06/21/millennials-and-robo-advisors-a-match-made-in-heaven.html (accessed February 21, 2019).

Porter, T. (2018). 'Why Robo-Advisory Services May Not be Worth the Investment,' *MyBanktracker*. February 20. https://www.mybanktracker.com/news/why-robo-advisors-may-not-be-worth-cost (accessed February 21, 2019).

Rappaport, A. M. and J. A. Turner (2010). 'How Does Retirement Planning Software Handle Postretirement Realities?' in R. L. Clark and O.S. Mitchell, eds., *Reorienting Retirement Risk Management*. Oxford, UK: Oxford University Press, pp. 66–85.

Regan, M. P. (2015). 'Robo Advisers to Run $2 Trillion by 2020 if This Model is Right,' *Bloomberg*. June 18. https://www.bloomberg.com/news/articles/2015-06-18/robo-advisers-to-run-2-trillion-by-2020-if-this-model-is-right (accessed February 21, 2019).

Reuter, J. and D. Richardson (2017). 'New Evidence on the Demand for Advice within Retirement Plans,' *Trends and Issues*, TIAA Institute. April. https://bit.ly/2ucC5TV (accessed February 21, 2019).

Riskalyze (2018). 'Risk Number.' https://blog.riskalyze.com/riskalyze-review-november-2018 (accessed March 25, 2019).Robo Advisors Europe (2018). http://robo-advisors.eu/ (accessed February 21, 2019).

Saacks, B. (2017). 'Wells Readies Robo Rollout (with Human Touch),' *Ignites*. March 29. http://bit.ly/2JBfmL4 (accessed February 21, 2019).

Skinner, L. (2017a). 'Raymond James to Deliver Robo Service for Advisers by Year End,' *Investment News*. January 30. http://www.investmentnews.com/article/20170130/FREE/170139992/raymond-james-to-deliver-robo-service-for-advisers-by-year-end (accessed February 21, 2019).

Skinner, L. (2017b). 'Robos Jumping into Socially Responsible Investing Space,' *InvestmentNews*. January 11. http://www.investmentnews.com/article/20170111/FREE/170119974/robos-jumping-into-socially-responsible-investing-space (accessed February 21, 2019).

Statista (2017). 'Forecast of Assets under Management of Robo-Advisors in the United States from 2016 to 2020 (in Billion U.S. dollars).' (Updated 2018.) https://www.statista.com/statistics/520623/projected-assets-under-management-us-robo-advisors/ (accessed February 21, 2019).

Stein, J. D. (2016). 'Test Driving Robo-Advisors: Their Recommended Portfolios and ETFs,' *Seeking Alpha*. June 13. http://seekingalpha.com/article/3981595-test-driving-robo-advisors-recommended-portfolios-etfs (accessed February 21, 2019).

Taulli, T. (2012). 'Interview: Wealthfront CEO and Founder Andy Rachleff,' *Investor Place*. February 7. http://investorplace.com/ipo-playbook/interview-wealthfront-ceo-and-founder-andy-rachleff/#.WZRqJoeWwck (accessed February 21, 2019).

Toonkel, J. and D. Randall (2015). 'Original Robo-adviser Financial Engines Seeks Life Beyond 401(k)s,' *Reuters*. May 26. https://www.reuters.com/article/us-financialengines-future-insight/original-robo-adviser-financial-engines-seeks-life-beyond-401s-idUSKBN0OC0BE20150527 (accessed February 21, 2019).

Turner, J. A., and B. W. Klein (2014). 'Retirement Savings Flows and Financial Advice: Should You Roll Over Your 401(k) Plan?' *Benefits Quarterly* 30: 42–54.

T. Rowe Price (2017). 'Enjoy the Convenience of Online Investing—Powered by Our Experts.' https://www3.troweprice.com/usis/personal-investing/products-and-services/activeplus-portfolios.html?v_linkcomp=aalink&v_link=ActivePlus%20Portfolios&v_linkplmt=TN (accessed February 21, 2019).

True Link (2017). 'Financial Services Built for You.' https://www.truelinkfinancial.com/ (accessed February 21, 2019).

US Department of Labor (2018). *Field Assistance Bulletin No. 2018–02*. Washington, D.C.: US DOL. https://www.dol.gov/agencies/ebsa/employers-and-advisers/guidance/field-assistance-bulletins/2018-02 (accessed February 21, 2019).

US Department of Labor (2016). *Definition of the Term 'Fiduciary'; Conflict of Interest Rule—Retirement Investment Advice (Final Fiduciary Definition)*. Washington, D.C.: 81 Fed. Reg. 20,946.

US Government Accountability Office (GAO) (2011). *Improved Regulation Could Better Protect Participants from Conflicts of Interest*. GAO-11-119. Washington, D.C.: USGAO. http://www.gao.gov/products/GAO-11-119 (accessed February 21, 2019).

US Securities and Exchange Commission (SEC) (2018). *Regulation Best Interest*. Washington, D.C.: US SEC. https://www.sec.gov/rules/proposed/2018/34-83062.pdf (accessed February 21, 2019).

US Securities and Exchange Commission (SEC) (2017). *Robo-Advisers, IM Guidance Update*. Washington, D.C.: US SEC. https://www.sec.gov/investment/im-guidance-2017-02.pdf (accessed February 21, 2019).

Wang, Y. and K. Padley (2017). 'Betterment Still Plans IPO But Not This Year, CEO Says,' *Mergermarket*. April 10.

Wealthfront (2017a). 'Here's How It All Started.' https://www.wealthfront.com/origin (accessed February 21, 2019).

Wealthfront (2017b). 'How Does Tax-loss Harvesting Relate to Rebalancing?' https://support.wealthfront.com/hc/en-us/articles/209348586-How-does-tax-loss-harvesting-relate-to-rebalancing- (accessed February 21, 2019).

Weisser, C. (2016). 'The Rise of the Robo-Adviser,' *Consumer Reports*. July 28. https://www.consumerreports.org/personal-investing/rise-of-the-robo-adviser/ (accessed February 21, 2019).

Wells Fargo (2016). 'Wells Fargo/Gallup Survey: Investors Curious about Digital Investing, More Optimistic about Economy Prior to Brexit.' July 19. https://newsroom.wf.com/press-release/innovation-and-technology/wells-fargogallup-survey-investors-curious-about-digital (accessed February 21, 2019).

Chapter 3

# The Transformation of Investment Advice: Digital Investment Advisors as Fiduciaries

*Jennifer L. Klass and Eric L. Perelman*

The landscape for investment advice is shifting, and an innovative model has emerged that combines technology and investment expertise to deliver high-quality advice at a lower cost than traditional investment advisory services. Digital or so-called 'robo-advisors' that use algorithms and technology to offer discretionary investment advice through a digital interface continue to experience a rapid growth in popularity. A recent survey of the industry found that digital investment advisory programs accounted for managed assets in excess of $200 billion globally (Eule 2018; AT Kearny 2015). The term 'digital advisor' encompasses a broad range of business models. Digital advisors include both independent investment advisors that focus on offering digital advice directly to retail consumers, as well as established financial industry incumbents who include a 'digital' offering among a broad suite of advisory and brokerage services. Other digital advisors pursue an intermediary model where they partner with financial institutions to develop 'white label' digital advisor programs, or serve as a sub-advisor or technology provider to such firms' proprietary digital programs.

Although humans are actively involved in the design of digital advisory offerings and formulation of investment advice, the degree to which humans are involved in the delivery of that advice varies depending on the business model. In its purest form, a digital advisor will only provide asset allocation advice and investment recommendations through a digital interface. Clients are able to contact the firm by e-mail, chat, or telephone only for technical support or to ask operational or administrative questions. Increasingly, however, digital advisors operate a so-called 'hybrid' model under which clients have the option to consult with financial advisors. Under the hybrid model, financial advisors supplement the digital advisor's automated functions and serve as an additional resource for clients.

Regardless of the business model, digital advisors generally leverage technology to automate both the client experience and the portfolio management process. Other common characteristics of digital advisors include:

- Primary reliance on a digital (web-based and mobile) interface to interact with clients, collect client profile information through an investor questionnaire, facilitate the account opening process and deliver account communications;
- Comparatively lower advisory fees than traditional advisory services and low or no account minimums. Digital advisors typically charge a single 'wrap' fee that covers discretionary management services and execution of client transactions. Many digital advisors have positioned themselves as a low-cost alternative to investment advisory products that offer a more comprehensive suite of services;
- A focus on goals-based investing where clients define their objectives based on specific life goals (e.g., saving for a house, retirement or a child's education) and measure performance based on progress toward that goal, rather than focusing exclusively on maximizing portfolio returns measured in relation to a benchmark;
- Personalized asset allocation recommendations generated by matching client profile information with a diversified portfolio of low cost, tax efficient, exchange-traded funds (ETFs);
- Discretionary investment advice that leverages algorithms to automatically monitor client positions against target asset allocation and risk thresholds associated with a client's investment strategy;
- Automated rebalancing designed to monitor for drifts from the intended asset allocation and generate trade orders for execution in order to 'rebalance' the client's account back to its intended asset allocation, as well as leveraging cash in-flows and out-flows to rebalance an account; and
- Implementation of certain investment strategies designed to minimize a client's tax burden (e.g., tax-loss harvesting[1] or asset placement[2]).

The emergence of digital advice is particularly significant for investors who were not previously able to access any advice because of the minimum balances required by other service models, but investors at every level of wealth have been drawn to the value, accessibility, and transparency offered by digital advice.

Many industry participants have commented on the transformative potential of digital investment advice. Of particular note, the former Chair of the US Securities and Exchange Commission (SEC) observed that digital investment advice holds the 'positive potential to give retail investors broader, and more affordable, access to our markets' (White 2016: n.p.). This chapter explores the application of fiduciary standards to digital advisors. It concludes that fiduciary standards, such as those incorporated into the Investment Advisers Act of 1940 (Advisers Act), are flexible principles that digital advisors and their nondigital counterparts (traditional advisors) are equally capable of satisfying. Investors benefit from this regulatory flexibility, which encourages innovation and permits the development of more varied services. Indeed, the Advisers Act already accommodates investment advisors with a wide variety of business models, investment strategies, and services. This chapter also explains that the products and services offered by digital advisors are not unique, but instead are technologically enhanced versions of advisory programs and services that have long been subject to this flexible regulatory framework. Finally, this chapter discusses the innovative and powerful ways that digital advisors can more effectively serve their clients, including by harnessing the efficiencies of technology and insights from behavioral finance.

## Drivers behind the Growth of Digital Advice

Americans find themselves in the midst of what many commentators and governmental officials have termed a 'retirement savings crisis' (USGAO 2017; Samuels 2018). On the one hand, people are increasingly responsible for managing their own retirement savings because of the disappearance of defined benefit plans, deteriorating confidence in the long-term viability of the social security system, and concern that social security payments will provide insufficient retirement income. Only 18 percent of American workers today reportedly are very confident that they will have enough money for a comfortable retirement, and participation in employee savings plans is at historic lows (Greenwald et al. 2017; USDOL 2017). Moreover, more than half of current households approaching retirement have no savings, and a large proportion of those with savings do not have enough to maintain their standard of living in retirement (USGAO 2017). Many of those able to maintain their standard of living may only be able to do so due to rising property values (Fox 2018). On the other hand, many investors who would benefit from professional advice are not able to meet the high account minimums that often accompany access to financial advisors (Fischer 2016).

Against this backdrop it is not surprising that there is tremendous hunger among the investing public for accessible, low-cost, and reliable advice. While some investors may still seek the services of a traditional advisor—and have sufficient assets to qualify for those services—others seek a different sort of advisory experience, at a different price point, to help them navigate the complexity of saving for retirement and other financial milestones. The availability of digital advice promotes the important policy objective of expanding access to retirement advice to a growing segment of underserved and undersaved Americans.

At the same time, the growing awareness of the importance of fees in driving investment outcomes has led both investors and digital advisors to focus on the benefits of exchange-traded funds (ETFs). The maturation and growth of the ETF market over the last two decades has produced a broad range of products covering different asset classes, markets, styles, and geographies (ICI 2017). ETFs, which are traded intraday and are offered without the sales loads and internal distribution costs that can drive up expense ratios in other investment products, are a transparent, low-cost, and tax-efficient investment option. In addition, the passive index bias that is prevalent in the ETF market fits well with the diversification tenets of Modern Portfolio Theory. The use of passive ETFs allows digital advisors to create and manage inexpensive, broadly diversified global portfolios correlated to particular risk and return characteristics.

The growth of digital advice has also been accelerated by advances in technology that allow for a more personalized, efficient, and seamless user experience. This appeals to the growing number of consumers who expect their financial providers to keep pace with the user experiences offered by other consumer services and who are comfortable relying on digital solutions to help manage their financial lives.[3] Banks and financial services firms are capitalizing on this trend by developing digital advice solutions designed to attract new clients and provide a broader range of services to existing clients (Desai 2016; Flood 2016). Like digital advisors, these traditional advisors also recognize that such solutions appeal to the investing needs and expectations of a previously underserved segment of the investing public (Terekhova 2017).

## Digital Advice is Fiduciary Advice

A key distinction between digital and traditional advisors is the more limited nature of the client interaction in the robo-setting. Nevertheless, the fact that digital advisors do not interface with their clients in the same way as traditional advisors does not mean that they are not fiduciaries to their clients, or that they cannot fulfill the fiduciary standards that govern an investment advisory relationship.

Fiduciary duties are imposed on investment advisors 'by operation of law because of the nature of the relationship between the two parties' (SEC 2013: n.p.). This is made enforceable by Section 206 of the Advisers Act, which applies to all firms meeting the Advisers Act's 'definition of investment adviser, whether registered with the [SEC], a state securities authority, *or not at all*' (SEC 2011a: n.p.). Investment advisors, including digital advisors, have an affirmative duty to act with the utmost good faith, to make full and fair disclosure of all material facts, and to employ reasonable care to avoid misleading clients (*SEC v. Capital Gains Research Bureau, Inc.* 1963). Sections 206(1) and (2) of the Advisers Act make it unlawful for an investment advisor 'to employ any device, scheme, or artifice to defraud any client or prospective client' or to 'engage in any transaction, practice, or course of business which operates as a fraud or deceit upon any client or prospective client' [Investment Advisers Act of 1940 § 206(1) and (2)].

The concepts of fraud in Sections 206(1) and (2) are based on common law principles[4] and include a duty of loyalty and a duty of care. The duty of loyalty refers to the obligation to act loyally for the client's benefit, which requires that the advisor place the client's interests ahead of its own.[5] The duty of care refers to the obligation to act with the care, competence, and diligence that would normally be exercised by a fiduciary in similar circumstances.[6]

As noted above, the Supreme Court has interpreted Sections 206(1) and (2) as establishing a federal fiduciary standard for investment advisors (*SEC v. Capital Gains Research Bureau, Inc.* 1963). Accordingly, it is an accepted legal principle that investment advisors, particularly advisors that are managing client assets on a discretionary basis, are fiduciaries (SEC 2011b). Below we explain the source and parameters of an investment advisor's fiduciary duties, and discuss how these duties—the duty of care and the duty of loyalty—apply to the contours of the digital advisory relationship.

Further, the Staff of the SEC's Division of Investment Management (SEC Staff) took a definitive step towards recognizing digital advisors as fiduciaries in guidance released in February 2017 (February 2017 Guidance) (SEC 2017). This guidance confirms that digital advisors registered as investment advisors with the SEC are subject to the substantive requirements and fiduciary obligations of the Advisers Act, even in the case of digital advisors with more limited business models.

## The Fiduciary Standard of Care is Defined by the Scope of the Relationship

As a threshold matter, no uniform or 'single' standard of care applies to all investment advisory relationships. Under both common law and the Advisers Act, the applicable standard of care may be defined by contract, and the concepts of reasonable care and skill that are at the heart of any standard of care necessarily must be judged in relation to the scope of services agreed to by the client (Frankel et al. 2018).

At common law, the standard of care an agent owes to a principal varies depending on the parties' agreement and the scope of their relationship [Restatement (Third) of Agency § 8.01 cmt. C]. An agent also owes to the principal a duty of care, which requires the agent to act with the care, competence, and diligence agents would normally exercise under similar circumstances. However, the agent and principal may agree to raise or lower the duty of care by contract. Even under trust law, which imposes higher obligations on trustees than exist under agency law, the scope of fiduciary duties is subject to the terms of the trust. A principal component of the common law duty of care is the requirement that a trustee act prudently in light of the purposes, terms, and other circumstances of the trust. The duty of prudence encompasses the duty to exercise reasonable care and skill and to 'act with a degree of caution suitable to the particular trust and its objectives, circumstances, and overall plan of administration' [Restatement (Third) of Trusts § 77, cmt. B]. While the trustee and beneficiary cannot agree to waive the trustee's fiduciary obligations under the duties of loyalty and care in their entirety, trust law, especially trust fiduciary law, is default law that can be modified by the terms of the trust (Laby 2008). Thus, the trustee and beneficiary may agree to modify or relax the default obligations of prudence through the terms of the trust so long as they do not 'altogether dispense with the fundamental requirement that trustees not behave recklessly but act in good faith, with some suitable degree of care, and in a manner consistent with the terms and purposes of the trust and the interests of the beneficiaries.'[7]

Consistent with the common law, an investment advisor may limit the scope of its relationship with a client. In fact, it is not uncommon for investment advisors of all types to limit the scope of their services and authority based on the nature of the advisory relationship with their clients. For example, many traditional advisors prepare financial plans that speak to clients' overall investment objectives and financial circumstances at a particular point in time, thus disclaiming the responsibility to update the information on an ongoing basis. They also may provide asset allocation services or recommend investment strategies by researching and monitoring managers or funds, yet disclaim responsibility for making the underlying investment decisions with respect to those investment strategies or funds. Traditional advisors provide advice in connection with particular transactions by providing transition assistance to institutional investors transferring assets from one investment manager to another, yet disclaim responsibility for selecting individual securities to be bought or sold; they also may provide discretionary investment management services for one segment of a client's overall investment portfolio, and simultaneously disclaim responsibility for the management of the client's remaining assets. Finally, advisors may provide nondiscretionary investment advice that cannot be implemented without the prior consent of a client; or provide pricing or evaluation services that are limited to judging the appropriate price of a particular security or basket of securities.

The SEC has long recognized that investment advisors come in many shapes and sizes (SEC 2011b). Rather than creating a prescriptive regulatory regime based on each discrete business model, the SEC has created a flexible, principles-based regulatory regime focused on an investment advisor's fiduciary duty to 'make full and fair disclosure' of all material facts, including conflicts of interest between the advisor and its clients and 'any other material information that could affect the advisory relationship.'[8] The SEC has generally viewed the negotiation of the terms of an advisory relationship to occur at arm's length, provided that the investment advisor has satisfied its disclosure obligations, including disclosure about the advisor's business, material conflicts of interest, disciplinary information, and other information, so that prospective clients can decide whether to enter into an advisory agreement with the advisor.[9]

Further, in the February 2017 Guidance, the Staff took a flexible, rather than one-size-fits all approach, emphasizing that digital advisors have a wide variety of business models and offer a range of advisory services, and consequently may have a 'variety of means' to meet their regulatory obligations. The SEC Staff therefore validates the concept that digital advisors may define and limit the scope of the advisory services they provide. In this regard, the SEC Staff provided a series of recommendations for how digital advisors may meet their fiduciary obligations under the Advisers Act. We discuss a number of these below.

## Establishing a Reasonable Basis for Digital Advice

Although there is no comprehensive list of the obligations that flow from fiduciary duty under the Advisers Act, it seems clear that part of that duty is to ensure that an advisor has a reasonable basis for its advice (Lemke and Lims 2018). The extent to which a digital advisor's client profiling process provides a reasonable basis for the advice it provides (i.e., its 'suitability') has been a central focus of regulatory guidance and industry commentary. In a typical digital advisory program, an initial asset allocation recommendation is made on the basis of a series of questions (an investor questionnaire) designed to gather information about the client's investment goals for the account. The length and types of information requested by a digital advisor's questionnaire vary from firm to firm. As discussed below, under established regulatory principles and the 2017 Guidance, the information captured in the client-profiling process should be evaluated in relation to the nature of the advice that is provided.

The Advisers Act does not dictate the minimum amount of information that must be collected to make a reasonable determination that investment advice is appropriate for a client. In fact, unlike the investment suitability rules promulgated by the self-regulatory organization for broker-dealers, the Financial Industry Regulatory Authority (FINRA), the Advisers Act does not prescribe the amount or types of client profile information that are required to be collected in any respect. In 1994 the SEC proposed, but did not adopt, a suitability rule[10] that would have required investment advisors to conduct a reasonable inquiry into a client's financial situation, investment experience, and investment objectives before providing advice.[11] However, the proposing release makes clear that 'the extent of the inquiry would turn on what is reasonable under the circumstances.' For instance, a 'comprehensive financial plan' may, according to the proposing release, require extensive personal and financial information about a client, including current income, investments, assets and debts, marital status, insurance policies and financial goals. The implication is that an advisory program that is not offering comprehensive financial planning would not require the collection of such extensive information.

What is required to make a reasonable determination is a qualitative rather than a quantitative inquiry, and the type or amount of information relied upon by an advisor to make a recommendation may vary without compromising the advice. Former SEC Chair Mary Jo White, in public remarks addressing digital advisors, has acknowledged that '[j]ust like a conversation with a "real person" about a client's financial goals, risk tolerances, and sophistication may be more or less robust, so too there is variation in the content and flexibility of information gathered by digital advisors before advice is given' (White 2016: n.p.). Even the more prescriptive FINRA suitability rules provide broker-dealers with the flexibility to omit certain information from a customer profile if the broker-dealer determines that information would not be relevant to making a suitability determination in light of the applicable facts and circumstances (FINRA Rule 2111.04).

The appropriate question is therefore not how *much* information an advisor is collecting, but rather whether the information the advisor decides to collect is appropriate in relation to the nature of the advice that is provided (FINRA 2016). It follows that where advisors, digital or otherwise, provide assistance with specific and identifiable investment goals such as college or retirement savings, they need not collect the same degree of information, or conduct comparable due diligence, to that which may be required for a more expansive investment strategy. In the February 2017 Guidance, the SEC Staff emphasized the importance of designing an investor questionnaire that permits the advisor to collect sufficient information on which to make an investment recommendation. The SEC Staff (2017) outlines the following as key considerations that digital advisors should evaluate when designing their investor questionnaires:

- Whether the questions elicit sufficient information to allow the digital advisor to conclude that its initial recommendations and ongoing investment advice are suitable and appropriate for that client based on his or her financial situation and investment objectives;

- Whether the questions are sufficiently clear, and whether the investor questionnaire is designed to provide additional clarification or examples to clients when necessary; and
- Whether steps have been taken to address inconsistent client responses, such as incorporating into the investor questionnaire design features to alert a client when their responses appear internally inconsistent or implementing systems that automatically flag any inconsistent information provided by a client for further review or follow-up by the digital advisor.

Further, digital advice must be understood in relation to its place in the market. Many clients who choose a digital advisor have affirmatively chosen *not* to enroll in a comprehensive financial planning or investment management service. Instead, these investors have opted for goal-based wealth management (e.g., accumulating for retirement, planning for college education, saving for a vacation home). Rather than lumping all assets together and managing them in relation to a particular benchmark, goal-based wealth management allows clients to create a separate 'bucket' of assets for each goal and define an investment strategy that is unique to that particular goal. Investors continue to have the option of working with an investment advisor that will provide a more comprehensive solution that considers outside resources, debt, financial history, career, anticipated medical expenses, and a myriad of other factors that could potentially influence the advice provided to an investor. However, the cost of such advisory programs will proportionally rise based on the scope of services provided.

## Digital Advisors and Conflict of Interest Mitigation

One of the positive features of digital advisors from a fiduciary perspective is that they typically present fewer conflicts of interest. As fiduciaries, all advisors owe their clients a duty of loyalty [Restatement (Third) of Agency § 8.01 and Restatement (Third) of Trusts § 78(1)]. In common law, this involves refraining from acting adversely or in competition with the interests of clients, and not using clients' property for the advisor's benefit or for that of a third party [Restatement (Third) of Agency§ 8.01–8.05].The duty of loyalty consists of the principles that advisors deal fairly with clients and prospective clients, seek to avoid conflicts of interest, disclose all material facts for any actual or potential conflicts of interest that may affect the advisor's impartiality, and not subrogate client interests to their own. Consistent with common law, the federal regulatory framework governing investment advisors is a disclosure-based regime that does not preclude an advisor from acting where there is an actual or potential conflict of interest, provided that full and fair disclosure is made to clients.

By emphasizing transparent and straightforward fee structures, prevailing digital advice business models inherently minimize conflicts of interest associated with traditional investment advisors. Digital advisory offerings are typically comprised of ETFs that, in comparison to mutual funds, offer little room for revenue streams and payment shares that would otherwise create a conflict of interest for investment advisors (e.g., 12b-1 fees, subtransfer agent fees). The absence of such compensation factors means that comparatively fewer conflicts of interest are present even where digital advisors are affiliated with some of the ETFs that they recommend, and independent digital advisors reduce such conflicts even further. Moreover, digital advisory solutions eliminate the representative-level conflicts of interest typically present in the nondigital advisory context because there is little or no role for financial advisors who receive incentive-based compensation in an online offering. Accordingly, digital advisory solutions are less susceptible to the financial incentives that create conflicts of interest, disclosure, and sales practice and supervisory issues resulting from the compensation paid on accounts recommended and managed by financial advisors (FINRA 2016; SEC 1995).

Importantly, digital advisors remain subject to the fiduciary norms of the Advisers Act and therefore have a duty to make full and fair disclosure of all material facts to, and employ reasonable care to, avoid misleading, clients. As stated by the SEC Staff in the February 2017 Guidance, the information provided by a digital advisor to its clients must be sufficiently specific so that clients are able to understand the advisor's business practices and conflicts of interest, and must be presented in a manner that clients are likely to read and understand (SEC 2017). The SEC Staff views the substance and presentation of disclosures as particularly important in the digital advisor context, because, in the absence of any human interaction, clients may look solely to electronic disclosures in order to make an informed decision about whether to enter into an investment advisory relationship with a digital advisor. As a result, the SEC Staff has noted that digital advisors should consider disclosing certain information regarding the limitations, risks, and operational considerations of certain defining aspects of their business model and advisory services. This includes disclosure about the following areas, among others:

**Methodology and services.** A description of the assumptions and limitations of algorithms used to manage client accounts, together with a description of the particular risks inherent in the use of an algorithm to manage client accounts, an explanation of the degree of human involvement in the oversight and management of individual client accounts (e.g., that investment advisory personnel oversee the algorithm but may not monitor each client's account); a description of how the digital advisor uses the information gathered from a client to generate a recommended portfolio and any limitations, such as whether responses to an informational questionnaire are the sole basis on which advice is provided.

**Limitations and scope of advisory services.** A description of any circumstances that might cause a digital advisor to override the algorithm used to manage client accounts. For instance, digital advisors should disclose whether they might suspend or delay trading or take other temporary defensive measures in stressed market conditions. Further, digital advisors should be precise about the nature and extent of the advisory services that are provided; digital advisors that do not offer a comprehensive financial plan should be precise about how advice is being provided with respect to specific financial goals identified by the client, and digital advisors should further not create the implication that their algorithms consider information outside of an investor questionnaire if that is not the case.

**Conflicts.** A description of any involvement by a third party in the development, management, or ownership of the algorithm used to manage client accounts, including an explanation of any conflicts of interest such an arrangement may create (e.g., if the third party offers the algorithm to the digital advisor at a discount, but the algorithm directs clients into products from which the third party earns a fee). Digital advisors should also disclose any financial incentives they may have to recommend particular investment products, including proprietary ETFs for which they or an affiliate receive advisory fees, licensing fees, distribution and servicing fees, revenue sharing or other compensation.

**Fees and expenses.** An explanation of any fees the client will be charged directly, such as advisory fees, as well as any other costs that the client may bear either directly or indirectly such fees and expenses investors bear in connection with an investment in the underlying investment products, custodial services, and brokerage and other transaction costs.

The SEC Staff further views the presentation of disclosures as a key component in meeting a digital advisor's fiduciary obligations to clients, given that the client relationship and display of key disclosures will take place primarily, if not entirely, through an online or application-based interface. With respect to the timing of disclosure, the SEC Staff suggests that digital advisors present 'key disclosures' prior to the sign-up process, so that information necessary to make an informed investment decision is available to clients prior to entering into an investment advisory relationship. The SEC Staff has also provided guidance on effective disclosure to clients can be made through the types of interactive online interfaces or mobile platforms that are commonly used. Specifically, the SEC Staff recommends that digital advisors emphasize key disclosures through design features such as pop-up boxes, or include interactive text (e.g., hover-over boxes that function as 'tooltips') or other means of providing additional details to clients who are seeking more information (for instance, through an FAQ section).

## Application of the Existing Regulatory Framework for Investment Advisory Services

Digital advisors are a disruptive and competitive alternative to traditional advisors, but the advisory services they offer build upon the traditional advisory framework and its regulatory structure, rather than depart from it. The range of advisory services offered by digital advisors—from online asset allocation recommendations to discretionary managed accounts comprised of diversified portfolios of ETFs—follow well-worn regulatory paths governing the use of electronic media, the use of interactive websites to deliver advice, and the governance of separately managed account and wrap fee programs. Further, the history of these services underscore that the Advisers Act is a flexible and technologically neutral regulatory regime that has accommodated technological change, innovation in products and services, and evolving business models.

**Electronic media.** In 1995, the SEC published its first interpretation on the use of electronic media to deliver regulatory communications. This release and the others that followed recognized the power of technology and, specifically, the electronic distribution of information, to 'enhance the efficiency of the securities markets by allowing for the rapid dissemination of information to investors and financial markets in a more cost-efficient, widespread, and equitable manner than traditional paper-based methods' (SEC 1995). In providing this guidance, however, the SEC also clearly established the principle that the securities laws are technologically neutral. The use of electronic media did not change the substantive provisions of the federal securities laws. In fact, the SEC specifically stated that the guidance set forth in the 1995 release 'addresses only the procedural aspects under the federal securities laws of electronic delivery, and does not affect the rights and responsibilities of any party under the federal securities laws.' In the 1995 release and in a subsequent release in 1996 extending the same principles to the delivery of required communications under the Advisers Act, the SEC was clear that the 'liability provisions of the federal securities laws apply equally to electronic and paper-based media.'

The SEC recognized the presence of digital advice and its compatibility with the framework of the Advisers Act when it adopted the so-called 'Internet Investment Advisers Exemption' in 2002 (SEC 2002). This exemption permits advisors that provide personalized investment advice exclusively through interactive websites to register as investment advisors at the federal level without necessarily meeting the regulatory assets under management threshold that is typically required of an SEC registered advisor. In adopting the exemption, the SEC acknowledged that it had to create a new basis for registration that captured investment advisors that did not technically have regulatory assets under management (the exemption assumed a business model under which advisors were not providing continuous and regular supervisory services). However, the SEC never considered changing the substantive provisions of the Advisers Act to address internet advisors solely because they provide advice through an interactive website.

**Safe harbor from investment company registration.** Digital advisors generally manage client assets on a discretionary basis through separately managed account and wrap programs,[12] which are subject to a longstanding regulatory regime under Rule 3a-4 of the Investment Company Act of 1940 (Company Act). Rule 3a-4 provides advisors that manage discretionary investment advisory programs with a nonexclusive safe harbor from being classified as operating an investment company (or mutual fund), which therefore requires the advisors to comply with extensive compliance and reporting requirements under the Company Act.[13] Rule 3a-4 was designed to address programs where advisors seek 'to provide the same or similar professional portfolio management services on a discretionary basis to a large number of advisory clients having relatively small amounts to invest.' Advisory programs that are organized and operated in accordance with the rule are not deemed to be de facto investment companies so long as they comply with a number of conditions designed to ensure that clients receive individualized treatment and there is no pooling of assets.

In a typical discretionary digital advice program, investors establish individual brokerage accounts to custody their assets, and the digital advisor selects and manages a portfolio of ETFs based on an asset allocation recommended by the advisor and selected by the client. Although many digital advisory services give clients the flexibility to change their asset allocation on a regular basis through a website or mobile application, the digital advisor retains the authority to manage the account based on the asset allocation parameters the client designates. This type of digital advisory service is not a radical departure from the norm. To the contrary, the wealth-management industry, which includes separately managed account and wrap fee programs, today accounts for $6.1 trillion in assets under management (MMI 2018).

Rule 3a-4 contains two key provisions that a digital advisor must satisfy in order to fit within the safe harbor. The first is that 'each client's account in the program is managed on the basis of the client's financial situation and investment objectives and in accordance with any reasonable restrictions imposed by the client on the management of the account'[17 C.F.R. § 270.3a–4(a)(1)]. The second is that the 'sponsor and personnel of the manager of the client's account who are knowledgeable about the account and its management are reasonably available to the client for consultation' [17 C.F.R § 270.3a–4(a)(2)(iv)].

With respect to the first provision relating to individualized advice, it is important to understand that this requirement of Rule 3a-4 is not a suitability rule that requires advisors to collect specific information concerning the financial situation and investment objectives of each client, nor does the rule dictate the quantity of information that must be collected. Rather, the intent of this provision is to negate the inference that the discretionary managed account program is operating as a pooled investment company. In many cases, digital advisors do far more than simply provide online tools that allow self-directed investors to determine their own risk tolerance and investment preferences and then subscribe to a model portfolio designed for investors with similar preferences. Digital advisors may permit customization by giving clients the ability to impose reasonable restrictions on the management of their accounts by designating certain ticker or security limitations. Moreover, digital advisors typically offer many features and tools that a client or financial advisor may use to customize managed account portfolios, including tools designed to optimize an existing portfolio; portfolio allocations that clients may customize to their desired asset class mix; options to select preferences for affiliated funds or apply ESG (environmental, social and governance investing) screens; the ability to retain legacy positions; sophisticated, technology-driven portfolio rebalancing based on market changes, cash in-flows and out-flows, and risk parameters; and asset placement and tax-loss harvesting services. The result is that the digital advisory model enables clients to receive investment advice that is customized to their particular investment goals and needs.

Moreover, digital advisors are 'reasonably available' to clients consistent with Rule 3a-4. The requirement that the manager of the account be reasonably available for consultation is one of many factors that distinguish a separate account holder from a mutual fund investor. A mutual fund investor generally would not have access to the portfolio manager of the fund. But, Rule 3a-4 does not dictate how that access needs to be accomplished. Digital advisors may satisfy this aspect of the safe harbor by making appropriate personnel reasonably available to clients by phone, e-mail, or platform-enabled chat services. In addition, there is no requirement that clients have the ability to discuss their portfolio with the individuals responsible for developing the advice algorithm. Rather, the focus is one whether the client has the ability to communicate with the advisor about questions relating to the management of his or her particular account. Further, Digital advisors typically provide their clients with around-the-clock access to a great deal of interactive real-time information about the holdings, performance and attributes of their accounts. Digital advisors generally make a great deal of information about their investment philosophy and approach available to investors through articles, blogs, and social media posts.

It is not surprising that the application of Rule 3a-4 looks different in the context of a digital offering, but that does not mean that digital advisors are operating unregistered investment companies. To the contrary, under digital offerings clients still receive the benefit of personalized advice and individualized treatment, and they maintain all of the indicia of ownership of the ETFs and other securities held in their accounts. It is important to note that, to date, the SEC Staff has not substantively addressed how digital advisors in particular may meet the Rule 3a-4 safe harbor. However, in the February 2017 Guidance the SEC Staff did remind digital advisors to consider their obligations under Rule 3a-4, and it encouraged them to contact the SEC for further guidance if they believe that their organizations and operations raise unique facts or circumstances 'not addressed' by Rule 3a-4 (SEC 2017).

**Algorithm governance and compliance considerations.** In its February 2017 Guidance, the SEC Staff provided a number of practical recommendations to digital advisors for how they may fulfill their fiduciary and substantive obligations under the Advisers Act. These recommendations are not a departure from the fiduciary standards within the regulatory framework for investment advisors, but rather provide the SEC Staff's perspective on the application of the existing regulatory and fiduciary framework to the digital advice model. In particular, the SEC Staff views the implementation of controls around the development, testing, and back-testing of the algorithmic code used by digital advisors, as well as the post-implementation monitoring of an algorithm's performance, as a key element of an investment advisor's compliance program. The SEC Staff recommends that digital advisors adopt and implement written policies and procedures that provide for testing of their algorithms before, and periodically after, they have been integrated into the digital advisor's platform. Testing should assess whether the algorithmic code is performing as represented, and should occur on all modifications to an algorithm that is currently being used to ensure that it does not adversely affect client accounts. Further, the staff recommends that digital advisors whose algorithms or software modules are developed, owned, or managed by a third party adopt written controls for appropriate oversight of such third parties.

# Digital Advice is Human Advice, with Certain Unique Advantages

Digital advisors possess unique advantages that strengthen the fiduciary relationship and promote the delivery of sophisticated, consistent advice. As discussed below, human intellect and judgment is an integral component of the digital advice model, which itself brings a number of positive features that help to serve clients in innovative and powerful ways.

First, the algorithms used by digital advisors are developed by humans, and they must be monitored and overseen by investment and technology professionals. Rather than take human judgment out of the equation, the skill and investment expertise of these professionals is reflected in the algorithms used to manage client accounts. Digital advisors thus leverage technology to make the value provided by talented portfolio managers and investment professionals available to the broadest universe of clients. Further, digital advice presents strong advantages with respect to the consistency, precision, and predictability of advice (Philippon 2019).Unlike advice delivered exclusively by individual human financial advisors, digital advice can mitigate instances of distraction, fatigue, or human bias that can lead to negative client investment outcomes or costly trade errors.

Additionally, digital advice tools can be used to rebalance portfolios, conduct daily portfolio reviews, and apply new investment insights across many different client accounts in a way that would not be economically or operationally feasible for individual human financial advisors. This promotes faster, smarter, and more effective investment decisions, which can help client portfolios stay on track and within applicable risk thresholds and efficiently allocate even the smallest cash flows across their investment portfolio. Moreover, automated investing enables digital advisors to more effectively implement their compliance programs and meet regulatory obligations. In contrast to advice delivered through individual human financial advisors, which may be offered ad hoc, by phone, or conducted without reliable documentation, digital advice enables the consistent application of investment methodologies and strategies to client accounts, providing transparency, improved recordkeeping, and ease of audit.

Second, humans are operationally present in the delivery of digital advice. A number of digital advisors offer live customer support to assist clients and answer service-related questions. Some digital advisors offer a so-called 'hybrid model' where clients have the ability to speak with live investment advisor representatives. Digital advisors also have the capability to communicate instantaneously through email, mobile applications and their web interfaces to clients at a scale that far surpasses what an individual human financial advisor would be able to accomplish. Such communication features can be used to provide real-time account data or tailored portfolio analysis to clients at intervals of their choosing. Whereas an individual human financial advisor may be unable to reach even a small subset of its clients in a timely manner, a digital advisor may provide important and personalized account updates to its clients on a real-time basis (Fisch et al. 2019).

Finally, digital investment advice platforms are able to leverage behavioral finance insights to offer innovative services and account features in a timely and consistent way. Digital advisors may collect data and observations based on a client's online behavior (either individually or in the aggregate) and use the information to enhance the client experience and promote positive investment outcomes (Barber and Odean 2000).For instance, digital advisors may observe that investors who look at their accounts frequently are more inclined to rebalance their portfolios in the event of minor losses that result from normal intraday market movements. In this way, digital advisors are able to focus on the actual behavioral patterns of clients, and this observed behavior tends to offer insights that clients are not aware of or may not voice to their financial advisors. Digital advisors may leverage such observations to guide investors away from missteps that could lead to negative investment outcomes. In response to actions involving contributions to or transfers from advisory accounts, for example, digital advisors can provide personalized recommendations and reminders that promote positive financial behaviors. These communications may take the form of reinforcement of savings and guidance around transfers that may have undesirable tax consequences (Barber and Odean 2013).

## Conclusion

Under established principles of fiduciary law, digital advisors are capable of fulfilling fiduciary standards that are consistent with the scope and nature of the advisory services they provide to clients. Rather than a radical departure, digital advice reflects the technological evolution of traditional advisory services and thus fits entirely within the existing regulatory framework governing investment advisors.

Digital advice offers the investing public a high-quality, transparent advisory product that entails a different blend of services, generally at a lower cost, than traditional advisors. Digital advice can help achieve the important policy objective of addressing the retirement crisis by providing advice that is accessible to individual investors—both financially and technologically. That includes investors who do not qualify for, or may not be able to afford, traditional advice. Digital advice presents the next step in the evolution of investment advisory services, and when offered pursuant to applicable fiduciary standards and the existing regulatory requirements imposed by the Advisers Act, provides a compelling mechanism to address the demand for low-cost advisory solutions for retirement savings.

## Notes

1. Tax loss harvesting is a strategy used to reduce capital gains tax exposure by selling one or more securities that can generate tax losses to offset capital gains. The proceeds of the sale are generally held in cash or, more commonly, invested in securities that provide similar market exposure.
2. Asset placement considers the tax treatment of different investments in determining whether to hold securities in taxable or non-taxable accounts.

3. A recent survey found that among affluent and high net worth investors, 64% expect their future wealth management relationships to be digital, and for those under the age of 40, 82% expect a digital relationship. A further 69% would be inclined to leave a wealth management firm if a digital component was not integrated into a wealth manager's offering. A separate survey by Wells Fargo/Gallup in found that 54% of investors would trust advice from an adviser that has 'good' applications and digital investing tools more than advice delivered by a less technologically savvy adviser (see Vakta and Chugh 2014; Wells Fargo 2016).

4. *See*, e.g., *In re Brandt, Kelly & Simmons, LLC & Kenneth G. Brandt*, SEC Administrative Proceeding File No. 3–11672 (Sept. 21, 2004) (alleging that respondent 'willfully violated Sections 206(1) and 206(2) of the Advisers Act, *which incorporate common law principles of fiduciary duties*' (emphasis added)).

5. *See* Restatement (Third) of Agency § 8.01 (2006) ('An agent has a fiduciary duty to act loyally for the principal's benefit in all matters connected with the agency relationship.'); § 8.01, cmt. b ('Although an agent's interests are often concurrent with those of the principal, the general fiduciary principle requires that the agent subordinate the agent's interest to those of the principal and place the principal's interests first as to matters connected with the agency relationship.'); *see also* Restatement (Third) of Trusts § 78(1) (2007) ('Except as otherwise provided in the terms of the trust, a trustee has a duty to administer the trust solely in the interest of the beneficiaries, or solely in furtherance of its charitable purposes.')

6. *See* Restatement (Third) of Agency § 8.08 ('[A]n agent has a duty to the principal to act with the care, competence, and diligence normally exercised by agents in similar circumstances.'); *see also* Restatement (Third) of Trusts § 77 (noting that a trustee has a duty to act with the exercise of 'reasonable care, skill, and caution').

7. *See* Restatement (Third) of Trusts § 76 cmt. b(1) ('A trustee has both (i) a duty generally to comply with the terms of the trust and (ii) a duty to comply with the mandates of trust law except as permissibly modified by the terms of the trust. Because of this combination of duties, the fiduciary duties of trusteeship sometimes override or limit the effect of a trustee's duty to comply with trust provisions; conversely, the normal standards of trustee conduct prescribed by trust fiduciary law may, at least to some extent, be modified by the terms of the trust.') See also Restatement (Third) of Trustsat § 77 cmt. d(3).

8. *See Amendments to Form ADV*, Investment Advisers Act Rel. No. 2711 (Mar. 3, 2008) (Mar. 14, 2008) [hereinafter, 'Form ADV Proposing Release'] (*see* General Instruction No. 3 & n.148); *Amendments to Form ADV*, Investment Advisers Act Rel. No. 3060 (July 28, 2010) [hereinafter, 'Form ADV Adopting Release']. The Form ADV Proposing Release reflects the SEC's view that investment advisers should do more than simply identify a potential conflict of interest and should also explain generally how they address that conflict.

9. The Advisers Act recognizes the arm's-length nature of the negotiation of an advisory relationship in not requiring that an investment advisory contract be in writing, or otherwise prescribing its terms, other than with respect to the receipt

of performance compensation, assignment of the contract, and change in ownership where the adviser is a partnership.

10. *Suitability of Investment Advice Provided by Investment Advisers,* Investment Advisers Act Rel. No. 1406 (Mar. 16, 1994).

11. Although the SEC did not adopt the proposed rule, the Staff of the Division of Investment Management has taken the position that 'the rule would have codified existing suitability obligations of advisers and, as a result, the proposed rule reflects the current obligation of advisers under the [Advisers] Act' (*see Regulation of Investment Advisers by the US Securities and Exchange Commission* at 23 n.134).

12. A wrap fee program, as defined by the SEC's Glossary of Terms to Form ADV, is 'any advisory program under which a specified fee or fees not based directly upon transactions in a client's account is charged for investment advisory services (which may include portfolio management or advice concerning the selection of other investment advisers) and the execution of client transactions.'

13. *Status of Investment Advisory Programs Under the Investment Company Act of 1940,* Investment Company Act Rel. No. 22579 [hereinafter, 'Rule 3a-4 Adopting Release'] (Mar. 24, 1997). Note that Rule 3a-4 formalized a long line of no-action letters that went back to 1980 that included conditions on which the rule was ultimately based.

# References

Barber, B. M. and T. Odean (2013). 'The Behavior of Individual Investors,' in G.M. Constantinides, M.Harris, and R.M.Stulz, eds., *Handbook of the Economics of Finance.* Amsterdam, NL: Elsevier.

Barber, B. M. and T. Odean (2000). 'Trading is Hazardous to Your Wealth: The Common Stock Investment Performance of Individual Investors,' *The Journal of Finance* 55(3): 773–806. https://faculty.haas.berkeley.edu/odean/Papers%20current%20versions/Individual_Investor_Performance_Final.pdf (accessed February 22, 2019).

Desai, F. (2016). 'The Great FinTech Robo Advisor Race,' *Forbes.* July 31. http://www.forbes.com/sites/falgunidesai/2016/07/31/the-great-fintech-robo-adviser-race/#267c5eee3812 (accessed February 22, 2019).

Eule, A. (2018). 'As Robo-Advisors Cross $200 Billion in Assets, Schwab Leads in Performance,' *Barron's.* https://www.barrons.com/articles/as-robo-advisors-cross-200-billion-in-assets-schwab-leads-in-performance-1517509393 (accessed February 22, 2019).

FINRA (2016). *Report on Digital Investment Advice.* March. https://www.finra.org/sites/default/files/digital-investment-advice-report.pdf (accessed February 22, 2019).

Fischer, M. S. (2016). 'Can Digital Advice Fill Advisor Gap for Small Investors?' *ThinkAdvisor.* June 20. http://www.thinkadvisor.com/2016/06/20/can-digital-advice-fill-advisor-gap-for-small-inve (accessed February 22, 2019).

Flood, C. (2016). 'Industry Heavyweights put Faith in Robo-Advisers,' *Financial Times*. September 11. https://www.ft.com/content/ba0ea8e4-652a-11e6-8310-ecf0bddad227. (accessed March 25, 2019).

Fox, J. (2018). 'Retirement Risks Keep Rising, and This Is Why,' *Bloomberg*. January 22. https://www.bloomberg.com/view/articles/2018-01-22/retirement-risks-keep-ris ing-and-this-is-why (accessed February 22, 2019).

Frankel, T., A. B. Laby and A. T. Schwing (2018). *Regulation of Money Managers: Mutual Funds and Advisers*. New York: Wolters Kluwer.

Greenwald, L., C. Copeland, and J. Van Derhei (2017). 'The 2017 Retirement Confidence Survey: Many Workers Lack Retirement Confidence and Feel Stressed About Retirement Preparations,' *Employee Benefit Research Institute Issue Brief No. 431*. Washington, DC: Employee Benefit Research Institute. https://papers.ssrn.com/sol3/papers.cfm?abstract_id=2941583 (accessed March 25, 2019). Investment Company Institute (ICI) (2017). *2017 Investment Company Fact Book*. April 26. https://www.ici.org/pdf/2017_factbook.pdf (accessed February 22, 2019).

Kearney, A. T. (2015). 'Robo-Advisory Services Study.' *AT Kearney Report*. http://www. atkearney.ca/documents/10192/7132014/Hype+vs.+Reality_The+Coming+Waves +of+Robo+Adoption.pdf/9667a470-7ce9-4659-a104-375e4144421d (accessed March 25, 2019).

Laby, A. B. (2008). 'The Fiduciary Obligation as the Adoption of Ends,' *Buffalo Law Review* 56 (99): 119.

Lemke, T. P. and G. T. Lins (2018). *Regulation of Investment Adviser*. Eagan, MN: Clark Boardman Callaghan.

Money Management Institute (MMI) (2018). 'Q1 2018 MMI Central – Investment Advisory Solutions Assets Top $6.1 Trillion,' June 12. http://www.mminst.org/mmi-news/investment-advisory-solutions-assets-top-61-trillion-%E2%80%93-q1-2018-mmi-central-now-available (accessed February 22, 2019).

SEC (US Securities and Exchange Commission) (1995). *Use of Electronic Media for Delivery Purposes*, Securities Act Rel. No. 7233. Washington, DC: USSEC.

SEC (US Securities and Exchange Commission) (2002). *Exemption for Certain Investment Advisers Operating Through the Internet*, Investment Advisers Act Rel. No. 2091. Washington, DC: USSEC.

SEC (US Securities and Exchange Commission) (2011a). *General Information on the Regulation of Investment Advisers*. Washington, DC: USSEC. https://www.sec.gov/divisions/investment/iaregulation/memoia.htm (accessed February 22, 2019).

SEC (US Securities and Exchange Commission) (2011b). *Study on Investment Advisers and Broker-Dealers*. Washington, DC: USSEC. https://www.sec.gov/news/studies/2011/913studyfinal.pdf (accessed February 22, 2019).

SEC (US Securities and Exchange Commission) (2013). *Regulation of Investment Advisers by the US Securities and Exchange*. Washington, DC: USSEC. https://www.sec.gov/about/offices/oia/oia_investman/rplaze-042012.pdf (accessed February 22, 2019).

SEC (US Securities and Exchange Commission) (2017). *Robo-Advisers, IM Guidance Update No. 2017–02*. Washington, DC: USSEC. https://www.sec.gov/investment/im-guidance-2017-02.pdf (accessed February 22, 2019).

Philippon, T. (2019). 'The FinTech Opportunity' in J. Agnew and O. S. Mitchell (eds.), *The Disruptive Impact of FinTech on Retirement Systems*. Oxford, UK: Oxford

University Press, pp. 190–217. Semuels, A. (2018). 'This is What Life Without Retirement Savings Looks Like,' *The Atlantic*. February 22. https://www. theatlantic.com/business/archive/2018/02/pensions-safety-net-california/553970/ (accessed February 22, 2019).

Terekhova, M. (2017). 'Morgan Stanley Launches a Robo-Adviser after 6-Month Pilot,' *Business Insider*. December 5. http://uk.businessinsider.com/morgan-stanley-launches-a-robo-advisor-after-16-month-pilot-2017-12?r=US&IR=T (accessed February 22, 2019).

US Securities and Exchange Commission (SEC) (1995). Report of the Committee on Compensation Practices. Washington, DC. https://www.sec.gov/news/studies/bkrcomp.txt

USDOL (US Department of Labor) (2017). *National Compensation Survey: Employee Benefits in the United States*. Washington, DC: Bureau of Labor Statistics. https://www.bls.gov/ncs/ebs/benefits/2017/ebbl0061.pdf (accessed March 25, 2019).

USGAO (US Government Accountability Office) (2017). *The Nation's Retirement System: A Comprehensive Re-Evaluation Is Needed to Better Promote Future Retirement Security*. Washington, DC: USGAO. https://www.gao.gov/assets/690/687797.pdf (accessed February 22, 2019).

Vakta, T. and Smit Chugh (2014). *Self-Service in Wealth Management: Remaining Competitive in a Fast-Changing World*. Paris, France: Capegemini. https://www.capgemini.com/wp-content/uploads/2017/07/self-service_in_wealth_management_whitepaper_2014.pdf (accessed March 14, 2019).

Wells Fargo (2016). *Investor and Retirement Optimism Index Q2 2016*. https://mms.businesswire.com/media/20160719005353/en/535372/5/3571706cInfographics_WF-Gallup_Investor_and_Retirement_Optimism_Index_2Q_2016_en+%281%29.jpg?download=1. (accessed March 14, 2019).

White, M. J. (2016). *Keynote Address at the SEC-Rock Center on Corporate Governance Silicon Valley Initiative*, US Securities and Exchange Commission. March 31. https://www.sec.gov/news/speech/chair-white-silicon-valley-initiative-3-31-16.html (accessed February 22, 2019).

# Part II
# FinTech and Retirement Security

## Chapter 4

# FinTech Disruption: Opportunities to Encourage Financial Responsibility

*Julianne Callaway*

Technology-enabled advancements in the financial services industry have allowed for improvements in customer engagement, education, and personalized product offerings. Investment in financial technology, or FinTech, has dramatically increased in recent years, to a record high $16.6 billion invested in more than 1,000 companies in 2017, according to CB Insights (Wong 2018). Investment in this space has the potential to disrupt the financial services industry and change the way traditional businesses operate. This chapter presents research gathered in support of business initiatives in the life insurance industry to adapt to FinTech disruption. These business plans focus on ways to improve the customer experience and encouraging financial responsibility.

## Drivers of the FinTech Revolution

One driver of the FinTech revolution is the significant generational change taking place: the retirement of the Baby Boom generation coinciding with larger numbers of the Millennial generation entering the workforce. The Baby Boom generation is typically defined as those born in the years following World War II through the early 1960s, and it is currently the largest generational demographic (Fry 2018). The Millennial generation has been referred to as the 'echo' boom, as many in this generation are the children of Baby Boomers. Millennials are those born between the early 1980s and the late 1990s, now 20–35 years old. According to the Pew Research Center (2015), they became the largest portion of the workforce in 2015. The Millennial generation also differentiated from previous generations by growing up in the digital age and attaining high levels of education, with over 60 percent attending college (Council of European Advisors 2014). The economic downturn of 2008 had a profound impact on both the near-retirement Baby Boomer cohort and the graduating Millennial generation. This shared experience means that these two large generations faced economic challenges to their financial security which may hinder their ability to achieve their retirement goals.

Another development with repercussions for the financial services industry is the emergence of data-enabled digital services, prompting a change in advice sources. Consumers can now obtain financial advice from a variety of channels, rather than only through in-person conversations. Consumers can read content online and ask questions within their social network communities. Data also enable consumers to benchmark themselves and compare their needs to those of 'people like me.' Technology has progressed to the point where consumers can ask questions any time of day and receive instantaneous answers. These advances allow for a more personalized consumer experience adapted to the needs of the individual.

An additional factor driving change in this industry is the evolution of employee benefits and the employment landscape. Traditionally, employee benefits provided people with resources to support a secure retirement, including health insurance coverage as well as group life insurance policies. Workers were also able to contribute to their retirement savings through pensions and 401k contributions. Today, by contrast, benefit packages less comprehensive than in the past, and a growing number of people are also employed outside of a traditional workplace. The workforce has changed, with more than one-third of the US workforce participating in the 'gig' economy (Pofeldt 2016). People can now earn money working freelance jobs or as entrepreneurs which provides greater flexibility but often lack traditional employment benefits, including retirement and insurance. These trends have contributed to the development of FinTech solutions and the disruption of the traditional financial services business model.

## Technological Change Democratized Financial Services

Financial advice and protection that were once reserved for the wealthy are now accessible to a greater number of people, due to lower costs to provide these services as well as an increase in the number of methods to communicate with consumers. This development has profoundly changed the life insurance industry, because even though insurance protection serves a social good, historical distribution methods have fallen short in reaching people who may most need coverage. We conducted many consumer interviews to understand how to most effectively adapt offerings to best meet their needs. Consumers explained that, without life insurance protection, loss of a family member would threaten their financial security and future financial stability.

The Life Insurance and Market Research Association (LIMRA) estimates that 30 percent of US households lack life insurance coverage and nearly half have insufficient protection to meet their needs, resulting in a $12 trillion coverage gap (Scanlon 2016). If the primary wage earner in a household were to die, 40 percent of households with children under age 18 report they would have immediate financial trouble, and nearly 70 percent of all households would struggle with everyday living expenses within a few months (LIMRA 2016).

There is tremendous opportunity for the financial services industry to leverage technological advances, which make financial information and tools more accessible, to help meet the needs of consumers who need financial protection.

## Barriers to Financial Protection

Insurance protection is largely an intangible benefit, especially if no claim is made while the customer has coverage. Additionally, consumers have many competing financial priorities, and coverage over a long time horizon can be difficult to conceptualize. The traditional sales process is also a barrier to many consumers, which can contribute to their inertia. A fully underwritten individual life insurance policy typically requires evaluation that can take several weeks before the application is approved. Further, policy language is complicated and time-consuming to research. Moreover, some consumers lack trust in the agent selling the policy and in the insurer to fulfill its claim payment obligations. Many people struggle to achieve their financial goals, and the financial services industry needs to understand the barriers consumers face in their quest for financial security.

## Technology Can Improve Customer Experiences

A subcategory of FinTech is Insuretech; technology solutions designed to address the needs of the insurance industry. Investment in Insuretech has grown 16 percent increase from 2016 to 2017, and more than $8 billion invested since 2012 (Wong 2018). Insuretech investments have focused on building platforms for underwriting, claims payments, and online quoting and application. The solutions are aimed at removing the above-mentioned barriers to obtaining life insurance coverage.

Insurance companies are adapting to the trends impacting the industry in other ways as well. Many are creating digital tools that satisfy consumers' desire for personalization and on-demand access. Data enable customizable product offerings designed to improve their relevance to an individual's particular coverage needs as well as to sustain engagement with the insurer. Simplicity in communication and transparency in the application and purchasing process have the potential to improve consumer trust in the insurance industry.

## Data Sources

The financial services industry has leveraged data from disparate sources to improve the customer experience. For instance, the traditional life insurance underwriting process considered many evidence sources, including the results of medical exams and blood profiles. The process was invasive, expensive, and lengthy—often taking several weeks to reach a decision to accept (or decline) a life insurance application. Life insurance consumers, as well as sales agents, wanted a more streamlined process for assessing risk. According to Art and Sondergeld (2017), half of the life insurers surveyed now have a process in place to utilize technology and additional data sources to accelerate the underwriting process, and only 10 percent of insurance company respondents lack plans to streamline the underwriting process.

Often this involves a triaged approach to assess risk, augmenting traditional data collection with additional information to accelerate acceptance of a subset of applicants based on the absence of concerning evidence. Some examples of data sources currently used include insurance application history, prescription history, driving history, and credit history. If no red flags are found, an individual consumer will be offered insurance at a competitive rate, while the remaining applications require further medical evidence.

Data on an applicant's insurance application history are available from the Medical Information Bureau (MIB), a member-owned organization established in 1902. Insurance company members submit application information to MIB with the intent to identify errors and omissions on an application and to prevent potential fraud. Participating insurers can use the MIB database to validate the accuracy of an insurance application relative to previous applications made by that same individual. MIB is a well-used data source in the life insurance underwriting process; it is used for nearly 90 percent of individual life insurance applications, and all of the widely used in accelerated underwriting programs (MIB 2017; Art and Sondergeld 2017).

Prescription drug data have long been available to pharmacy companies for drug research and development. In recent years, Pharmacy Benefit Managers (PBMs) and PBM aggregators have also provided these data to the life insurance industry to assist in the assessment of mortality risk. This information is valuable to insurers because prescription history is closely related to medical history. Studies have shown that predictive models designed to assess risk can utilize this type of data to segment mortality and enable policy application acceptance without the need to depend on slower, more costly, and invasive tests. Art and Sondergeld (2017) report that more than two-thirds of insurers use prescription drug records to inform their accelerated underwriting programs.

Actuarial studies have also found a statistical relationship between motor vehicle records (MVR) and all-cause mortality experience. Researchers at the Reinsurance Group of America (RGA) analyzed the relationship between mortality and motor vehicle driving records (Rozar and Rushing 2012). Figure 4.1 demonstrates the extra mortality from higher-risk individuals solely due to their driving history. People with one or more major driving violations, such as driving in excess of 30 miles per hour above the speed limit, exhibit higher overall mortality experience. Further, this extra risk increases with the number of violations.

Underwriters have relied on MVRs to assess mortality risk for years; however, MVRs also provide value in accelerated underwriting decisions. For example, a driving record that includes major violations could require additional underwriting evidence to support policy acceptance, while a clean driving record may support an accelerated decision. Similar to prescription drug data, Art and Sondergeld (2017)reported that more than two-thirds of insurers use MVRs to inform their automated underwriting programs.

Following the lead of property and casualty insurers, the life insurance industry has also begun to employ financial credit data provided by the US major credit bureaus to better applicants' mortality risk. Actuarial studies

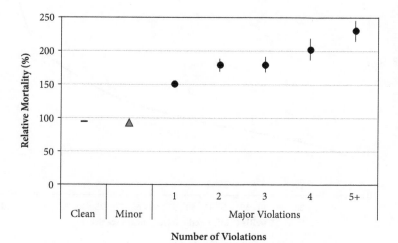

**Figure 4.1**  Relative mortality by number of major violations
*Source*: Data from Rozar and Rushing (2012).

have found an association between an applicant's credit history and his or her mortality risk. For instance, TransUnion and RGA have developed a tool called TrueRisk® Life using components of individual consumer credit data that effectively segments mortality risk even without further underwriting. As shown in Figure 4.2, people with the best 5 percent of TrueRisk® Life scores (96–100), have five times lower mortality than those with the worst percent of scores (1–5) (Kueker 2015).

The use of credit data in accelerated underwriting programs is growing in popularity among insurers. Only 18 percent of companies surveyed by LIMRA use credit data in their accelerated underwriting programs in 2017, but an additional 38 percent of surveyed companies have plans to include this data as an evidence source in the future (Art and Sondergeld 2017). This is significant for life insurance consumers because it reduces the need for intrusive underwriting evidence to assess risk for a segment of applicants. Insurers are able to provide a faster decision to insurance applicants who score well in the model.

The universe of data used to accelerate underwriting decisions continues to expand, as insurers are investigating the protective value of other sources such as electronic health records, fitness data obtained from wearable

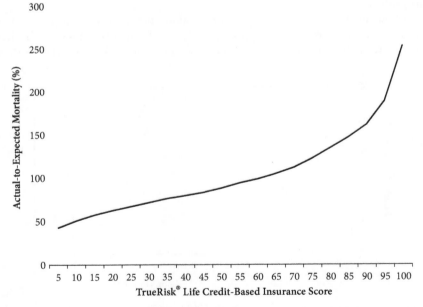

**Figure 4.2** Twelve-year study of US population mortality segmented by a credit-based score

*Source:* Data from Kueker (2015).

Table 4.1  Comparing life expectancy for a 65-year-old man with different conditions

| Description | Estimated life expectancy | Difference from clean |
|---|---|---|
| Clean health | 22 years, 10 months | 0 |
| High blood pressure; cholesterol | 21 years, 10 months | 1 year |
| Prostate cancer | 21 years, 3 months | 1 years, 7 months |
| Diabetes | 19 years, 10 months | 3 years |
| Smoker; BMI 35 | 18 years, 8 months | 4 years, 2 months |
| Recent heart attack | 17 years, 3 months | 5 years, 7 months |
| Decompensated heart failure | 11 years, 1 month | 11 years, 9 months |
| Lung cancer stage IV | 0 years, 11 months | 21 years, 11 months |

*Notes*: Technology, such as RGA's AURA underwriting system is at the heart of our Annuity Risk and Rating Tool (ARRT). ARRT calculates individual life expectancy based on detailed medical history, treatment and symptoms; it has been the bedrock of the UK enhanced annuity market.

*Source*: Life expectancy calculations are based on RGA's Annuity Risk and Rating Tool. In this example, a healthy 65-year-old man could expect to live to age 87 and 10 months.

devices, and connected devices (known as 'the internet of things'). Data and technology used to streamline the life insurance underwriting process also have the potential to improve the financial planning industry. Retirement savings plans will benefit from improvements in longevity projections that are supported by new data sources. For instance, projections for how much money an individual will need to save for retirement often include a life expectancy used to estimate the necessary amount of savings. However, these projections are often oversimplified and based on longevity projections of average individuals. More information can be used to do a better job with retirement planning, as demonstrated in Table 4.1.

A healthy 65-year-old man can expect to live to age 87 and 10 months. By contrast, when specific health conditions are factored in, they have a clear impact on his expected life expectancy. For example, half of overweight smokers will live to 83 years and 2 months. The accuracy of retirement projections could improve if they were based on the more individualized life expectancy projections utilized in life insurance underwriting. In this way, technological advances can help the financial planning process, as customers and advisors seek to better match their wealth trajectories with their longevity.

## End-of-Life Planning Tools

Consumers increasingly want to research financial options on their own schedule. Millennial consumers, in particular, are interested in utilizing technology such as video conferencing and tech services in lieu of financial advisors. Nevertheless, many consumers remain interested in purchasing life insurance with an advisor. According to Finnie et al. (2017), more than half of consumers use the internet to research policy options, but fewer than one-third purchase life insurance online. Our own consumer research highlighted the need for simplicity in financial educational tools and a desire for personal assistance. According to one of the consumers interviewed, 'The insurance information my husband brought home was just charts, charts, charts. I feel overwhelmed with all this information. I would like someone to read it to me.'

While the majority of consumers still rely on the advice of a salesperson to complete the purchase of life insurance products, the network of trusted advisors has expanded. People are increasingly relying on the recommendations and advice of their friends and family, as well as their broader social network. Online content, assessment tools, and calculators all contribute to the financial education support system. That said, navigating the myriad of planning tools remains overwhelming to many consumers. Consequently, end-of-life planning tools are gaining popularity, both as employee benefits and as value-added services from insurers and agents.

Even though the majority of consumers know financial planning is important, many postpone taking steps to protect their future financial security, which in turn becomes a source of stress. In a survey conducted by Allianz, 61 percent of survey participants indicated they were more afraid of outliving their assets than they were of death (Allianz 2010). Yet, in spite of the fear and stress that result from financial uncertainty, there is still a gap between those that intend to buy life insurance and those who actually purchase. This inertia creates emotional and financial costs for consumers.

Financial planning needs extend beyond simply educating consumers about the insurance purchasing decision. They also include services that help families manage the full portfolio of assets associated with an estate plan. Because so much of people's lives is conducted digitally, consumer assets have grown beyond account balances and monthly statements, and as a result are becoming more difficult to manage. Digital assets likely to be lost or destroyed without a digital estate plan include:

(1)  Online accounts, including email and social media;
(2)  Personal documents such as photos and videos;
(3)  Financial and investment accounts;
(4)  Loyalty reward points; and
(5)  Digital data that requires a password to access.

Companies exist that provide estate plan management digitally, offering users the organization of important information, educational support, and clear communication to friends and family during a time of grief. End-of-life planning tools often include a variety of services such as digital storage, wishes that go beyond information in a will, appointing deputies, communicating financial information as well as digital information to family, checklists, and pet care. Companies in this space prominently feature data security. Nevertheless, there are differences in the scope of services provided. For example, Docubank focuses on secure storage of important end-of-life planning files and documents, whereas Everplans offers educational content and financial advisor communication tools in addition to data repository services. Current offerings vary in their format and level of educational detail, from providing a mobile app with simple swipe features for consumers to indicate end-of-life wishes to full-service guidance, storage, and communication tools (Bednar 2017).

End-of-life planning tools can also fill a need for financial planning, helping families navigate confusing financial areas by providing guidance. RGA's consumer research also found that some people are concerned about their loved ones' ability to responsibly manage a life insurance benefit without guidance. This consumer concern is another justification for an expanded financial planning tool kit.

Competiscan reviewed consumer feedback on several 'final wishes' planners and evaluated feedback on ease of understanding, demonstration of expertise, and emotional appeal. It concluded that service providers must be able to strike a balance between providing overly simplistic materials, versus and overwhelming consumers with too much detail. Many consumers value the ability to digitally save documents in a single location, including personal genealogy information.

While finding the right balance of practicality and emotional appeal poses a challenge to creators of end-of-life planning tools, there is tremendous need for financial guidance. Lack of end-of-life planning costs American families an estimated $58 billion in unclaimed benefits that are unknown to beneficiaries. The unclaimed property includes abandoned bank accounts and stock holdings, unclaimed life insurance payouts, and forgotten pension benefits (Hicken 2013). Millennials and Gen-X consumers are attracted to digital self-service platforms, and given that the average age of financial advisors is 50, an expanded service offering would help the financial services industry maintain relevance with digital-savvy consumers (Touryalai 2017).

## Challenges to Saving

Financial challenges that inhibit people's ability to save for retirement also affect whether they can afford life insurance protection. Allison and Harding (2017) note that 52 percent of American workers are stressed about their finances, and 54 percent of those stressed about finances plan to postpone retirement.

Debt is a burden for many Americans. According to the Federal Reserve Bank (2018), non-mortgage debt in 2017 estimated at $3.8 trillion. For many Millennials, this debt is due to a heavy student loan burden, but it also includes debt from home improvement projects, car loans and paying for consumer goods. High levels of debt also compromise budgets with principal and interest payment obligations. Noble (2018) found that nearly half of survey participants stated that too much of their annual income goes toward paying off debt, and 61 percent of survey respondents indicated that debt payment responsibilities negatively impacted their ability to save for retirement.

According to the Common Cents Lab (2017), 90 percent of Americans lack personal savings. Further, 40 percent of those who will reach retirement age in the next 5–10 years report having no money saved for retirement (Common Cents Lab 2017). Because an inability to save is related to spending behaviors, our research evaluated spending needs arising from life events that often coincide with a need for life insurance. We found that those life events included marriage, buying and improving a home, and having a baby.

This research revealed that very few people understand the full cost of purchases related to one of these life events. Even diligent savers without debt felt unsure about how much they would have to save to prepare for such events.

Competing financial priorities is one of the many obstacles to saving, yet consumers have suggested a few techniques financial services companies could employ to help encourage saving. Tools designed to encourage saving can remind consumers of their savings goals, giving a purpose to their saving. This could be as simple as including a picture related to their saving need (such as a baby) on their digital saving tool.

Common Cents Lab (2017) found that consumers save more when they are given a visual representation of the progress they have made toward their saving goals. Our consumer interviews supported the use of positive reinforcements such as a bonus associated with attainment of interim goals.

A number of companies compete in this area of financial technology. One such, Qapital, seeks to help consumers increase savings accounts by 'rounding up' payments to add a small amounts over time to their savings. Other companies, such as Acorns and Stash, utilize technology to democratize services and allow middle-income consumers to formulate their own investment strategies (Murakami-Fester 2017). In order to engage with consumers, such firms must have a strong mobile presence.

FinTech can also provide new tools designed to help consumers spend more wisely. Many financial service offerings are geared only toward saving for a future point in time, without consideration for how to spend money efficiently in the present. To help fill this gap, United Income helps consumers establish a wise post-retirement spending plan (Hughes 2017).

## Wellness

Many insurers are beginning to adopt a holistic view of wellness that includes financial well-being along with physical health. This helps send consumers a message about living longer, more productive, and financially responsible lives supported by insurance-provided wellness benefits. Wellness programs that contribute to healthy lifestyle behaviors may also lead to shorter periods of ill health and disability as people age.

Over 70 percent of the US population is overweight or obese, and this contributes to more than half of the early deaths from related conditions including heart disease, diabetes, and certain cancers (Centers for Disease Control 2016; Macha 2017). Good nutrition, sleep, and exercise all contribute to healthy living, and to the extent that wellness programs can motivate healthy changes, insurance customers will benefit from them as well as improve the financial returns of life insurers. Additionally, the wearable device technology used to verify wellness program activity can also help in earlier detection of conditions such as heart disease and diabetes, which can lead to earlier interventions and extend quality of life.

Technology-driven wellness solutions have many possible applications in the life insurance industry. For instance, people who suffer from chronic conditions often struggle to obtain affordable insurance protection. Consumers seeking to demonstrate responsible management of their health conditions may be able to use a wellness program to differentiate their risk from people who are not active in improving their health. Similarly, technology can enable drug-adherence programs, which also contribute to the improved heath of their users.

Thoughtfully wellness programs can also play a part in healthy aging. Programs focused on mobility can prevent falls and improve strength, thereby enabling seniors to live independently longer at home. Indeed, connected devices in the home can extend this period of independent living, which benefits individuals as well as providers of long-term care insurance coverage.

It is also important for insurers to understand a given technology's capabilities and usability before including it in an insurance wellness program. A wearable technology study of 1,000 employees, their family, and friends, employed five different fitness devices worn for 12 weeks. The researchers found that there was a difference in the metrics captured by the wearable devices. Moreover, comfort of the device contributed to sustained usage;

this was especially true for those wearing the device to measure sleep (Falkous 2016).

Insurance wellness programs have potential to increase the years of healthy independent living as well as lower healthcare costs as people age and move through retirement.

## Conclusion

Technological advances are enabling the financial services industry to develop data-driven, personalized products that are responsive to consumer expectations. The availability of new data sources can improve the customer purchase experience and enable digital sales of financial products, such as life insurance, that historically required invasive and lengthy evaluation.

Helping consumers improve their saving habits as well as fostering informed spending with FinTech will remove some of the barriers that threaten financial responsibility. Programs focused on promoting wellness can improve participants' quality of life. This increases the value of insurance offerings beyond simple financial protection.

## References

Allianz (2010). *Reclaiming the Future: Challenging Retirement Income Perceptions*, Munich, Germany: Allianz White Paper. https://www.allianzlife.com/-/media/files/allianz/documents/ent_991_n.pdf?la=en&hash=22B9CE8151AB813C34696723818B40C4 AF46D62D (accessed February 28, 2019).

Allison, K. E. and A. J. Harding (2017). *2017 Employee Financial Wellness Survey*, London, UK: PWC Report. https://www.pwc.com/us/en/industries/private-company-services/library/financial-well-being-retirement-survey.html (accessed February 28, 2019).

Art, M. M. and E. T. Sondergeld (2017). *Transforming Underwriting*. Windsor, CT: LIMRA Report.

Bednar, J. (2017). 'Web Services Take End-of-life Planning into the Smartphone Age,' BusinessWest.com. http://businesswest.com/blog/web-services-take-end-life-planning-smartphone-age (accessed February 28, 2019).

Centers for Disease Control and Prevention (2016). *Obesity and Overweight*, Washington, D.C.: CDC. https://www.cdc.gov/nchs/fastats/obesity-overweight.htm (accessed February 28, 2019).

Common Cents Lab (2017). *2017 Annual Report—Common Cents Lab*, Center for Advanced Hindsight.

Council of Economic Advisers (2014). '15 Economic Facts About Millennials.' Washington, D.C. https://obamawhitehouse.archives.gov/sites/default/files/docs/mil lennials_report.pdf (accessed February 28, 2019).

Falkous, C. (2016). *Wearable Wellness*, New York, NY: Reinsurance Group of America (RGA). http://www.rgare.com/knowledge-center/media/articles/wearable-wellness (accessed February 28, 2019).

Federal Reserve Bank of New York (2018). *Household Debt and Credit Report*. New York, NY: Center for Microeconomic Data. February: https://www.newyorkfed.org/microeconomics/hhdc.html (accessed February 28, 2019).

Finnie, L., J. Scanlon, and M. Leyes (2017). '2017 Insurance Barometer Study,' LIMRA.

Fry, R. (2018). *Millennials Projected to Overtake Baby Boomers as America's LargestGeneration*. Washington, DC: Pew Research Center. http://www.pewresearch.org/fact-tank/2018/03/01/millennials-overtake-baby-boomers/ (accessed February 28, 2019).

Hicken, M. (2013). '$58 Billion Unclaimed: Is Some of it Yours?' *CNN Money*. January 27. https://money.cnn.com/2013/01/24/pf/unclaimed-money/index.html (accessed February 28, 2019).

Hughes, N. C. (2017). 'The FinTech Startup Helping Retirees with Spending, Not Saving,' *The Next Web*. September 27. https://thenextweb.com/contributors/2017/09/27/united-income/ (accessed February 28, 2019).

Kueker, D. (2015). 'The Power of Big Data: An RGA Case Study,' *RGA Quarterly: Europe*.

LIMRA (2016). *Facts About Life 2016*. LIMRA Report. Windsor, CT. https://www.limra.com/uploadedFiles/limra.com/LIMRA_Root/Posts/PR/_Media/PDFs/Facts-of-Life-2016.pdf (accessed February 28, 2019).

Macha, R. (2017). 'Association between Dietary Factors and Mortality from Heart-Disease, Stroke, and Type 2 Diabetes in the United States,' *Journal of American Medical Association*, 317(9): 912–24.

Medical Information Bureau. (2017). 'Facts about MIB,' MIB Report. Braintree, MA. https://www.mib.com/facts_about_mib.html (accessed February 28, 2019).

Murakami-Fester, A. (2017). 'NerdWallet's Best Money Saving Apps.' *Nerdwallet*. November 8. https://www.nerdwallet.com/blog/banking/best-money-saving-apps/ (accessed February 28, 2019).

Noble, E. (2018). 'Danger Ahead? Impact of Debt on Retirement Saving.' LIMRA Report. Windsor, CT.

Pew Research Center (2015). *Millennial Ssurpass Gen Xers as the Largest Generation in U.S. Labor Force*. Pew Research Center. http://www.pewresearch.org/fact-tank/2015/05/11/millennials-surpass-gen-xers-as-the-largest-generation-in-u-s-labor-force/ (accessed February 28, 2019).

Pofeldt, E. (2016). 'Freelancers Now Make Up 35% Of U.S. Workforce.' *Forbes*. October 6. https://www.forbes.com/sites/elainepofeldt/2016/10/06/new-survey-freelance-economy-shows-rapid-growth/#140052fc7c3f (accessed February 28, 2019).

Rozar, T. and S. Rushing (2012). *An Analysis of Motor Vehicle Records and All-CauseMortality*. St. Louis, MO: Reinsurance Group of America (RGA).

Scanlon, J. T. (2016). *Life Insurance Ownership In Focus—U.S. Household Trends 2016*. LIMRA. September 28. https://www.limra.com/Research/Abstracts_Public/2016/Life_Insurance_Ownership_in_Focus__U_S__Person-Level_Trends_(2016).aspx (accessed February 28, 2019).

Touryalai, H. (2017). 'America's Top Next-Gen Wealth Advisors: Millennials Who Survived 2008 Are Now Managing Billions.' *Forbes.* July 25. https://www.forbes.com/sites/halahtouryalai/2017/07/25/americas-next-gen-wealth-advisors-millennials-who-survived-2008-are-now-managing-billions/#5fb7cea42d1a (accessed February 28, 2019).

Wong, M. (2018). 'Fintech Trends to Watch in 2018,' *CB Insights.* https://www.cbinsights.com/reports/CB-Insights_Fintech-Trends-2018.pdf (accessed February 28, 2019).

# Chapter 5

# Ethics, Insurance Pricing, Genetics, and Big Data

*Robert Klitzman*

Dramatic technological advances in computers and genomics are radically transforming countless aspects of contemporary life, including health care, life expectancy, retirement and financial planning, posing opportunities, but also profound ethical and public policy challenges. In the future, genetic testing promises to affect many aspects of health care and estimates of life expectancy in ways that can significantly shape decisions about various aspects of financial planning. Data that include genetic information are, for instance, yielding new insights on how best to diagnose, prevent, and treat many diseases, from cancer to Alzheimer's, and revealing factors associated with aging and longer or shorter lifespans. Such data can thus potentially influence perceived needs for, and pricing of, life, disability, and long-term care insurance (Callaway 2019), and various other financial products and services. Individuals who have genes that increase risks for Alzheimer's, for example, may decide to retire earlier and/or try to purchase more insurance than they would otherwise, and have different investment goals or needs. Based on genetic information, individuals may also decide not to have children, or to try to screen embryos for certain diseases, which may or may not succeed.

As scholars and others probe how technologies may disrupt and alter financial services and pension planning, it is vital to consider how computer, genetic, and other technologies are combining and transforming each other to refashion these domains.

## The Case of Life Insurers

The effects on life insurance raise many of these issues in stark relief, and are thus explored below, as a case-in-point. Critical questions emerge, for instance, regarding whether companies selling life, disability, and long-term care insurance should have access to consumers' genetic information, and whether certain individuals, due to their genetics, will consequently be denied coverage or face unaffordable prices. In deciding whether to sell such insurance policies and at what price, insurers routinely consider applicants' risk factors such as smoking and obesity, but society is now beginning to ask whether genetic information should be treated differently.

## Background Concerning Genetics

Genes consist of deoxyribonucleic acid (DNA) that in turn is composed largely of four nucleotides: guanine, cytosine, thymine, and adenine (abbreviated GCTA). Sequences of thousands of these nucleotides (commonly described using these abbreviations of four 'letters') code particular proteins that have various functions in the human body. Periodically, one such letter mistakenly replaces another—a misspelling. Some such misspellings are benign, while others may selectively harm or help the organism, significantly increasing or decreasing morbidity and mortality.

Technological advances have yielded inexpensive genetic testing, including whole genome sequencing. Over the past two decades, the cost of sequencing one individual's genome has fallen dramatically from several hundred million to less than one thousand dollars (though that current cost does not include interpretation of the information). Yet questions of privacy, confidentiality, and potential stigma and discrimination emerge. Direct-to-consumer genetic testing companies such as 23andme have sold their files on one million customers' genomic information to pharmaceutical companies for $60 million (Herper 2015). This raises additional ethical questions regarding ownership of such data. The rapid spread and expansion of big data have thus made genetic information more cheaply and easily shared, sold, and resold, either with or without individuals' knowledge, understanding, willingness, or explicit permission. Questions surface regarding how readily these data can identify individuals, whether the uses of these shared data sets should be limited in any ways, and if so, who and how they should decide.

With just a few other bits of data about an individual (e.g., date of birth and zip code), genomic data can be identifying, raising possibilities of discrimination (Erlich and Narayanan 2014). Science fiction scenarios as in the film *Gattaca* highlight public fears of potential misuses of genetic data. In the US, the Genetic Information Nondiscrimination Act (GINA; US Equal Employment Opportunity Commission 2008) currently bars use of genetic information for health insurance underwriting decisions, but not for life, long-term care, or disability insurance.

The plummeting cost and widening use of genetic testing make these issues ever more pressing. Individuals at risk of serious diseases that are associated with genetic tests may fear loss of insurance coverage or higher costs, and thus avoid genetic tests that might aid the prevention, diagnosis, or treatment of the disease. In the future, for instance, hospitals may sequence the genes of all patients who enter the institution, using left over blood samples, and store the information in large databanks. Questions therefore emerge of who should have access to such information—whether any researcher, pharmaceutical company, law enforcement official, school, insurer should potentially see the data and if so, to what specific information—for example, if certain identifiers should first be removed, and if so, which. US policymakers recently wrestled with a few of these dilemmas in revising the so-called Common Rule (Office for Human Resource Protections 2009, 2016), regulating human subjects research, including use of large biobanks. The revised Common Rule (2016) allows for broad onetime consent for unspecified future research uses, provided certain privacy protections are met. What remains to be determined is how exactly such regulations will be implemented, what unanticipated challenges may arise, what kinds of patient consent may be needed in other situations, and whether any restrictions should be placed on data sharing. Questions also persist regarding whether all patients will find these situations acceptable or might avoid certain tests or medical care as a result.

Problems also arise of potential misinterpretation by both providers and patients of genetics, statistics (e.g., absolute vs relative risks), and genetic tests (concerning relatively large numbers of variants of uncertain significance). Levels of understanding of genetics are low among providers, including most physicians. Most internists rate their knowledge as very/somewhat poor concerning genetics (73.7 per cent) and guidelines for genetic testing (87.1 percent), and most felt they need more training on when to order tests (79 percent), how to counsel patients (82 percent), interpret results (77.3 percent), and maintain privacy (80.6 percent) (Klitzman et al. 2013).

Concerns arise, too, given noted examples of hacking of data from major corporations and institutions. Violations of confidentiality have occurred through various means, both intended and accidental (Rouse et al. 2019).

## Challenges Concerning Life Insurance

Life insurance permits pooling of the financial risks of unanticipated disability, chronic disease, or premature death, providing a key social value, preventing survivors from becoming impoverished after a wage-earner dies. Large numbers of policyholders come to share these risks.

But as more consumers obtain genetic testing, often on their own, actuarial risk assessments will become more complicated (Klitzman et al. 2014). Consumers may discover that they possess genes that increase their risks of sudden cardiac or other premature death or Alzheimer's disease or other conditions that may require long-term care. These individuals may not disclose these test results to insurers, but buy insurance. People with highly penetrant genes for diseases that lack effective prevention or treatment report being advised to undergo anonymous testing, and if they learn they have the mutation, to purchase life, disability, and long-term care insurance (Klitzman 2012). Individuals who learn that they have genes associated with increased risks of Alzheimer's, for instance, are 2–3 times more likely to purchase long-term care insurance or to plan to do so (Taylor et al. 2010). Another study of individuals testing for genes associated with Alzheimer's disease found no significant differences in health, life, or disability insurance purchases, but individuals who learned that they had these genes were 5.76 times more likely to alter their long-term care insurance (Zick et al. 2005). Knowledge asymmetry can result if consumers have such information while insurers do not, causing 'adverse selection' and uneven playing fields.

Rothschild and Stiglitz (1976) have suggested that asymmetric information could significantly affect insurance markets. Yet in analyzing data on annuities in the UK, Finkelstein and Poterba (2004) found that asymmetric information may affect certain aspects of consumer behavior, but not others. Specifically, individuals who expected to live longer tend to purchase more 'back-loaded' policies (that, over time, pay more per year), while people who expect to live for shorter periods tend to purchase policies that provide payouts to the consumer's survivors. Nevertheless, asymmetric selection did not appear to affect the size of the annuities purchased (Finkelstein and Poterba 2004). These results suggest the need to look at multiple aspects of life insurance policies that such asymmetric knowledge can affect. As one strategy for diminishing potential adverse selection, Brown and Warshawsky (2013) have suggested combining annuities and long-term care insurance policies, pooling these products. Whether such an approach will reduce adverse selection due to genetic testing is unclear.

If insurers decide to access genetic information, they could potentially do so in several ways: through family history, medical records, asking applicants if they or family members have had genetic tests performed, and asking applicants to undergo such tests. The growth of electronic health records (EHRs) heightens the accessibility of such data. Genetic test results are increasingly becoming parts of EHRs, and insurance applications regularly request releases of medical records.

Indeed, insurers are currently debating how to address these issues. In the UK, life insurers have accepted a moratorium on using genetic information (Association of British Insurers 2011). In the US, one American life insurance executive has stated that his company would ask for such genetic information but did not wish to be the first to do so (Peikoff 2014).

A group of Canadian and European authors (Joly et al. 2014) has articulated a set of broad questions requiring further examination along these lines.

In the US, however, life insurers remain uncertain what to do. Scientific understandings of genomics are rapidly evolving. Though some have argued that 'genomic information about currently known common variants seldom substantially affects mortality risk estimation that is already based on phenotype and family history' (Klitzman et al. 2014: 2), genomic risk assessments can be more accurate for highly penetrant disorders, than prognostications based on family history. Even in a family whose parents both had breast cancer and carry a BRCA gene, for example, a woman may be found to not have the mutation, thereby lowering her risk significantly. Many consumers' genomic information may ultimately assist diagnosis, treatment and prevention, reducing risks. Knowledge of the presence of certain genes can motivate individuals to reduce their risk behaviors and pursue enhanced medical interventions. Insurers will need to appreciate how individuals without mutations for lethal disorders have lower risks than do the general population.

As seen in Table 5.1, nations differ considerably in how they confront these issues. For instance, France and Germany have established full moratoria on insurers' use of genetic test results, while Australia and Canada have instituted partial moratoria (Knoppers et al. 2004).

TABLE 5.1   Moratoria on the use of genetic information by life insurance companies

| Yes | No | Partial |
|---|---|---|
| Canada | Austria | Australia |
| Finland[a] | Belgium | Canada |
| France[a] | Bulgaria | Greece |
| Germany[a] | Chile | New Zealand |
| Ireland[a] | Cyprus | South Africa |
| New Zealand | Czech Republic | |
| South Africa | Denmark | |
| Sweden[a] | Estonia | |
| Turkey | Georgia | |
| The United Kingdom[a] | Hungary | |
| | Iceland | |
| | India | |
| | Israel | |
| | Italy | |
| | Japan | |
| | Luxembourg | |
| | South Korea | |
| | Spain | |
| | Switzerland | |

*Note.* [a] The amounts and expiration dates vary
*Source*: Knoppers et al. (2004).

US federal legislation does not directly comment on life, disability, or long-term care *insurers using genetic information,* and state laws range considerably. Vermont and a few other states prohibit use of genetic information, while others bar use of genetic tests for certain conditions such as sickle-cell trait (e.g., in North Carolina). New York requires specific informed consent for genetic testing. Wisconsin requires that underwriting reflects actual risks (National Human Genome Research Institute 2018). States thus range from 'strong' to 'no protection.'

Insurers should avoid unfair discrimination, but the meaning of this concept can differ, especially in the context of genetics (Klitzman et al. 2014). Definitions of 'unfairness' can involve weighing the competing interests of consumers vs. insurers. Insurance companies that know consumers' genetic test results can stratify risks more accurately. At the same time, insurers may make conservative business decisions, overestimating risks in ways that lead to denials of coverage or significantly increased costs for certain consumers.

While scientific knowledge about the roles and predictiveness of many genes is rapidly advancing, many uncertainties persist. Studies suggesting that particular genes are highly associated with certain diseases have frequently failed to be replicated. Genetics research is often biased, selectively focusing on severely ill patients, rather than the general population, thus leading to overestimations of risks. Use of genetic information could thus result in many individuals unjustifiably being priced out of the life insurance market.

## Possible Solutions

To address these concerns, several solutions are possible. First, government policies could prohibit all insurers from using any genetic information. In such a case, however, asymmetrical knowledge and adverse selection could ensue. Presumably, insurance companies would then seek to amortize the effect, increasing rates for all consumers. And some consumers may object, wary of individuals with mutations who disproportionately buy insurance. Research is thus needed to gauge how potential customers would view these trade-offs.

Second, insurers could be allowed access to all genetic information they seek. Unfortunately, some consumers might then be unable to obtain insurance.

Third, insurers could be permitted to obtain genetic information only about certain pre-defined, well-characterized, highly-penetrant genes. Consumers with certain genes who reduce their risks through effective treatment or prevention would have prices lowered accordingly. A list of such highly predictive tests could be determined, and clearly listed. The number of applicants excluded from coverage would thus presumably be reduced. Extreme care and caution would be needed, however, since most genes are not very penetrant, and environmental and other factors are involved in whether, when and how symptoms may occur. How much insurance prices would vary based on the presence or absence of these genes is also unclear.

Fourth, all individuals could be allowed to obtain a certain modest amount of insurance, with insurers able to obtain genetic test results from consumers who wish to buy additional coverage. This situation currently exists in the UK, for instance, since individuals there must have life insurance to obtain a mortgage.

Since life insurance provides a social benefit, public policy makers can seek to maximize its availability. Accordingly, the option of providing a certain modest amount of insurance to everyone may have certain advantages. Currently, in the US, social security offers some retirement annuity, disability insurance, and survivors' insurance to all who contribute. Medicaid and Supplemental Security Income also provide some long-term care coverage and disability benefits, but they favor lower-income individuals and families. Moreover, the benefits provided for living expenses (as opposed to health care) are relatively limited for many individuals. Some employers also offer varying degrees of life insurance coverage, though policies range widely in generosity and cost.

If life insurers do access genetic information, input from genetic and policy experts and public transparency will be crucial in establishing which genes should be included. More population-based research is also vital to determine accurately the unbiased prevalence and natural history of these genetic markers and disorders. If insurers request information on results of genetic tests, significant caution is needed since patients may consequently be wary of undergoing such testing, even when it may potentially aid their heath. Insurance policies could disincentivize patients from pursuing genetic testing that may be medically helpful, because of concerns about consequent diminished future insurability. Genetic test results differ from other medical data since individuals cannot alter their genes, as they can their weight, diet, and amount of physical exercise. An individual's genetic test results can also unfairly impede family members' insurability.

Key questions arise, too, regarding how companies allowed to access genetic information would or should do so. Insurers might only inquire whether individuals or family members have histories of certain specific conditions, or ever undergone genetic testing, and if so, to self-report the results. Alternatively, insurers might require potential customers to undergo genetic testing and submit the data.

Major challenges would also arise because many individuals have variants of uncertain significance. Given the thousands of letters in each DNA sequence, scientists remain unsure whether certain gene variants in fact impose major dangers, cause only slight impairments, are in fact benign, or even are protective against a disease. Thus genetic test sequencing yields high amounts of uncertainty, and deep questions arise regarding how insurers will view and handle such ambiguities. Companies may want to drastically raise costs for, or exclude many consumers, but such decisions may be unwarranted since genetic risks may be minor, unlikely, and/or potentially offset by other biological or environmental factors.

Economic models of the impact of using genetic testing tend to show that outcomes depend on the assumptions imposed (Macdonald and Yu 2011; Howard 2014). One model, for instance, assumed that 100 percent of people with a particular high-risk gene will be tested over their lifetimes (Howard 2014). Yet this figure seems unrealistically high, at least presently, as well as in the near future. Indeed, rates of lifetime uptake of genetic testing in the US remain very low: no more than 20 percent of individuals at risk of HD have undergone testing, with only 14.7 percent of at-risk individuals doing so over 20 years in Northern Ireland (Morrison et al. 2011). For diseases such as breast cancer, the rates are below about 20 percent (Childers et al. 2017). Granted, such rates may increase if insurance company policies change, yet many people are wary of undergoing genetic tests, due to fears of stigma and discrimination. Moreover, the US has very few genetic counselors, making it unlikely that consumers could get the information needed when they are tested (Bureau of Labor Statistics 2018).

## Conclusion

Federal and state policymakers, industry stakeholders, academic researchers, and others need to examine these questions carefully. Public policy in this area could influence whether patients opt to undergo genetic tests for medical reasons, ultimately helping or impeding individual and public health.

These issues also have critical implications for future research, underscoring needs to assess consumer attitudes regarding these tradeoffs. For instance, it is not yet known how much consumers would pay to avoid genetic testing. Additional research can elucidate views and attitudes in ways that might inform government and industry decisions. An examination of insurance company policies and decisions regarding genetics is also important. It may also be important to establish an independent ombudsoffice to receive and review claims of unfair discrimination, when they arise. Public trust in health care providers and institutions, government policymakers, and insurers is crucial, as the lives and welfare of countless individuals are at stake. Future research is also critical on how these technologies will affect other consumer and industry choices as well. For example, it would be important to learn whether and to what degree certain consumers will be more or less likely to seek certain kinds or amounts of financial products or services, and whether genetic data will affect decisions about financial portfolios and annuity pricing, and if so, how, and what challenges will emerge as a result.

In short, to understand the impact of new technologies on individual and company decisions regarding financial products, several complexities need to be considered. Computer technologies may alter not only the types of products offered, but also consumers' preferences based on information about themselves that technology provides. The term 'FinTech' should, arguably, thus be expanded from the way it is now sometimes used, to address how a wide variety of new technologies have financial implications for both individuals and financial institutions. Given how rapidly computer capabilities and analytics and genomic technologies are advancing and evolving, these domains will continue to be critical to monitor and examine.

## Acknowledgements

This research was funded in part by a grant from the National Human Genome Research Institute: P50HG007257. The author has no financial conflicts of interest to disclose. The authors would like to thank Kristina Hosi, Charlene Sathi, and especially Patricia Contino, for assistance in preparation of this manuscript.

## References

Association of British Insurers (2011). *Concordat and Moratorium on Genetics and Insurance.* UK: Association of British Insurers. https://webarchive.nationalarchives.gov.uk/20130123204306/http://www.dh.gov.uk/en/Publicationsandstatistics/Publications/PublicationsPolicyAndGuidance/DH_4105905 / (accessed March 25, 2019).

Brown, J. and M. Warshawsky (2013). 'The Life Care Annuity: A New Empirical Examination of an Insurance Innovation that Addresses Problems in the Markets for Life Annuities and Long-term Care Insurance.' *The Journal of Risk and Insurance,* 80(3): 677–703.

Bureau of Labor Statistics (2018). 'Occupational Outlook Handbook Genetic Counselors.' *US Department of Labor.* https://www.bls.gov/ooh/healthcare/genetic-counselors.htm (accessed March 1, 2019).

Callaway, J. (2019). 'FinTech Disruption: Opportunities to Encourage Financial Responsibility' in J. Agnew and O. S. Mitchell eds., *The Disruptive Impact of FinTech on Retirement Systems.* Oxford, UK: Oxford University Press, pp. 61–74.

Childers, C. P., K. K. Childers, M. Maggard-Gibbons, and J. Macinko (2017). 'National Estimates of Genetic Testing in Women with a History of Breast or Ovarian Cancer.' *Journal of Clinical Oncology*, 35(34): 3800–6.

Erlich, Y. and A. Narayanan (2014). 'Routes for Breaching and Protecting Genetic Privacy.' *Nature Reviews Genetics*, 15(6): 409–21.

Finkelstein, A. and J. Poterba (2004). 'Adverse Selection in Insurance Markets: Policyholder Evidence from the UK. Annuity Market.' *Journal of Political Economy*, 112(1): 183–208.

Herper, M. (2015). 'Surprise! With $60 Million Genentech Deal, 23andMe has a Business Plan.' *Forbes.* January 6. https://www.forbes.com/sites/matthewherper/2015/01/06/surprise-with-60-million-genentech-deal-23andme-has-a-business-plan/#40dc97f02be9 (accessed March 1, 2019).

Howard, R. C. W. (2014). *Report to CIA Research Committee: Genetic Testing model: If Underwriters Had No Access to Known Results.* Document 214082: Canadian Institute of Actuaries. http://www.cia-ica.ca/docs/default-source/2014/214082e.pdf (accessed March 1, 2019).

Joly, Y., H. Burton, B. M. Knoppers, I. N. Feze, T. Dent, N. Pashayan, N. S. Chowdhury, W. Foulkes, A. Hall, P. Hamet, N. Kirwan, A. Macdonald, J. Simard, and I. Van Hoyweghen (2014). 'Life Insurance: Genomic Stratification and Risk Classification.' *European Journal of Human Genetics*, 22(5): 575–9.

Klitzman, R., W. Chung, K. Marder, A. Shanmugham, L. J. Chin., M. Stark, C.-S. Leu, and P. S. Appelbaum (2013). 'Attitudes and Practices Among Internists Concerning Genetic Testing.' *Journal of Genetic Counseling*, 22(1): 90–100.

Klitzman, R., P. S. Appelbaum, and W. K. Chung (2014). 'Should Life Insurers Have Access to Genetic Test Results?' *JAMA*, 312(18): 1855–66.

Klitzman, R. (2012). *Am I My Genes? Confronting Fate and Family Secrets in the Age of Genetic Testing.* New York: Oxford University Press.

Knoppers, B. M., Godard, B., and Joly, J. (2004). 'A. Comparative International Overview,' in M. A. Rothstein, ed., *Genetics and Life Insurance: Medical Underwriting and Social Policy (Basic Bioethics).* Cambridge: The MIT Press, pp. 173–94.

Macdonald, A. S., and Yu, F. (2011). 'The Impact of Genetic Information on the Insurance Industry: Conclusions from the 'Bottom-Up' Modelling Programme.' *ASTIN Bulletin: The Journal of the IAA*, 41(2): 343–76.

Morrison, P. J., Harding-Lester, S., and Bradley, A. (2011). 'Uptake of Huntington Disease Predictive Testing in a Complete Population.' *Clinical Genetics*, 28: 1–6.

National Human Genome Research Institute. (2018). Genome Statute and Legislation Database. https://www.genome.gov/policyethics/legdatabase/pubsearch.cfm (accessed March 1, 2019).

Office for Human Research Protections. (2009; 2016). *Federal Policy for the Protection of Human Subjects* ("Common Rule", revised January 15, 2009; effective July 14, 2009; content last reviewed February 16, 2016). https://www.hhs.gov/ohrp/regulations-and-policy/regulations/common-rule/index.html (accessed March 25, 2019).

Peikoff, K. (2014). 'Fearing Punishment for Bad Genes.' *The New York Times.* April 7. https://www.nytimes.com/2014/04/08/science/fearing-punishment-for-bad-genes.html (accessed March 1, 2019).

Rothschild, M., and Stiglitz, (1976). 'Equilibrium in Competitive Insurance Markets: An Essay on the Economics of Imperfect Information.' *The Quarterly Journal of Economics*, 90(4): 629–49.

Rouse, T., D. Levine, A. Itami, and B. Taylor (2019). 'Benefit Plan Cybersecurity Considerations: A Recordkeeper and Plan Perspective,' in J. Agnew and O. S. Mitchell (eds.), *The Disruptive Impact of FinTech on Retirement Systems*. Oxford, UK: Oxford University Press, pp. 86–103.

Taylor, D. H., Cook-Deegan, R. M., Hiraki, S., Roberts, J. S., Blazer, D. G., and Green, R. C. (2010). 'Genetic Testing for Alzheimer's and Long-Term Care Insurance.' *Health Affairs*, 29(1): 102–8.

US Equal Employment Opportunity Commission (2008). *The Genetic Information Nondiscrimination Act of 2008*. https://www.eeoc.gov/laws/statutes/gina.cfm (accessed March 1, 2019).

Zick, C. D., Mathews, C. J., and Roberts, J. S. (2005). 'Genetic Testing for Alzheimer's Disease and its Impact on Insurance Purchasing Behavior.' *Health Affairs (Millwood)*, 24(2): 483–90.

Chapter 6

# Benefit Plan Cybersecurity Considerations: A Recordkeeper and Plan Perspective

*Timothy Rouse, David N. Levine, Allison Itami, and Benjamin Taylor*

Plan sponsors and fiduciaries[1] have traditionally relied on advisers—from attorneys to accountants to benefit consultants—to help guide decisions with respect to their retirement plans. For decades, a cornerstone of this assistance has been making recommendations about retirement plan investment portfolios. With the rise of both defined contribution (DC) plans and cyberattacks on financial institutions, a number of plan sponsors and their advisers have started to focus more time and resources on the security of their plan data, including the participant information held by service providers.

As plan sponsors and their advisers ask these providers more questions about cybersecurity, resistance to answering those inquiries has also risen. Service providers recognize the right of plan sponsors to confirm their participants' data is protected but fear the information, if distributed, could help cybercriminals breach systems.

Government regulators continue to grapple with how to develop workable regulatory structures. Rules by nature limit how providers can operate, which in turn helps cybercriminals focus their efforts at undermining those regulations. The United States Department of Labor (DOL) and the Employee Retirement Income Security Act of 1974 (ERISA) Advisory Council have, consistent with the flexibility adopted in other parts of ERISA, not required one single approach to ensure cybersecurity. States too have entered the cybersecurity discussion but, given ERISA preemption standards and the multistate nature of many retirement plans, face many challenges in imposing their own requirements upon ERISA plans.

The retirement industry itself has begun to develop its own solutions by working with all stakeholders—service providers of all shapes and sizes as well as plan sponsors. In this chapter, we present a solution for the challenge of verifying the cybersecurity capabilities of providers without revealing information that could help cybercriminals. The potential solution we present in this paper relies on attestations provided by trusted third parties to audit the providers with a consistent set of standards. Since it is not a regulated solution, this approach is flexible enough to allow industry members to use whatever data security frameworks they feel are most appropriate for their organizations. Yet while providers are free under this potential solution to use frameworks of their choosing, the reporting of the controls used and how these controls were tested is designed to fit a uniform basic framework.

This chapter discusses the development, the components, and the communications process for this uniform basic framework, incorporating the perspectives of an investment consultant, a data security professional, and two lawyers. Retirement plans commonly employ advisers to assist with fiduciary oversight tasks such as selecting funds, benchmarking fees, and choosing third-party vendors such as recordkeepers, trustees, and custodians. These advisers include investment consulting firms, accountants, attorneys, and other industry experts. The vendor selection process is often led by investment consulting firms. The core competencies of these consulting firms are typically services such as asset allocation, capital market research, investment manager selection, monitoring, and other affiliated services. For many of these firms, the optimal approach to conducting vendor due diligence on complex administrative tasks has been to rely on third parties—whether auditors, attorneys, or other services—to verify the accuracy and thoroughness of the vendor's procedures. As DC plans have grown to be a larger part of the marketplace, these consulting firms shifted focus from defined benefit (DB) to DC services, and that shift included developing the ability to select and monitor recordkeepers and custodians.

Until now, firms conducting most of the vendor search and due diligence services in the marketplace have not had a primary focus on matters such as cybersecurity. Yet a handful of leading-edge firms has been developing ways to help plan sponsors evaluate the cybersecurity protocols of their service providers.

At present, there is no consensus within the industry regarding which cybersecurity framework constitutes a 'best practice' approach. Additionally, the major frameworks address the matter slightly differently, and the implementation of each framework introduces additional variability.

The process of assessing security is further complicated by a destructive information cycle. Recordkeepers have significant incentives to reveal only a limited amount of information about their cyber defenses, because hackers can learn from extensive revelations to adapt their methods and avoid detection. This means that recordkeepers often rationally respond with only limited information about cyberattacks. This, in turn, causes some plan sponsors and consultants to react with renewed vigor in their efforts to confirm the adequacy of defenses, which can lead to either frustration or to recordkeepers complying with the requests, weakening their defenses.

There is significant room to improve the measurement of security within the vendor community, and later sections of this chapter will address the efforts SPARK and the ERISA Advisory Council, among others, have made in that direction. Ultimately, it is clear that the lack of cybersecurity expertise in the adviser community, the need for plan sponsors to protect participant data, and the lack of a uniform standard or process for third-party audits of cybersecurity measures, all call for a solution. That solution will ultimately very likely include an industry standard that permits third-party audit.

## Existing Regulatory Structure

**Gramm Leach Bliley.** The 'Safeguard Rule' of the Gramm-Leach-Bliley Act of 1999 (GLBA) requires that covered US financial institutions safeguard sensitive data (15 U.S.C. 6801). Businesses that are significantly engaged in providing financial products or services, such as banks and brokers, are covered financial institutions that must safeguard customers' personal information. This personal information includes nonpublic information that is personally identifiable financial information (known as National Provider Identifier, or NPI) collected by the financial institution. Items such as names, social security numbers, debt and payment history, and account numbers can be NPI when provided by the customer to the financial institution.

According to the law, the goal of the Safeguard Rule is to:

> Ensure the security and confidentiality of customer records and information; protect against any anticipated threats or hazards to the security or integrity of such records; and protect against unauthorized access to or use of such records or information that could result in substantial harm or inconvenience to any customer.    (5 U.S.C. 6801(b)).

It establishes standards relating to physical, technical, and administrative information safeguards. It also requires a written information security program that contains certain basic elements, has a continuous life-cycle, and is subject to revision as experience warrants.

The written plan must include (16 C.F.R. § 314):

(1) The appointment of a person responsible for coordinating the program;
(2) Identification of reasonably foreseeable internal and external risks, and an assessment of the sufficiency of any safeguards against those risks in these areas:
   a) Employee training and management
   b) Information systems, including information processing, storage, transmission and disposal, network software and design

    c) Detection, prevention, and response to attacks, intrusions, or other systems failures
(3) The procedure for designing, implementing, and testing of information safeguards
(4) Protocols for overseeing service providers capable of maintaining appropriate safeguards
(5) Rules for evaluating and adjusting the security program to react to any material business changes.

Under the Safeguard Rule, it is interesting to note, there is no obligation for a financial institution to disclose its information security program.

**Title V privacy.** Under GLBA's 'Privacy Rule,' financial institutions in possession of NPI must also provide customers with notices regarding the use of their NPI and give them the opportunity to opt out of sharing that data with unaffiliated third parties, unless subject to an exception (15 U.S.C. § 6802).

**Prudent protections.** ERISA imposes a standard of care on plan fiduciaries. One becomes a plan fiduciary either by being named as such, or through actions that result in the exercise of discretionary authority or control with respect to the management of a plan or its assets; providing investment advice for compensation; or having discretionary authority or responsibility in the administration of a plan (ERISA § 3(21)).

Fiduciaries are subject to the prudent expert standard of care and owe a duty of loyalty to the plan participants. A prudent expert acts with the care, skill, and diligence that the circumstances call for a person of like character and like aims to use. Fiduciaries must discharge their duties solely in the interest of plan participants and beneficiaries for the exclusive purpose of providing benefits to those participants and beneficiaries (ERISA § 404).

ERISA also requires that plan assets be held in trust by one or more trustees and that the indicia of ownership of such assets be held within the jurisdiction of the district courts of the United States (ERISA §§ 403 and 404).

Undeniably, the monetary assets of the participant accounts are plan assets and a fiduciary must undertake prudent steps to protect them from theft, including theft by means of a cyberbreach. However, unlike the HIPAA rules (45 C.F.R. 160, 162, and 164) that apply to health care data for ERISA-covered health care plans, there is no clear ERISA regulatory scheme governing the protection of financial information in retirement plans.

Whether a failure to protect retirement-related financial data results in a fiduciary breach turns on whether the financial data is considered a plan asset. If it is a plan asset, then failure to take prudent steps to prevent its loss or misuse likely results in a fiduciary breach.

Several different tests could be applied to determine whether plan data is a plan asset, although none have been applied by a court directly to personal financial data. It has been the DOL's position that 'the assets of a plan generally are to be identified on the basis of ordinary notions of property rights under non-ERISA law' (DOL Adv. Op. 92-02A (January 17, 1992)). Courts have applied other tests such as whether the data have any value and whether the assets were viewed or treated as plan assets (*Patient Advocates, LLC v. Prysunka*, 316 F. Supp. 2d 46, 49 (D. Me. 2004)). In *Acosta v. Pacific Enterprises,* the court said that

> [i]n order to determine whether a particular item constitutes an 'asset of the plan,' it is necessary to determine whether the item in question may be used to the benefit (financial or otherwise) of the fiduciary at the expense of the plan participants or beneficiaries.   (950 F.2d 611, 620 (9$^{th}$ Cir.1990)).

Another court found that plan assets must have some sort of inherent value, be capable of the assignment of value, or otherwise be subject to market forces (*Grindstaff v. Green*, 133 F.3d 416, 423, 425 (6th Cir. 1998)).

The need to protect the privacy of certain participant information has been directly addressed by the USDOL. For example, information relating to participant actions related to employer securities is briefly touched upon in the context of ERISA section 404(c). Additionally, the concept of securing private participant information in connection with a retirement plan is also raised by DOL Technical Release No. 2011-03 addressing certain electronic disclosures.

Given the focus on the value of personal data in our society, a conservative approach is to treat plan participant financial data as being a plan asset and take prudent steps to protect it as such.

**International regulations.** The European Union General Data Protection Regulation (GDPR) is the foremost set of European rules on information privacy,[2] with requirements applying as of May 2018. 'Data subjects' are persons that provide their individual information to companies, if they are identifiable from that information. Personal data includes financial data. These data subjects have rights under the GDPR with regard to companies that 'process' the data. Processing data has a very broad definition that includes collection and storage. There are core principles that apply to the companies that possess the data including: lawfulness, fairness, and transparency; purpose limitation; data minimization; accuracy; storage limitation; integrity and confidentiality; and accountability. These principles encompass many of the goals found in the separate privacy laws in the United States, but they are combined into a single scheme that is applicable much more broadly than any current US law. Under the GDPR, data subjects have many rights, including the right to be 'forgotten,' or erased from a company's data; the right to portability of the data; and the right not to be profiled if this has legal effects on the data subject.

The GDPR imposes many rules on the companies that act as a data controller and data processer regarding the safeguarding of personal data aimed towards achieving the core principles. These range from required contractual provisions to notifications of a breach.

This regulatory scheme is acknowledged as being one of, if not the most, comprehensive data protection regimes in the world. The GDPR has some extraterritorial implications applying to data from Europeans outside of Europe that are less likely to apply to a US-based retirement plan, but potentially could apply.

## Regulatory Directions

There is no comprehensive federal regulatory scheme governing cybersecurity for retirement plans in the US. Likewise, there is no comprehensive federal scheme that covers their service providers, as not all are subject to GLBA. ERISA is silent on data protection in the form of electronic records, and the US courts have not yet decided whether managing cybersecurity risk is a fiduciary function. Many providers that service the retirement market are covered by federal rules based on their industry. However, these same retirement plan service providers often cross several different industries, making compliance more of a patchwork.

To address these gaps, some states have started to create their own laws which typically address breach notifications and private rights of action for any unauthorized disclosures of protected personal information. While several state attorneys general have been active in enforcing these laws in cyberbreach cases, a state-by-state framework remains a patchwork solution.

**ERISA Advisory Council.** Despite a lack of federal regulation, the DOL and the ERISA Advisory Council (2016) recently recommended that the DOL communicate to the employee benefits community the cybersecurity risks and potential approaches for managing those risks (ERISA 2016). The ERISA Advisory Council's proposal to the DOL included guidance for plan sponsors on how to evaluate cyber-risks for their benefit plans, requiring them to: understand the plan's data; know the different security frameworks used to protect data; build an adaptive cybersecurity process that includes implementation and monitoring, testing and updating, reporting, training, controlling access, data retention and destruction, and third-party risk management. Additionally, the guidance required these sponsors to: customize a strategy to fit the unique needs of the plan sponsor; balance the plan sponsor's threats based on size, complexity, and risk exposure; and address state law considerations.

While ERISA does not outline specific rules for protecting data, the DOL did recognize the risks associated with electronic communications of plan information. For instance, in Regulation Section 2520.104b-1(c),the DOL addressed electronic distribution of plan information to participants, by saying that plan administrators must take appropriate measures to 'protect the confidentiality of personal information relating to the individual's accounts and benefits.' These measures were designed to prevent unauthorized receipt of information or access to such information by individuals other than the intended user. Additionally, DOL Technical Release No. 2011-03 addressed participant information available on administrators' websites and required the plan administrator to take appropriate and necessary measures reasonably calculated to ensure that the electronic delivery system protects the confidentiality of all personal information. How best to achieve the confidentiality of personal information relating to individuals' accounts and benefits is not well defined.

Despite the ERISA Advisory Council's recommendations on how to evaluate risks, important questions remain unanswered. For example, is cybersecurity an ERISA fiduciary responsibility? If so, does ERISA preempt state cybersecurity laws? Plan sponsors and service providers already take seriously their responsibilities to protect participant data, but where are the lines of responsibilities and accountability in the event of a breach?

## Other Legal Considerations

For some plans, such as state and local government-sponsored plans, ERISA and its preemption do not apply. Moreover, even for ERISA-covered plans, it is not clear that state privacy or cybersecurity statutes would be preempted by ERISA.

**Governmental plans.** Many governmental plans, especially on the state level, have adopted ERISA statutory language nearly word-for-word. For example, retirement systems in numerous states such as the District of Columbia, Illinois, and Ohio, have used substantially the same language as ERISA to govern state plans (7 DCMR 15; 40 ILCS 5/; ORC145.01). Most of these plans will look to how an ERISA plan or an ERISA service provider would address the same situation, in order to determine what actions and remedies are appropriate. A court would also do the same in these jurisdictions. In other jurisdictions, the fiduciary concepts are similar to ERISA even when the statutory language is different, and courts are again likely to look to ERISA precedent.

**State statutes.** While ERISA was intended to prevent a patchwork of state law requirements from applying to the same plan, it is not clear that personal privacy and cybersecurity statutes would be preempted by ERISA. Clearly

ERISA predates the widespread use of the internet and the general awareness of cyberthreats. The lack of comprehensive financial privacy protections in ERISA could lead courts to determine that no ERISA preemption
occurs with respect to state protections. A majority of states have statutes
regarding privacy, cybersecurity, financial information, or all of the above.
For example, Massachusetts has its 'Standards for the Protection of Personal
Information of Residents of the Commonwealth' (201 CMR 17.04).
A written information security program is required for entities including
employers that maintain personally identifiable financial information about
a Massachusetts resident. Statutes and regulations such as those adopted by
Massachusetts can provide plan sponsors, fiduciaries, and service providers
with additional reference points for constructing their own cybersecurity
protocols for retirement plans.

Another prominent example is the New York Department of Financial
Services regulation, considered to be one of the most comprehensive cybersecurity regulations at the state level. Entitled Cybersecurity Requirements
for Financial Services Companies, the ruling was promulgated in 2017 and
covers financial services companies operating under a license or certification
issued under the New York Banking, Insurance, or Financial Services laws
(23 NYCRR 500). It aims to set certain minimum standards for cyber-security
programs that keep pace with technological advances, while promoting the
protection of customer information. It requires involvement from senior
level management to file an annual statement of compliance with the New
York Department of Financial Services. While there are staged deadlines,
compliance generally requires having a cyber-security program, policies,
penetration testing, an incident recovery plan, risk assessment, encryption
of non-public information, and training and monitoring (*Id.*).

**Cybersecurity breach examples.** Cyberbreaches have become an unfortu-
nate part of commerce today. Whenever and wherever value has been
stored, thieves have always tried to take it. The motives remain the same,
but the methods and means of stealing have adapted to where and how we
store value. The United States is by far the number one target, followed by
the United Kingdom (Tech World 2017). Some of the most infamous
breaches of the last several years have exposed millions and in a few cases,
billions of individuals to identity theft. Well-known cases include:

(1)  Uber: Over 57 million customers and drivers had their names, emails,
     and phone numbers stolen in 2016;
(2)  Target: In 2013, the firm's customers had their names, credit/debit
     card numbers, expiration dates, and card values stolen. The theft
     involved over 70 million retail customer accounts. Investigations
     showed the thieves entered the retailer's systems through a third-party

refrigeration company hired by Target to help renovate some stores; and

(3) Equifax: This firm's 2017 breach is one of the most serious ever because it included the names, social security numbers, dates of birth, and addresses for more than 143 million.

Cyberattacks tend to fall into several general categories which information security officers use to identify countermeasures and solutions based on the different types of attacks:

Phishing. Hackers pose as a trusted vendor or third party and request data, often providing a link for victims to enter personal data. While phishing emails have gotten much more sophisticated in recent years, consumers have also become more sophisticated. Many consumers verify such requests directly with their financial institutions before clicking on links or providing information. Nevertheless, a vulnerable population and a favorite target for hackers are the elderly. To combat these attacks, most companies stress to clients that they will not ask for personal information via email, and tell them that if they receive such a request they should report it immediately to the firm.

Malware. This term includes several cyberthreats such as trojans, viruses, and worms. In simple terms it refers to any code with malicious intent that typically steals or destroys data or locks a computer. Recordkeepers protect against such attacks through firewalls that catch malware programs before they get into a system, or by educating employees not to click on suspicious links or download attachments from unknown senders. This is sometimes done by deploying robust and updated firewalls, which prevent the transfer of large data files over the network to weed out attachments that may contain malware. It is also important to continually ensure all computer operating systems are updated and use the most recent security programs.

Rouge software. This is a newer type of malware that masquerades as legitimate security software. The criminal designs the software to make pop-up windows and alerts that look authentic. Once a user downloads the new security software, the corrupt software is downloaded to the user's computer. An organization's information technology practices can help prevent these attacks with updated firewalls or trusted anti-virus or anti-spyware software.

Password attacks. These happen when a thief gains access to a customer's account by cracking the user's password. This type of attack is often simple and does not usually require any type of malicious code or software. Hackers use software to guess passwords by comparing various word combinations against a dictionary file. Recordkeepers typically require their clients to use sophisticated passwords that include a combination of letters, numbers, and special characters, as well as limiting the number of failed login attempts.

Denial-of-Service (DoS) attacks. A DoS attack disrupts the service to a network. Attackers will send a high volume of data requests to a network until it becomes overloaded and can no longer function. Attackers typically use several means of attack, but the most common is the distributed-denial-of-service (DDoS) attack: this involves the attacker using multiple computers to send the traffic or data to overload the system. Often computer users do not even realize that their computers have been hijacked. Many of these types of attacks are not intended to steal data or money, but to protest something. Although recordkeepers are not typically the targets of these types of attacks, they help prevent them by monitoring security as well as data flows to identify any unusual or threatening spikes in traffic before these become a problem. DoS attacks can also be accomplished by physically cutting cables or disconnecting servers, which is why firms also protect their physical properties and systems.

'Man in the Middle' (MITM). Sophisticated hackers will often impersonate an organization's login page or endpoint. From here they will ask the client for online information. For example, if you are banking online, the man in the middle would communicate with you by impersonating your bank, and communicate with the bank by impersonating you. The man in the middle would then receive all the information transferred between both parties, which could include sensitive data such as bank accounts and personal information. Recordkeepers and other financial firms usually require clients to use only encrypted access points.

Drive-By Downloads. Through malware on a legitimate website or detachable drive, a program is downloaded to a user's system just by visiting the site or connecting to the target's system. Typically, a small snippet of code is downloaded to the user's system and that code then reaches out to another computer to get the rest of the program. It often exploits vulnerabilities in the user's operating system or in other programs. Some thieves have even labeled thumb drives with 'payroll' and dropped them in an organization's parking lot. The intent is for an unsuspecting employee to pick up the thumb drive and connect it to a secure computer. Once that happens, the malware code is released. Organizations protect against these attacks in various ways such as education, strict rules against use of detachable drives, and restrictions on web browsing.

## Data Security Best Practices

The Data Security Oversight Board (DSOB) of Spark Institute has developed standards to help recordkeepers communicate the full capabilities of their cybersecurity systems to plan sponsors, consultants, and others. These standards are not intended to provide a recommended level of cyber protection or guarantee against a data breach or loss. Instead, these standards are intended to help establish a uniform communications tool to assist plan sponsors and service providers in properly assessing and comparing retirement plan vendors.

Plan sponsors and their consultants generally understand that recordkeepers need to maintain a level of secrecy around the products and processes used to secure client data. Conversely, recordkeepers know that clients and prospects have legitimate needs to understand how their data are protected. These standards establish a base of communication between recordkeepers and sponsors using independent third-party audits of cybersecurity controls. With this tool, vendors can properly validate the robust nature of their cybersecurity systems and provide assurances to clients and prospects that their systems are protected against hackers.

A firm's overall data security capabilities identify recommended control objectives in 16 areas critical to data security as defined by SPARK. The resulting audit reports identify the primary applications and processing systems that support the services offered. Recordkeepers and service providers can report their results in two ways. First, they can generate a Service Organization Control (SOC 2) report, conducted under the AICPA audit standards. This focuses on controls at a firm relevant to security, availability, processing integrity, confidentiality, or privacy (AICPA 2017). Second, they can produce an Agreed Upon Procedures (AUP) report, in which an auditor is contracted to issue a report or findings based on specific agreed-upon procedures with the client applied to cybersecurity controls for use by specified parties (AICPA—AT-C Section 215).[3]

Section III of the SOC 2 or the cover page of an AUP would be used to address which systems are within the scope of the audit and which are not. The scope of these audits includes anywhere customer or plan-provided NPI or Personally Identifiable Information (PII) is processed or stored. PII is defined as (US Department of Labor 2017, n.p.):

> Any representation of information that permits the identity of an individual to whom the information applies to be reasonably inferred by either direct or indirect means. Further, PII is defined as information: (i) that directly identifies an individual (e.g., name, address, social security number or other identifying number or code, telephone number, email address, etc.) or (ii) by which an agency intends to identify specific individuals in conjunction with other data elements, i.e., indirect identification. (These data elements may include a combination of gender, race, birth date, geographic indicator, and other descriptors) ... Additionally, information permitting the physical or online contacting of a specific individual is the same as personally identifiable information. This information can be maintained in either paper, electronic or other media.

NPI is defined as (Federal Trade Commission 2002: 4–5):

> Any information an individual gives you to get a financial product or service (for example, name, address, income, social security number, or other information on an application); Any information you get about an individual from a transaction involving your financial product(s) or service(s) (for example, the fact that an individual is your consumer or customer, account numbers, payment history, loan or deposit balances, and credit or debit card purchases); or Any information you get about an individual in connection with providing a financial product or service (for example, information from court records or from a consumer report).

The detailed control objectives section of the auditor's report must include each control objective, the test procedures, and the results. The format for this report should follow a format similar to that outlined in Table 6.1. Table 6.2 shows each of the required categories of control objectives, provides a description of the category and gives an example of a control that might apply.

How cybersecurity testing results are reported can differ in several ways. First, firms can choose to perform an AUP engagement. This is one in which an auditor is engaged to issue a report and findings based on specific agreed-upon procedures that apply to certain subject matters for use by specified parties. In this case, the specified parties would typically be a client plan sponsor that requires independent proof of cybersecurity capabilities. Under AICPA guidelines, the specified parties determine the procedures they believe appropriate to be used by the auditor. This creates a slight challenge when using the SPARK Industry Best Practices, since these 16 categories and the controls aligned to these categories by the recordkeeper must be accepted as appropriate by the client. Client acceptance of the procedures can take several forms and be a formal letter or a simple email.[4]

A SOC 2, or Service Organization Control report 2, addresses a firm's controls related to operations, availability, security, processing integrity, confidentiality, and privacy. The report follows the five AICPA Trust Services principles and includes detailed descriptions of the auditor's test of controls and results.

TABLE 6.1  Sample format: SPARK Data Security Report

| Controls | Test Procedures | Results |
| --- | --- | --- |
| Each control tested is defined and aligned to one of SPARK's 16 key areas of security focus. | Test parameters: Define what was tested and how test was performed. | Summarize test results (i.e., no exceptions noted or exception noted and provide details). |

*Source*: The SPARK Institute (2017).

TABLE 6.2 Spark Institute 16 control objectives for communicating cybersecurity capabilities

| Control objective | Description | Sample controls[a] |
|---|---|---|
| (1) Risk assessment and treatment | The organization understands the cybersecurity risk to organizational operations (including mission, functions, image, or reputation), organizational assets, and individuals. | *Technology risk assessments are completed.* |
| (2) Security policy | Organizational information security policy is established. | *Security policies are approved and communicated.* |
| (3) Organizational security | Information security roles and responsibilities are coordinated and aligned with internal roles and external partners. | *A CISO or ISO has been assigned.* |
| (4) Asset management | The data, personnel, devices, systems, and facilities that enable the organization to achieve business purposes are identified and managed consistent with their relative importance to business objectives and the organization's risk strategy. | *IT application records are maintained in a formal system of record.* |
| (5) Human resource security | The organization's personnel and partners are suitable for the roles they are considered for, are provided cybersecurity awareness education and are adequately trained to perform their information security-related duties and responsibilities consistent with related policies, procedures, and agreements. | *Personnel are subject to initial and periodic background checks* |
| (6) Physical and environmental security | Physical access to assets is managed and protected. | *Data centers are secured 24× 7× 365 with on-site physical security controls.* |
| (7) Communications and operations management | Technical security solutions are managed to ensure the security and resilience of systems and assets, consistent with related policies, procedures, and agreements. | *Networks and systems include standard data security tools such as firewalls, antivirus, intrusion detection, and patch management.* |
| (8) Access control | Access to assets and associated facilities is limited to authorized users, processes, or devices, and to authorized activities and transactions. | *Unique, complex passwords are assigned to all employees.* |
| (9) Information systems acquisition development | A system development life cycle (SDLC) to manage systems is implemented; a vulnerability management plan is developed and implemented, and vulnerability scans are performed. | *Regular penetration tests are conducted on customer-facing applications.* |

| (10) Incident and event communications management | Response processes and procedures are executed and maintained to ensure timely response to detected cybersecurity events. | *Cyber incident procedures are documented and routinely tested.* |
|---|---|---|
| (11) Business resiliency | Response plans (IncidentResponse and Business Continuity) and recovery plans (Incident Recovery and Disaster Recovery) are in place and managed. | *The organization maintains and tests BCP and DR plans.* |
| (12) Compliance | Legal requirements regarding cybersecurity, including privacy and civil liberties obligations, are understood and managed | *Policies and procedures are in place to enforce applicable privacy obligation.* |
| (13) Mobile | A formal policy shall be in place and appropriate security measures shall be adopted to protect against the risks of using mobile computing and communication facilities. | *A mobile policy is approved and enforced.* |
| (14) Encryption | Data-at-rest and data-in-transit are protected. | *External transmissions are encrypted using FIPS-approved algorithms.* |
| (15) Supplier risk | Ensure protection of the organization's assets that is accessible by suppliers. | *Suppliers are subject to periodic security reviews.* |
| (16) Cloud security | Ensure protection of the organization's assets that are stored or processed in cloud environments | *Cloud providers are subject to periodic security reviews or can provide independent security assessments of their environment.* |

*Notes*: For illustrative purposes only; not intended to be a list of controls.

*Source*: The SPARK Institute (2017).

## The Role of an ERISA Attorney

While investment consultants often play a lead role, ERISA attorneys are regularly deeply involved in the Request for Proposal (RFP) process when a retirement plan puts services out to bid and in the response to such requests. By understanding the SPARK Best Practices prior to entering into the RFP process, the ERISA attorney can facilitate communication between the parties. ERISA attorneys for recordkeeping institutions can use this knowledge to respond to RFPs that may, at first, not necessarily focus on cybersecurity in a coherent manner. By providing thoughtful responses and information to an RFP request, the ERISA attorney can focus plan sponsors on the items most appropriate for a benefit plan. While procurement and technology personnel are adept at cybersecurity as it relates to the plan sponsor's business, the ERISA attorney will be able to provide guidance regarding norms for benefit plans, which will help align a plan fiduciary's behavior with that of other prudent experts in similar circumstances in keeping with ERISA's standard of care. By facilitating understanding of the standards and practices, an informed ERISA attorney can help the benefit plan seek and obtain cybersecurity protection appropriate for particular needs of a retirement plan, while also reducing liability exposure for the plan's fiduciary.

## The Road Ahead for Cyber Security and Employee Benefits

**Plan sponsor next steps.** Plan sponsors will need to quickly educate themselves about the benefit plan cybersecurity environment. This could involve a presentation to plan sponsor personnel with responsibility for a retirement plan, or by attending a conference for human resource professionals regarding plan cybersecurity. Awareness of the issue can help obtain buy-in to expend resources so as not to lag behind other plan stewards. Education can also help set realistic expectations, because total prevention is not achievable, and total outsourcing of cybersecurity is also unlikely. With these fundamentals established, a plan sponsor can begin or further a productive endeavor towards retirement plan data security that meets the applicable fiduciary standards.

Moreover, plan fiduciaries might consider going on a 'data diet' to reduce the amount of retirement plan information shared among the plan, the plan sponsor, and service providers. Like any diet, the first step is to identify what data are currently being collected, produced, retained, and shared. From there, it is likely that a plan sponsor may be able to identify excess at each of these stages. As part of this process, plan sponsors might evaluate whether each recipient truly requires the full scope of data being shared to accomplish the task at hand, and if not, whether there is an operationally efficient manner to reduce the creation, transfer, and storage of excess data. By reducing the data at play, a plan sponsor can limit the plan's exposure to a cybersecurity attack. Of course, the degree to which a plan sponsor will have leverage to modify existing practices is likely to depend on the size and assets of its plan.

ERISA does not mandate a written cybersecurity or financial information policy, and there is no one-size-fits-all approach that must be taken. Instead, a plan sponsor must act prudently. The easiest way to show that a plan sponsor has followed a prudent process is to document that process. Creating any prescriptive document beyond those required by ERISA can carry significant challenges and risks, so cybersecurity documents should focus on process items rather than attempting to lay out any hard and fast rules.

Cybersecurity incidents or breaches involving plan sponsors are a question of when, not if. Therefore, plan sponsors might also consider a response-and-recovery plan. The timing of the development of such a plan can vary widely—from proactively or after-the-fact. Fiduciary insurance is typically triggered when a lawsuit is filed or regulatory investigation is commenced (or sometimes when a regulator asserts a deficiency), while cyber insurance is often triggered by a data breach. This means that while existing fiduciary insurance may help after a lawsuit is filed, but prior to that point, the plan and/or plan sponsor may be responsible for the costs and mechanics associated with a breach (depending on the terms of the insurance policy). These include finding, hiring, and paying for experts to assess the scope of the breach and develop a mitigation plan, as well as finding the capacity to notify and respond to participant inquiries regarding an incident.

Plan sponsors may wish to seek specific cyber insurance policies or riders to existing policies (some of which are available in the market today) to cover the employee benefit plan(s). Policies that provide benefits upon a breach can offer assistance in locating the appropriate personnel to address each step of the process, from determining the scope of the breach, to notifying the appropriate individuals or entities, to providing resources to mitigate, or making whole any damages suffered as a result of the breach, such as identity monitoring or replacing stolen assets. Plan sponsors will also wish to consider how to evaluate and update their plan-related cybersecurity approach on a periodic basis.

## Conclusion

The cybersecurity environment for retirement plans is undergoing significant evolution, and this evolution is likely going to continue to accelerate. While the precise fiduciary obligations of plan sponsors with respect to plan and participant information are not yet clearly defined, it is clear that multiple efforts are underway to define those obligations, and to respond to the increasing need to strengthen protections. Presently, the SEC, the DOL, multiple states, and key industry organizations like SPARK are working to regulate cybersecurity and develop increased protections.

As these efforts proceed, it is essential that plan sponsors work together with their vendors, including recordkeepers, consultants, accountants and attorneys to put in place adequate safeguards. For these safeguards to be successful, it will also be essential to develop common practices for conducting due diligence with respect to these safeguards while also avoiding disclosures that may help malicious actors. The SPARK standards, applied via a SOC2 or AUP, can serve as an essential starting point and provide the opportunity to receive assurance of industry-vetted practices via a trusted third party. Plan sponsors may also benefit from careful review of their insurance coverages with respect to cybersecurity, as there is a wide range of available protections including common gaps with respect to when policies are triggered or what they provide.

# Notes

1. This chapter refers to 'plan sponsors' as including both plan sponsors and plan fiduciaries. Although there are important lines between plan sponsor 'settlor' advice and fiduciary activities, for ease of communication we have used the term 'plan sponsor' throughout.
2. Regulation (EU) 2016/679 (General Regulation of the European Parliament and the Council on the protection of natural persons with regard to the processing of personal data and on the free movement of such data, and repealing Directive 95/46/EC 25).
3. Under AICPA standards, an AUP is only to be used by the parties that agreed to the procedures. Any AUP that is used over again for new clients would first require that client to accept the original agreed upon procedures.
4. A self-assessment using the SPARK Institute's Cyber Security Best Practices is only a stopgap process to help aid in industry adoption. Recordkeeping firms can use the SPARK 16 Cyber Security Categories and report their controls and test results without third-party attestation, but only until they can contract with their audit firms to do independent reporting.

# References

AICPA (2017). *AT-C Section 215: Agreed-Upon Procedures Engagements.* Association of International Certified Professional Accountants. https://www.aicpa.org/research/standards/auditattest/downloadabledocuments/at-c-00215.pdf (accessed March 1, 2019).

ERISA Advisory Council (ERISA) (2016). *Cybersecurity Considerations for Benefit Plans.* Report to the Honorable Thomas E. Perez, United States Secretary of Labor. https://www.dol.gov/sites/default/files/ebsa/about-ebsa/about-us/erisa-advisory-council/2016-cybersecurity-considerations-for-benefit-plans.pdf (accessed March 1, 2019).

Federal Trade Commission (2002). *How to Comply with the Privacy of Consumer Financial Information Rule of the Gramm-Leach-Bliley Act.* Washington, DC: FTC. https://www.ftc.gov/system/files/documents/plain-language/bus67-how-comply-privacy-consumer-financial-information-rule-gramm-leach-bliley-act.pdf (accessed March 1, 2019).

Tech World (2017). 'The Most Infamous Data Breaches.' *Tech World*. December 6. https://www.techworld.com/security/uks-most-infamous-data-breaches-3604586/ (accessed March 1, 2019).

The SPARK Institute (2017). 'Industry Best Practice Data Security Reporting.' *SPARK Institute Release 1.0*. September 20. http://www.sparkinstitute.org/pdf/SPARK%20Data%20Security%20Industry%20Best%20Practice%20Standards%209-2017.pdf (accessed March 1, 2019).

US Department of Labor (2017). *Guidance on the Protection of Personal Identifiable Information*. https://www.dol.gov/general/ppii (accessed March 1, 2019).

## Chapter 7

# Designing for Older Adults: Overcoming Barriers to a Supportive, Safe, and Healthy Retirement

*Cosmin Munteanu, Benett Axtell, Hiba Rafih,*
*Amna Liaqat, and Yomna Aly*

Older adults[1] are often considered to be technologically less savvy than the average population (Grimes et al. 2010), which is due to several factors: declining tech savviness as seniors retire from the workforce, or social isolation which reduces the available peer support that can provide assistance and encouragement in adoption online technologies. This can affect several aspects of their security and well-being, such as increased risks of exposure to financial loss (e.g., through scams) (Garg et al. 2011; CFAC 2014).

At the same time, numerous seniors are or feel socially isolated (Nicholson 2012). These two issues may be in fact co-dependent: our own research (Munteanu et al. 2015) has revealed that seniors[2] rely on their social network for support with Internet-related problems and that they avoid many online activities as a consequence of their lack of digital confidence or concerns with exposure to risks (e.g., fraud).

Older adults tend to acquire most of their digital knowledge from family (Boothroyd 2014). However, socially isolated seniors may have limited contact with family or friends that can provide such knowledge, so instead they rely on mass-media for information, often presented in alarming terms (Boothroyd 2014). This lack of support limits opportunities that would allow them to learn about online practices (e.g., safety), which in turn may deter older adults from participating in online activities such as shopping or banking. This puts older adults at a disadvantage, as the Internet can provide them with relevant resources (Czaja et al. 2009), and more importantly, access to means that can aid in reducing the social and digital isolation (Czaja and Lee 2007) from which this issue may stem.

## Background

The issue of digital marginalization that emerges from the combination of lack of access to social support and the uneven technological literacy may be further compounded by aspects of usability (ease of use) and perceived utility of digital (online) technologies. The Technology Acceptance Model (TAM) (Venkatesh and Davis 2000) indicates several factors that affect the adoption of (potentially beneficial) technologies, particularly by older adults (Venkatesh et al. 2012). TAM is a widely used theoretical framework that examines how people accept and use a specific technology. While not without its shortcomings (Salovaara and Tamminen 2009), TAM has been successfully used in the (scant) work studying the factors affecting the adoption of technologies by older adults (Neves et al. 2013).

Two of the key adoption factors captured by the TAM are usability and perceived value (usefulness/utility). Grudin (1992) defines usability as the property of a software system to be 'easily learned and handled' by its intended users, with usefulness referring to the attribute of 'serving a recognizable purpose.' Within this context, the TAM is typically interpreted to indicate that, in order for seniors to adopt a software system (or more broadly, digital technology), such a system must be highly usable by them, but also offer a recognizable purpose. The latter factor is often reduced to the notion of offering older adults the motivation to learn how to use that system and potentially overcome usability barriers—motivation that is intrinsically tied to the system being perceived as offering a value. Such motivation (value) is prompted by a variety of factors, among the most frequent being the desire to maintain family connections or the need to leverage such connections (Neves et al. 2015; Dang 2016). Many of the most ubiquitous software tools widely used for daily activities (e.g., online banking) are often not designed to be usable by older adults (Franz et al. 2015; Munteanu et al. 2015). This further marginalizes seniors with respect to the adoption of digital technologies, as the perceived value of these tools needs to be relatively higher in order to motivate older adults' in investing efforts as required to overcome usability issues.

## Barriers to Designing FinTech for Older Adults

Designers and developers of essential digital services and tools intended for older adults (such as online banking or other online financial tools) must therefore find solutions that address the barriers to adoption as related to usability, perceived usefulness, and lack of (or reduced) digital literacy. These are interconnected with issues of older adults' social isolation and digital marginalization, which in turn further amplify such barriers. In this chapter we argue that, at the core of these barriers, lies one of the most fundamental concepts related to designing (interactive) digital tools: mental models.

Present in many disciplines (Rouse and Morris 1986), mental models can be seen as intrinsically related to the aspect of perceived usefulness and usability in the TAM. Within a technology space, mental models define what a user believes about how an interactive system or digital technology works (Nielsen 1990). That is, a mental model captures what users 'know (or think they know) about a system such as a website' (Nielsen 2010: n.p.). For example, the ability of being able to type in search terms in the 'address bar' of modern (as of 2018) browsers is a feature added in response to users' mental model of entering terms into browser or website elements that have the appearance of a search box—this mental model likely developed as the results of users' accessing the websites of online search engines such as Google (Mental Models in Design 2018).

Mental models are influenced by many non-technological factors, including users' socio-demographic background or cultural norms and expectations (Moffat 2013; Neves et al. 2015). For designers of such systems, the challenge is to minimize the mismatch between users' mental models and how the system is designed. A large gap between designers' mental models and users' models can result the technology adoption factors established by the TAM to be degraded—namely the perceived usefulness and usability. This is due to the appearance of two 'gulfs' caused by this mismatch, as defined by Norman (2013): the 'gulf of evaluation' and the 'gulf of execution.' The gulf of execution is the difference between what users think a system can do and what the system can actually do, while the gulf of evaluation captures how difficult it is for users to interpret a system's internal state. In particular, the gulf of evaluation captures the connection between mental models and the perceived usability/usefulness as defined by the TAM—for example, does the system provide easy to understand information that matches the way the user thinks of the system? A typical (albeit simplistic) practical example of the gulf of evaluation is the use of either 'on' or 'off' labeling on a Bluetooth connection sliding switch, which when the label shows 'off' but the slider position is opposite the 'off' label, this can interpreted as either 'status: off, slide to turn on,' or just 'slide to turn off' (Whitenton 2018).

If designers of essential digital services fail to fully understand the mental models of older users, including their use of alternative ways of accessing the service, not understanding how the proposed service works, and not understanding the benefits the proposed new service is offering, then this may lead to older users' non-adoption of a new digital service. In particular, we look at mental models and adopting online services from the perspective of trust, especially in relative terms between the trust in online platforms and the trust in established ('traditional') services.

## Solutions to Designing FinTech for Older Adults

Numerous design approaches exist that aim to improve the user experience with new digital tools or services. Yet many of these design methods are activated only later in the service development cycle, often after assumptions about users' needs are already drafted from a variety of sources and methods. By contrast, the design of essential services (e.g., within the space of FinTech for older adults) can lead to increase adoption rates if more in-depth methods are employed that build an extensive understanding of users' specific practices. We make the case for the use of Contextual Inquiry (CI), a method successfully used in domains like the workplace for predesign stages, but not widely explored when designing for older adults. We evaluate how employing such requirement-collecting methods, complemented with user-centered design strategies such as Participatory Design (PD) can lead to a reduction in the gap between older users' mental models and those of the system's or service's designers, and subsequently, to an increase in adoption. We then discuss how this is particularly relevant for the design of FinTech for older adults, such as online banking or other online financial services.

## Barriers to FinTech Adoption by Older Adults

Financial security in retirement is one of the most pressing concerns faced by older adults (Kemp and Denton 2003). As such, many older adults are actively pursuing strategies to ensure this goal is attained (Kemp and Denton 2003; Sixsmith et al. 2014). This seems to be a universal concern independent of several other factors, including the availability of government-funded or government-backed retirement plans that are found in countries with social safety programs such as Canada (Raphael et al. 2001).

Some of the concerns with respect to the financial aspects of retirement are due to the complexity of planning long-term strategies that ensure income security in retirement (Vettese 2015). Additionally, retirees face the prospect of uncertainties at older ages, especially if income sources are not from government-backed or government-funded defined benefit plans. This can lead to seniors resorting to other strategies (e.g., drastic reductions in spending and thus in quality of life) as a precautionary mechanism to ensure financial security (Vettese 2016). Many older adults face increased difficulty in managing their financial plans, even if otherwise they planned well for life events (Denton et al. 2004). Some researchers suggest that cognitive decline, alongside other ageing-specific factors (e.g., lack of financial literacy), contributes to the older adults' difficulty in managing their finances and planning for a secure retirement (Loibl 2017). However, others disagree with the role of cognitive decline in older adults' financial planning, and instead suggest that 'domain-specific knowledge and expertise provide an alternative route to sound financial decisions' (Li et al. 2015:

65). This indicates that designing services to support, encourage, and educate older adults with respect to their financial practices may provide a
solution to this problem (Lusardi and Mitchell 2007).

Several policymakers have called upon financial institutions to provide
educational programs or resources for older adults in order to assist them
with planning for a secure retirement, including protecting their financial
assets from fraud (Blazer et al. 2015). Yet, such recommendations may be at
odds with industry trends that see a shift from 'brick and mortar' banking
and financial services to the online space (Campbell 2017). Such a shift may
disproportionately affect older adults, since recent research has shown that
seniors are the demographic group that has the lowest adoption of online
banking and financial services (Alhabash et al. 2015). Yet, there is some
evidence that adoption of online FinTech can be increased if factors other
than convenience are considered—for example, the establishment of a
relationship of trust with a 'brick and mortar' financial institution can be
successfully (albeit slowly) transferred to the online services offered by the
same institution (Montazemi and Qahri-Saremi 2015).

Barriers to the adoption of online FinTech services by older adults have
been explored in other fields as well. In particular, research in Human-
Computer Interaction (HCI) and within this, User Experience (UX)
Design, have recently started addressing the barriers faced by this demographic. These research and design fields are concerned with understanding users in relation to technology, and with designing solutions that make
interactions with technology easier, more meaningful, and more relevant to
users (Interaction Design Foundation 2018).

An example of such research is work by Vines et al. (2012), who have
conducted an ethnographic-like qualitative study of how older adults envi-
sion and engage with electronic payments. The study has revealed significant issues with respect to how older users perceived online FinTech
services, such as lack of trust (in both the provider of the service and in
the underlying technology) or lack of confidence in using the online version
of these services (e.g., 'Electronic records are seen as ephemeral', as quoted
in the above-mentioned paper). This suggests that, in addition to the
dimensions established by the TAM (namely, perceived usefulness), a significant barrier is represented by the mismatch between how online Fin-
Tech services work and how older users perceive them: that is, their mental
models of these services.

Mental models have been extensively explored in behavioral economics
and financial research, most recently from the perspectives of individuals'
relationship with economic and financial policies and developments (World
Bank 2015), and within the contexts of (financial) decision making (Denzau
and North 1994; De Bondt and Thaler 1995). New perspectives have also
emerged linking individuals' mental models to how financial services work,

and the consequences of mismatch between these (Acemoglu 2009), such as consumers' perception of how a company operates within a market space. This, together with the UX research of (Vines et al. 2012) that identified differences of perception about how online financial services work, further supports our argument that the design and development of FinTech for older adults must focus on addressing the barriers represented by older adults' mental models of such services (in addition to other UX-related barriers, such as perceived usefulness and usability).

## Designing for Mental Models

We offer three case studies supporting our central argument that mental models are a key component of the barriers to older adults' adoption of online FinTech. These are drawn from our own qualitative and field research on understanding older adults' information practices in three key areas related to their retirement: social isolation, health information access, and online safety. We elaborate on two methodological aspects related to designing for mental models: understanding older user needs with respect to an online service, and engaging users in the design process in order to ensure the final service matches their mental models.

## Understanding Users' Needs

There is a long history of methods in Human–Computer Interaction that include user input in the process of designing technologies. Most methods engage users through various approaches to elicit requirements for the design of interactive applications; such engagement aims to produce designs that meet users' needs. However, as older adults are often less familiar with technology or are reticent to adopt new technologies, designing for these users may benefit from initial research that does not ask seniors to directly join in the design process or respond to the technology right away. For this, data about users' information practices needs to be gathered outside of the design context, before a design solution is even considered. That is, an ethnographic approach is needed to build such an understanding of users' current practices. Ethnography is a social science research method that facilitates the understanding of issues affecting people as they engage in their daily lives or in specific activities (e.g., workplace); this understanding is drawn from either over or covert extensive observations by the researchers (Hammersley and Atkinson 2007).

Grounded in on our own research experience, we argue that Contextual Inquiries as a form of Ethnographies are a suitable approach for understanding users (and subsequently, their mental models) in the context of activities essential to maintaining a financially safe, socially-connected, and healthy retirement for seniors.

## Contextual Inquiry

Contextual Inquiry (CI) is a method for Human–Computer Interaction research and requirements gathering, similar to ethnography, that seeks to observe and understand how a new design can fit within a current practice with minimal disruption. This method presents a particular way of doing observations that builds an understanding of user practices. These observations lead to the creation of a design that supports or improves upon the observed actions and is more likely to be adopted (Wixon et al. 1990; Beyer and Holtzblatt 1997). The observations for a CI are focused on the relevant activities and can be prompted by the researcher for the purpose of observation, with participants being encouraged to explain what they are doing and why.

This method is helpful in developing an in-depth, focused understanding of a user's practices, their related motivations and attitudes, and how a new design can fit with those practices. While it was initially intended for use in the workplace, it is also useful when working with any specific group of target users in a given setting, including to building an understanding of older adults' practices as a prerequisite for designing a technological solution. Yet, it is only recently that CI has started being used for this demographic. For example, this approach was taken by Muskens et al. (2014) to understand how older adults may use mobile devices as a replacement for TVs, which resulted in the design of an entertainment-focused media consumption tablet app that mimics many of the channel-browsing features of traditional TVs. In our own work we have employed CI methods to gain insights into the role that paper or digital photographs play in prompting older adults to share stories about past memories—this lead to the design of an intuitive tablet app that increases social connectivity by engaging older adults in oral storytelling around digital photographs (Axtell 2017).

## Contextual Inquiry Methods for Older Adults

Contextual Inquiry (CI) is a qualitative field method that employs in-situ observations of users, combined with thematic analysis of these observations to build a detailed understanding. Beyer and Holtzblatt (1999: 34) describe CI as 'an explicit step for understanding who the users really are and how they work on a day-to-day basis.' Users often have difficulty expressing what they do in detail and explaining their motivations, so CI observations expose the elements of the work that would not otherwise be articulated by a participant, but are an essential part of their process. These observations are around the tasks, activities, practices, and uses of artefacts (technological or not) relevant to the participant's process. Directly observing these allows the researcher to identify how a new design could be introduced within a participant's current practices with minimal disruption. To support these observations, Contextual Inquiries are guided by four core principles:

(1) Context: observations in the natural setting to get the best and most relevant data.
(2) Partnership: researcher and participant collaborate in understanding the work as only the participant knows everything about their practices.
(3) Interpretation: analyzing the results for themes and meaning which leads to a new design.
(4) Focus: sharing a common starting point to guide the observations and conversation and move towards a common goal.

These principles guide the process in order to understand what matters to users and analyze the results for themes that can lead to new design ideas. Through these, the observations expose more than the participant's actions, but also their knowledge, abilities, and attitudes. This process can also expose details about their particular practices that may not be conscious choices on their part.

The usual steps of a CI study are to: observe the relevant practices in the participant's environment, follow the observations with interviews guided by the users to expand on their actions and motivations, analyze the observations and the interviews to find themes and build understanding leading to an initial design, and evaluate the resulting design with the target users performing their actual tasks, if possible (Wixon et al. 1990). From a methodological perspective, these steps implement the four major phases of a CI, which are, as per (Wixon et al. 1990):

(1) Phase 1 (Inquiry): Talk to specific participants in target areas.
(2) Phase 2 (Interpretation): Interpret the data to capture the key issues emerging from the inquiry.
(3) Phase 3 (Models): Consolidate data across participants and build models that provide a holistic understanding of the identified issues.
(4) Phase 4 (Visioning): Redesign the way the tasks are performed, through the use of new technology.

The first three phases represent the requirement gathering part of designing new technology, focused on understanding what matters to users and on characterizing what users do (Wixon et al. 1990); the fourth phase helps with the concrete steps of designing solutions.

## Contextual Inquiry Case Studies

Many of the issues affecting older adults' UX when interacting with current interactive technologies are known—for example, deteriorating visual acuity or decline of cognitive function, leading to current websites' or interfaces' lack of accessibility for older adults (Johnson 2015). Such issues further risk digitally marginalizing older adults, as prior research has revealed that usability is a key factor for the successful long-term adoption of potentially beneficial technologies by older adults (Venkatesh et al. 2012). However, the tools and methodologies employed in the research and commercial development of Internet and mobile technologies at best follow UX design principles that are largely the same as those used for any other user group. In most cases, some of the current practices of technology development only marginally incorporate UX design approaches (and often only in name). At worst, some such approaches have been downright questionable—even described as 'snake oil' by some scholars (Sauro et al. 2017). While this is in part due to a lack of industry awareness or knowledge about UX design and development, more often this is in fact due to a widespread lack of adequate tools to support senior-focused design and development.

The consequences of this are twofold: a further widening of the digital divide facing older adults, and a barrier toward market adoption of beneficial technologies such as online banking. As outlined in the previous section, richer UX methods are needed to overcome these barriers, amongst which some of the stronger ones are mismatched mental models. We have proposed updates and refinements to one such rich method—CI—which facilitate the design of technologies that are more usable by older adults and that lead to a better user experience for them. In our lab, Technologies for Ageing Gracefully, we have applied this method to several of the short and long-term user experience studies on designing interactive technologies to support older adults' essential activities. We describe here the results of three such recent projects, demonstrating the suitability of our CI adaptions for collecting design requirements (grounded in an understanding of mental models) for this demographic. The projects address three essential aspects related to quality of life in retirement: safety, wellness (health), and social connectivity. We then draw parallels and implications for the FinTech industry, and outline recommendations for employing this method for the design of senior-centered digital financial tools. In the next section we elaborate on how additional user experience research methods (namely Participatory Design) can assist with implementing the design requirements collected through CI investigations with older adults.

## Staying Safe and Avoiding Financial Scams (Online)

The number of Canadian adults aged 65 or older who are active users of the Internet is constantly increasing. The 2011 Census (Stats Canada 2011) indicate that 66 percent of such adults are daily Internet users. Yet such users are also the most vulnerable—often seen as 'novice' and lacking 'security awareness' (Grimes et al. 2010). The Canadian Anti-Fraud Centre (CFAC) estimates that older adults are the preferred target of various Internet scams, with more than $10 million being reported lost annually to online financial fraud.

Prior research on this topic showed that older adults typically adopt technologies upon encouragement from family members, and they tend to acquire most of their knowledge about the device or tool from family as well (Boothroyd 2014). This applies to financial tools as well, such as online banking. However, the limited contact older adults have with family or friends limits opportunities that would allow seniors to learn about online safety and instead forces them to rely on mass-media for information, often presented in alarming terms (Boothroyd 2014). This may further exacerbate the mental models employed by older adults when interacting with online technologies, especially with respect to financial concerns. In our research (Munteanu et al. 2015) we have found that, lacking a strong social network that seniors can use to troubleshoot Internet-related security problems, they avoid many online activities due to concerns about financial losses or breaches targeting their private data. This can have significant implications for FinTech designers and developers.

Our research conducted a cross-disciplinary investigation consisting of a mixed-methods approach, which aimed to answer several questions related to the information practices of older adults with respect to online safety. The study was conducted using our adaption of Contextual Inquiries. Ten older adults participated in the study, each of them taking part in an extensive (2+ hour) session consisting of CI observations, interviews, and questionnaires. The CI observations were structured around several tasks, such as processing email messages, some crafted by the research team to mimic a variety of common templates used by financial scammers posing as legitimate businesses. Additional messages were used that were legitimate but which were flagged as potential threats, such as emails from established but lesser-known charities. The main activity of the CI session consisted of engaging in typical tasks with a banking website—the website was designed to match the look and feel of a real bank but with some elements suggesting that this may not be the case.

The thematic analysis of data collected during these sessions revealed several interesting findings with respect to our participants' mental models of online financial tools and the barriers toward their adoption, particularly as related to safety concerns. The most salient theme was that of resistance to the use of online banking and similar applications. This was mostly driven by low trust, among other factors, in the online process of transacting both monetary value and private information. This varied depending on the entities involved in such transactions, with higher trust being placed in financial institutions having a recognizable physical presence. This confirms some of the themes captured in the prior research on investigating barriers to transitioning from paper checks to online tools (Vines et al. 2012).

In terms of mental models, we have identified a preference for interacting with 'real people' for financial transactions. Performing such tasks online competes with their current mental models—there is no 'safety net' online (as participants mentioned to us: 'if something goes wrong, whom can I talk to? Where do I go?').

Finally, aspects of the TAM were visible in other themes, such as the lack of motivation for adopting a new way of performing activities that were done 'in person' before. Some participants did not feel the need to migrate financial activities online and were satisfied with the status quo. Our observations also confirmed the usability aspects of the TAM—the new (online) tool must be not only easy to use, but instill confidence. Even for participants that saw a measurable benefit (e.g., increased convenience such as form not having to walk outside during winter), there were concerns about making mistakes and 'breaking things'. In some cases, these were mitigated by an approach to learning that was hands-on, with encouragement and support from family or friends.

Recommendations for FinTech. Contextual Inquiries can expose older users' mental models with respect to how they trust an online platform that transacts both monetary values and personal (financial) information, and how they perceive the benefit/effort trade-off with respect to learning how to use a new tool.

## Accessing Essential Information Online

Although there has been much research in the last two decades on technology for knowledge acquisition and sharing, little of this has considered seniors and their sense of independence and control as the primary target. Moreover, where research has focused on older adults, it has predominately studied them as consumers of content, knowledge and care, rarely focusing on their capacity to manage and even contribute to knowledge creation. To address this gap, we have engaged in a mixed-methods study to develop a more integrated approach to acquiring, managing, and sharing increasingly-complex information by older adults. For this, we have focused on online health information access as a representative case, in particular investigating the privacy aspects of older adults' mental models with respect to online information access and sharing. This is grounded in prior research (Prasad et al. 2012) which showed that seniors are willing to share private information (such as health) depending on whom it will be shared with.

In a study with twelve older adults we sought to answer several questions, such as: Who do seniors trust within their care or social circle when discussing private information and concerns (such as health)? How do seniors seek answers to questions and concerns they have? And, how do seniors judge the reliability and credibility of online sources of information?

The thematic analysis of data collected from contextual inquiries of typical online health information access activities (e.g., accessing information repositories) revealed several key findings. We found that seniors are active information seekers, actively engaged in reading several sources of information. When they lacked understanding of the information presented, they preferred to seek answers by themselves, out of both their desire to safeguard their privacy and their concern for not burdening their social or care circle. However, their expectation of full privacy and control over their health information was often at odds with their preference for prompt answers to their questions about the information found, especially when encountering technical jargon.

With respect to trust, we (unexpectedly) found that almost all participants in this study were aware of the reputation and trustworthiness of various online repositories of health information as well as online discussion forums. Our observations suggested a higher level of trust in website that had 'name recognition' but which also had information written in a more professional (but also technical) manner.

Implications for FinTech. When conducting Contextual Inquiries with older adults, it is crucial to focus on activities that are related to information seeking (including question-answering tactics) with respect to the (technical) domain of the application that is to be designed. Such activities may reveal the mental models with respect to trust in information sources.

## Sharing of Personal Artefacts

The last of the three cases studies we discuss here is centered around social connectivity. We followed the CI method in an observation of nine older adults and their interactions with family pictures, with the goal of creating a digital tool that supported casual picture interactions. Existing digital pictures solutions were not being adopted by older adults, particularly for use in reminiscence activities. To better understand why this was and what might support their reminiscence in digital spaces, we wanted to first understand what they get out of sharing stories around paper pictures and their practices with physical pictures, so CI was a natural choice for this study. We conducted CI sessions in participants' homes to prompt casual oral reminiscence in its natural setting.

Across participants, we observed many different choices in how they stored and accessed their pictures, from photo albums to tablets. We also encountered common themes across participants, such as a curated wall of family pictures in a commonly accessed space. The prompt for the observation was intentionally open, allowing the participant to guide the experience. They were asked to show the different ways they stored and shared their family pictures, to guide the researcher through some of these storage items, and to freely reminisce from them. Nearly all participants used traditional photo albums, though some preferred framed pictures or tablets. As the observed practice involved speech, participants were not able to describe what they were doing in the process. Some research has also shown that these 'think-aloud' methods are less effective with older adults (Franz 2017). Instead, we followed the observation with an interview expanding on their recent reminiscence. This built on the observations to expose user motivations and requirements without biases or assumptions that may come with the expectation of new technology.

While this project was focused on designing novel interactive technologies that enhance social connectivity through storytelling based on digitized pictures, the analysis of data collected from the CI sessions revealed some interesting aspects about the participants' mental models. In particular, we found that participants' mental models of online cloud storage for digital pictures show that this is considered less permanent than paper options. This is aligned with other preliminary prior work (Petrelli et al. 2009; Keightley and Pickering 2014) which revealed that older users' mental models of online storage is perceived to be insecure.

Implications for FinTech. Older adults' mental models of online technologies, especially as applicable to storage of valuable artefacts or information (e.g., cloud storage), may not fully reflect the risk-benefit ratio of such technologies as compared to their non-digital equivalents. When designing FinTech solutions that require safeguarding of valuable information or digital artefacts (e.g., pension documents), Contextual Inquiries can help identify the mental models held by older adults with respect to their perceptions of risk of losing this valuable information.

# A UX Approach to FinTech Adoption

As we have illustrated earlier, designing technologies that support older adults' access to essential services in retirement needs to overcome barriers related to mismatched mental models. This was evident in our research investigating a wide range of services, from access to online health info and to cloud-based social sharing of photos. Moreover, it was particularly salient in our work on understanding older adults' practices with respect to online safety such as avoiding financial scams. Extracting these insights into how older adults may interact with digital technologies that complement or replace existing services (such as banking or financial support) was greatly facilitated by our use of methods that more deeply expose users' mental models. Contextual Inquiries can reveal hidden elements of user's mental models that result from the difficulty associated with verbalizing one's process (Liaqat et al. 2018). Accordingly, we have illustrated the value of ethnographic gathering methods such as Contextual Inquiries as a critical component of the design and development of technologies to support older adults' essential retirement services.

Studying users in context and being able to understand their mental models is an essential design step, but this in itself is not sufficient to ensure that the resulting design is fully adoptable by older users. Nor is there a single design method that can address all usability and adoption aspects. We suggest that methods that engage users more deeply at all stages of the design process be used—in particular, Participatory Design (PD), which can complement and augment many of the methods typically employed in User Experience Design (Preece et al. 2015).

Participatory Design integrates users into the technology creation process through a variety of methods such as interviews, observations, or design activities (Muller and Kuhn 1993; Muller 2003). While Participatory Design is used to elicit requirements throughout several stages of the design-development cycle, its core method (collaborative design) is most useful in the early stages of this cycle, as this prompts users to propose and visualize a potential design. PD involves users at all stages of the design, and elicits their direct input for specifying the design and the functional requirements of a system (Schuler and Namioka 1993). Typically this is conducted in the form of small workshops, during which participants work in groups of two to four to complete sketching activities around the design of a low-fidelity user interface prototype on paper, using a variety of design props such as sticky notes, printed icons, markers, etc. (Liaqat et al. 2018).

While Participatory Design has been extensively used to designing a wide range of applications for older adults, including in our own research—from fall prevention monitoring (Yu and Munteanu 2018) to learning support tools (Liaqat 2018)—its role in designing FinTech for older adults is only recently receiving attention. The most notable such research is that of (Vines et al. 2012) who employed Participatory Design with older adults to design digital alternatives to paper checks. Older adults' mental models of financial services was identified as the most significant barrier to the migration of such services to an online space, but the use of PD to design an alternative to a financial instrument as common and entrenched as paper checks was critical in overcoming such barriers. This suggests that Participatory Design is a promising method for the design of FinTech for older adults.

## Considerations for Older Adults

User Experience (UX) researchers face methodological challenges when working with older adults. For example, focus groups (a widely employed UX research method), is more difficult to run with senior users due to the participants' declining communication abilities (Barrett and Kirk 2000). Other common UX methods such as interviews or usability assessments can result in inaccurate data by encountering issues such as participants responding with what they think the researcher wants to hear (Franz 2017). While these methods continue to be used, CI may better support early research with older adults without these challenges.

In particular for FinTech, CI has the potential to exposure older adults' mental models that otherwise may not be uncovered through other elicitation techniques. This is due to the 'master-apprentice' model employed by CI, in which the researcher not only observes the users performing tasks in their own environment without being influenced, but is 'coached' by the user in how to perform those tasks. This is particularly useful when designing a new application that aims to replace an existing service, such as is common when transitioning financial services to an online-only operation. Often in such cases, the research or the design team may have their own mental models which are different than those of the target users with respect to how the service (and the application) works. This is an issue that may be very relevant to (online) FinTech, due in part to different generational perspectives on how financial services are or should be delivered. In addition to addressing the issues caused by generational differences in mental models, using Contextual Inquiries in the early stages of designing such technologies may also mitigate other barriers that older adults face in adoption digital technologies. One of these is the stigma associated to (lack of) technology use, which may influence how older adults respond when questioned directly about their activities during the requirements gathering stages of UX design (Franz 2017).

Earlier in this chapter we have presented the findings of CI studies with older adults that reveal an understanding of key practices that would have otherwise been more difficult to develop. These findings are relevant to several dimensions that define a positive retirement experience: financial safety, health knowledge, and social connectivity. These also illustrate how CI can help designers better understand older adults' mental models with respect to adopting solutions which are technologically similar to those found within FinTech. Based on these, we detail here three new methodological considerations shaping how to apply Contextual Inquiries to the early stages of designing with older adults:

**Observations separate from technology.** To support CI observations in as natural a setting as possible, participants should not be biased by introducing issues of technology and its adoption before they have had the chance to demonstrate their current practices. CI observations should be completed before introducing the idea of a new or modified technology, to avoid the potentials for stigma and limited access. Introducing the concept of new technology before the observation can bias how senior participants demonstrate their activities.

**First support current practices.** New technologies often leave behind older adults and their preferred practices, so the understanding and resulting design should first aim to support current practices, and second to improve on potential existing setbacks or limitations. In our studies, we have observed seniors maintaining time-consuming or difficult but familiar practices rather than adopt a new technology that forces them to change their process. Technology adoption is more likely if older adults do not need to adjust their current activities or learn new processes, though this should not lead designers to consider emerging technologies as not adoptable. One of the case studies discussed in this chapter shows CI findings lead to designs supporting current activities (family picture reminiscence prompted by looking at photographs) along with expansions such as features supporting the creation of multimedia digital stories.

**Realistic side-by-side comparison.** When assessing the design, after completing the four phases of a CI, participants should be able to experience the new technology in as realistic a setting as possible and be given the chance to compare that to their current activities. Providing a practical example of how they might use a new design, ideally with their own data (e.g., their calendar, pictures, etc.), and enabling them to compare that to current practices provides concrete experience and contextualizes that experience within their familiar activities. This recommendation is based in our own experience running studies where we have noticed how seniors benefit from relating the new design to their prior practices. Older adults should be asked to first assess just the parts that support the existing practices before being introduced to potential improvements or other changes in the new design.

## Conclusion

Several barriers exist when designing interactive applications for older adults to support them in their retirement. We propose that mental models are such a key barrier, and we have found that CI—an often-overlooked UX research method—may be used by designers of critical services such as FinTech to better expose older adults' mental models to designer. Based on three cases studies of research on older adults engaging with essential digital services, we suggest several adaptations to CI that may increase its applicability to FinTech design:

1. Observe and interview older adult users as they engage with the relevant activity without introducing new technologies;
2. Build and understanding of their current practices in order to ensure these are first and foremost supported in any new technology or digital service that is to be developed;
3. Evaluate new designs in realistic settings with older adults using their own artefacts;
4. Compare these to users' existing processes in the same session so they can provide direct feedback about the new experiences.

The evaluation should separate existing practices and any potential opportunities provided by the new technology in order to remove the potential biasing effect of these new tools.

## Notes

1. We consider older adults as being 65 years old or older, as per Statistics Canada's definition (Stats Canada 2012), while also capturing research that includes adults age 55 to 64 if relevant, such as for studying longer-term concerns (e.g., retirement, health), as per Statistics Canada's reporting (Schellenberg and Turcotte 2007).
2. We acknowledge that there is a significant debate on the appropriate term to describe such a broad user group (Taylor 2011; Smith 2012). In this work, we interchangeably use the terms 'older adults' and 'seniors', as we have informally found that our participants (in studies conducted in our lab) refer to themselves by either of these two terms. Additionally, the present study was exploratory in nature and not aimed at a particular subset of this demographic. It should be noted that, in the region we are located, the term 'senior' is the most commonly used to denote 'older adults' without a more specific age definition, including by the relevant funding agency and government ministry that supports our work.

# References

Acemoglu, D. (2009). The Crisis of 2008: Lessons for and from Economics. *Critical Review*, 21(2–3), 185–94.

Alhabash, S., Brooks, B. A., Jiang, M., Rifon, N. J., Robert, L., and Cotten, S. (2015). Is It Institutional or System Trust?: Mediating the Effect of Generational Cohort Membership on Online Banking Intentions. *iConference 2015 Proceedings*.

Axtell, R. B. (2017). *Frame of Mind: Bringing Family Photo Interaction into Speech-Enabled Digital Spaces to Support Older Adults' Reminiscence*. Master of Science Thesis. Toronto, ON: University of Toronto.

Barrett, J., and Kirk, S. (2000). 'Running Focus Groups with Elderly and Disabled Elderly Participants.' *Applied Ergonomics*, 31(6), 621–9.

Beyer, H., and Holtzblatt, K. (1997). *Contextual Design: Defining Customer-Centered Systems*. San Francisco, CA: Morgan Kaufmann.

Beyer, H., and Holtzblatt, K. (1999). Contextual Design. *ACM interactions*, 6(1), 32–42.

Blazer, D. G., Yaffe, K., and Karlawish, J. (2015). Cognitive Aging: A Report from the Institute of Medicine. *Jama*, 313(21), 2121–2.

Boothroyd, V. (2014). *Older Adults' Perceptions of Online Risk*. Master of Arts Thesis. Ottawa, ON: Carleton University.

CFAC (2014). *Annual Report*, 2014. North Bay, Ontario: The Canadian Anti-Fraud Centre. http://www.antifraudcentre-centreantifraude.ca/reports-rapports/2014/ann-ann-eng.htm#a2 (accessed March 1, 2019).

Campbell, T. (2017). 'How Canadians are harnessing the technological revolution in banking,' *The Hamilton Spectator*. March 2. https://www.thespec.com/opinion-story/7168266-how-canadians-are-harnessing-the-technological-revolution-in-banking/ (accessed March 1, 2019).

Czaja, S. J., and Lee, C. C. (2007). 'The Impact of Aging on Access to Technology.' *Universal Access in the Information Society*, 5(4): 341–49.

Czaja, S. J., Sharit, J., Nair, S. N., and Lee, C. C. (2009). Older Adults and Internet Health Information Seeking. *Proceedings of the Human Factors and Ergonomics Society Annual Meeting* 53(2): 126–30.

Dang, Y. (2016). *Engaging Seniors through Automatically Generated Photo Digests from their Families Social Media*. Master of Science Thesis. Toronto, ON: University of Toronto.

De Bondt, W. F., and Thaler, R. H. (1995). Financial Decision-Making in Markets and Firms: A Behavioral Perspective. *Handbooks in Operations Research and Management Science*, 9, 385–410.

Denton, M. A., Kemp, C. L., French, S., Gafni, A., Joshi, A., Rosenthal, C. J., and Davies, S. (2004). 'Reflexive Planning for Later Life. *Canadian Journal on Aging/La Revue Canadienne Du Vieillissement*, 23(5), S71–S82.

Denzau, A. T., and North, D. C. (1994). Shared Mental Models: Ideologies and Institutions. *Kyklos*, 47(1), 3–31.

Franz, R. L. (2017). *I Knew That, I Was Just Testing You: Understanding Older Adults' Impression Management Tactics during Usability Studies*. Master's Thesis. Toronto, ON: University of Toronto.

Franz, R. L., Munteanu, C., Neves, B. B., and Baecker, R. (2015). 'Time to Retire Old Methodologies? Reflecting on Conducting Usability Evaluations with Older Adults.' *Proceedings of the 17th International Conference on Human-Computer Interaction with Mobile Devices and Services Adjunct,* pp. 912–15.

Garg, V., et al. (2011). 'Designing Risk Communication for Older Adults.' *Symposium on Usable Privacy and Security (SOUPS),* ACM.

Grimes, G. A. et al. (2010). 'Older Adults' Knowledge of Internet Hazards.' *Journal of Educational Gerontology,* 36(3): 173–92.

Grudin, J. (1992). 'Utility and Usability: Research Issues and Development Contexts.' *Interacting with computers,* 4(2), 209–17.

Hammersley, M., and Atkinson, P. (2007). *Ethnography: Principles in Practice.* Abingdon, UK: Routledge.

Interaction Design Foundation (2018). 'User Experience (UX) Design.' *Interaction Design Foundation.* https://www.interaction-design.org/literature/topics/ux-design (accessed March 1, 2019).

Johnson, J. A. (2015). 'Designing Websites for Adults 55+: Toward Universal Design.' *Proceedings of the 33rd Annual ACM Conference Extended Abstracts on Human Factors in Computing Systems* ACM, pp. 2449–50.

Keightley, E., and Pickering, M. (2014). 'Technologies of Memory: Practices of Remembering in Analogue and Digital Photography'. *New Media & Society,* 16(4), 576–93.

Kemp, C. L., and Denton, M. (2003). 'The Allocation of Responsibility for Later Life: Canadian Reflections on the Roles of Individuals, Government, Employers and Families.' *Ageing & Society,* 3(6): 737–60.

Li, Y., Gao, J., Enkavi, A. Z., Zaval, L., Weber, E. U., and Johnson, E. J. (2015). 'Sound Credit Scores and Financial Decisions despite Cognitive Aging'. *Proceedings of the National Academy of Sciences,* 112(1), 65–9.

Liaqat, A. (2018). *Design Requirements for a Tool to Support the Writing Development of Mature ELLs.* Master of Science Thesis. Toronto, ON: University of Toronto.

Liaqat, A., Axtell, B., Munteanu, C., and Demmans Epp, C. (2018). 'Contextual Inquiry, Participatory Design, and Learning Analytics: An Example.' *Companion Proceedings 8th International Conference on Learning Analytics & Knowledge* (LAK18), pp. 1–5.

Loibl, C. (2017). 'Living in Poverty: Understanding the Financial Behaviour of Vulnerable Groups.' In R. Ranyard (ed.), *Economic Psychology.* Hoboken, NJ: John Wiley & Sons, Inc. 421–34.

Lusardi, A., and Mitchell, O. S. (2007). 'The Importance of Financial Literacy: Evidence and Implications for Financial Education Programs'. *Policy Brief.* The Wharton School.

Moffatt, K. (2013). 'Older-Adult HCI: Why Should We Care?' *ACM interactions,* 20(4), 72–5.

Montazemi, A. R., and Qahri-Saremi, H. (2015). 'Factors Affecting Adoption of Online Banking: A Meta-analytic Structural Equation Modeling Study.' *Information & Management,* 52(2), 210–26.

Muller, M. J. (2003). 'Participatory Design: The Third Space in HCI.' *Human-Computer Interaction: Development Process,* 4235: 165–85.

Muller, M. J., and Kuhn, S. (1993).' Participatory Design.' *Communications of the ACM*, 36(6): 24–8.

Munteanu, C., Tennakoon, C., Garner, J., Goel, A., Ho, M., Shen, C., and Wind-eyeret, R. (2015). 'Improving Older Adults' Online Security: An Exercise in Participatory Design.' *Proceedings of the ACM Symposium on Usable Privacy and Security (SOUPS)*, pp. 1–2.

Muskens, L., van Lent, R., Vijfvinkel, A., van Cann, P., and Shahid, S. (2014). 'Never Too Old to Use a Tablet: Designing Tablet Applications for the Cognitively and Physically Impaired Elderly,' in K. Miesenberger, D. Fels, D. Archambault, D. Penaz, and P. Zagler (eds.), *Computers Helping People with Special Needs*. New York, NY: Springer Publishing, pp. 391–8.

Neves, B., Franz, R., Munteanu, C., Baecker, R., and Ngo, M. (2015). 'My Hand Doesn't Listen to Me! : Adoption and Evaluation of a Communication Technology for the 'Oldest Old'.' *Proceedings of the ACM SIGCHI Conference on Human Factors in Computing Systems*. CHI, Seoul, South Korea, April 2015, pp. 1–10.

Neves, B. B., et al. (2013). 'Coming of (Old) Age in the Digital Age: ICT Usage and Non-Usage among Older Adults.' *Journal of Sociological Research Online*, 18(2): 6.

Nicholson, N. R. (2012). 'A Review of Social Isolation: An Important but Under-assessed Condition in Older Adults.' *The Journal of Primary Prevention*, 33(2–3): 137–52.

Nielsen, J. (1990). 'A Meta-model for Interacting with Computers'. *Interacting with Computers*, 2(2), 147–60.

Nielsen, J. (2010). 'Mental Models,' *Nielsen-Norman Group*. https://www.nngroup.com/articles/mental-models/ (updated October 18, 2010; accessed March 1, 2019).

Norman, D. (2013). *The Design of Everyday Things: Revised and Expanded*. New York, NY: Perseus Basics Books.

Petrelli, D., Van den Hoven, E., and Whittaker, S. (2009). 'Making History: Intentional Capture of Future Memories.' *Proceedings of the SIGCHI Conference on Human Factors in Computing Systems*, pp. 1723–32.

Prasad, A., Sorber, J., Stablein, T., Anthony, D., and Kotz, D. (2012). 'Understanding Sharing Preferences and Behavior for Health Devices.' *Proceedings of the 2012 ACM Workshop on Privacy in the Electronic Society*, pp. 117–28.

Preece, J., Rogers, Y., and Sharp, H. (2015). *Interaction Design: Beyond Human–Computer Interaction*, 4th Edition, Hoboken, NJ: John Wiley & Sons.

Raphael, D., Brown, I., Bryant, T., Wheeler, J., Herman, R., Houston, J., and McClelland, B. (2001). 'How Government Policy Decisions Affect Seniors' Quality of Life: Findings from a Participatory Policy Study Carried out in Toronto, Canada.' *Canadian Journal of Public Health*, 92(3): 190–5.

Rouse, W. B., and Morris, N. M. (1986). 'On Looking into the Black Box: Prospects and Limits in the Search for Mental Models.' *Psychological Bulletin*, 100(3): 349.

Salovaara, A., and Tamminen, S. (2009). 'Acceptance or Appropriation? A Design-Oriented Critique of Technology Acceptance Models,' in H. Isomäki and P. Saariluoma (eds.), *Future Interaction Design II*. Springer London, UK: Springer, pp. 157–73.

Sauro, J., Johnson, K., and Meenan, C. (2017, May). 'From Snake-Oil to Science: Measuring UX Maturity.' *Proceedings of the 2017 CHI Conference Extended Abstracts on Human Factors in Computing Systems* (pp. 1084–91). ACM.

Schellenberg, G., and M. Turcotte. (2007). 'A Portrait of Seniors in Canada.' *Statistics Canada Journals and Periodicals.* Catalogue No. 89–519–X.

Schuler, D. and Namioka, A. (1993). *Participatory design: Principles and practices.* CRC Press: Boca Raton, FL.

Sixsmith, J., Sixsmith, A., Fänge, A. M., Naumann, D., Kucsera, C., Tomsone, S., Haak, M., Dahlin-Ivanoff, S., and Woolrych, R. (2014). 'Healthy Ageing and Home: The Perspectives of Very Old People in Five European Countries.' *Social Science & Medicine*, 106, 1–9.

Smith, A. (2012). 'Elders? Older Adults? Seniors? Language Matters.' *GeriPal—A Geriatrics and Palliative Care Blog.* March 21. https://www.geripal.org/2012/03/elders-older-adults-seniors-language.html (accessed March 1, 2019).

Stats Canada (2011). *Statistics Canada 2011 Census of Population* https://www12.statcan.gc.ca/census-recensement/index-eng.cfm (updated June 15, 2018; accessed March 1, 2019).

Stats Canada (2012). *Statistics Canada 2012 Canada Year Book* 11-402-X http://www.statcan.gc.ca/pub/11-402-x/2012000/chap/seniors-aines/seniors-aines-eng.htm (updated October 7, 2016; accessed March 1, 2019).

Taylor, A. (2011). 'Older Adult, Older Person, Senior, Elderly or Elder: A Few Thoughts on the Language we use to Reference Aging.' *British Columbia Law Institute.* October 30. https://www.bcli.org/older-adult-older-person (accessed March 1, 2019).

Venkatesh, V., and Davis, F. A. (2000). 'A Theoretical Extension of the Technology Acceptance Model: Four Longitudinal Field Studies.' *Journal of Management Science*, 46(2): 186–204.

Venkatesh, V., Thong, J. Y. and Xu, X. (2012). 'Consumer Acceptance and Use of Information Technology: Extending the Unified Theory of Acceptance and Use of Technology.' *MIS Quarterly*, 36(1): 157–78.

Vettese, F. (2015). *The Essential Retirement Guide: A Contrarian's Perspective.* New York, NY: John Wiley & Sons.

Vettese, F. M. (2016). 'How Spending Declines with Age, and the Implications for Workplace Pension Plans.' *Essential Policy Intelligence E-Brief.* Toronto, ON: C. D. Howe Institute.

Vines, J., Blythe, M., Dunphy, P., Vlachokyriakos, V., Teece, I., Monk, A., and Olivier, P. (2012). 'Cheque Mates: Participatory Design of Digital Payments with Eighty Somethings.' *Proceedings of the SIGCHI Conference on Human Factors in Computing Systems*, pp. 1189–98.

Whitenton, K. (2018). 'The Two UX Gulfs: Evaluation and Execution.' *Nielsen Norman Group Technical Report.* California: Neilson Norman Group. https://www.nngroup.com/articles/two-ux-gulfs-evaluation-execution/ (accessed March 1, 2019).

Wixon, D., Holtzblatt, K., and Knox, S. (1990). 'Contextual Design: An Emergent View of System Design.' *Proceedings of the SIGCHI Conference on Human Factors in Computing Systems*, pp. 329–36.

World Bank. (2015). 'Thinking with mental models'. In *World Bank—World Development Report 2015: Mind, Society, and Behavior*. World Bank Group. Chapter 3, pp. 62–75.

Wu, A. Y., and Munteanu, C. (2018, April). 'Understanding Older Users' Acceptance of Wearable Interfaces for Sensor-based Fall Risk Assessment'. *Proceedings of the 2018 CHI Conference on Human Factors in Computing Systems*, paper no. 119. ACM, pp. 1–13.

# Part III

# New Roles and Responsibilities for Plan Sponsors and Regulators

# Chapter 8

# The Big Spenddown: Digital Investment Advice and Decumulation

*Steven Polansky, Peter Chandler, and Gary R. Mottola*

As the Baby Boomers retire and pivot to generating an income in retirement, many of them will seek easy and inexpensive ways to manage their investments to this end. Whether digital investment advice providers, often called 'robo-advisors' or 'robos,' can meet this need is the subject of our chapter. We begin with a brief overview of the development of digital investment advice services, followed by a review of the challenges of asset decumulation in retirement, many of which apply to both traditional and robo-advisors. Yet because robos operate primarily in a realm of electronic communications, they face a number of unique demands. Next we briefly discuss the issues with which digital advice providers wrestle as they try to provide decumulation services for their clients; and end by discussing implications for the robo marketplace.

## A Brief History of Automated Financial Advice

Technology has played a major role in driving development of the financial services industry in the US for hundreds of years. In the nineteenth and early twentieth centuries, trades were entered longhand into a New York Stock Exchange ledger. Electronic tickers then replaced ledgers, and in the early 1960s, Bunko Ramo Corporation developed a computerized quote system that laid the groundwork for the introduction of the automated, high-speed markets we know today. Advances in technology also led to advances in the types of investment tools available to financial advisors.

Beginning in the early 2000s, several firms offered a variety of online, client-facing tools that presaged some of the functionality available through today's robos (Ameriks 2001; Agnew 2006). Broadly speaking, those tools provided two main elements: (1) limited financial or investment planning functionality, such as calculators and budgeting tools to assist investors in determining how much they need to save for a particular goal or objective within a timeframe (e.g., retirement or purchase of a new home in five years); and (2) asset allocation tools, frequently provided by online broker-dealers to their clients to help investors determine how to allocate their investments based on their investment profiles. Beyond that, some online broker-dealers offered additional tools to assist self-directed investors in screening or filtering securities.

In the aftermath of the 2008–2009 financial crisis, a new type of investment intermediary emerged: the client-facing digital investment advisor or robo-advisor. As the industry has developed, some firms offered robo service directly to consumers, while others offered their product on a white-label basis through a third-party advisor and/or employer-provided retirement plans. Some did both.

Robos typically ask customers a limited set of questions about their investment objectives, investment time horizon, and risk tolerance, as well as other questions, and then process the responses through algorithms to profile the investors and place them into low-cost portfolios, usually made up of exchange-traded funds (ETFs; see FINRA 2016). In addition, some robos offer portfolio rebalancing and tax loss harvesting functionality. In their earliest incarnations, the robo-advisors typically did not provide access to a human investment advisor. As will be discussed below, this has changed, and many robos now offer access to a technology help desk and, typically at additional cost, to a human advisor.

Of course, digital functionality is by no means new to the securities industry. Sophisticated resources have long been available to the professional advisory community, often in the form of proprietary 'in house' services that run simulations, customize portfolios, and more. What has changed is that this functionality is becoming available directly to retail investors in a simplified, accessible form. Moreover, advisory firms have long used investment models, Modern Portfolio Theory, and other models seeking to reassure investors that their services were rigorous.

Despite the common academic foundation driving investment advice, it is clear that robo portfolios can differ, even for a given investor (Polansky and Sibears 2016; Deschenes and Hammond 2019). Further, there is no generally accepted investment methodology around which firms can anchor their approaches to decumulation.

## Why Generating Retirement Income Is a Challenge

Many Americans have a difficult task before them, and so do financial advisors seeking to offer decumulation services: it is not simple to generate a stable retirement income stream. For one reason, people may need to generate income from several employer-based retirement accounts, individual retirement accounts (IRAs), traditional defined benefit pensions, taxable investment accounts, and savings accounts, all of which may be held by different financial institutions. Retirees must also consider their social security options, since deciding when to claim social security benefits is affected by a number of behavioral factors and can have a considerable impact on retirement income (Knoll 2011). There is also the question of whether to tap home equity (if any exists). Tax treatment of retirement income is yet another factor retirees must consider: taxes vary depending on the type of account or investment tapped for retirement income, the amount received, and other factors.

Complicating matters further, people must make a number of important assumptions when planning their retirement incomes. These include inflation rates, equity returns, bond returns, expected health in retirement, and life expectancy—assumptions that, if wrong, could impact the quality of life people experience in their later years.

Equally importantly is the matter of how much risk a retiree can take. Lifecycle funds and other products that automatically rebalance generally involve increasingly lower levels of risk over time (reducing exposure to stocks, for instance, and increasing exposure to bonds and cash). At the same time, some older investors may feel a need to take on additional risk in the hope of catching up if they lack sufficient funds for retirement. This can lead to practices such as 'yield reaching' or, worse, make them vulnerable to financial fraud. Several studies have, in fact, found an association between risk taking and fraud susceptibility, as well as debt and fraud susceptibility (Kieffer and Mottola 2017; Kircanski et al. 2018).

As a result, generating a retirement income by decumulating assets is arguably more difficult than accumulating assets destined for retirement. The accumulation phase involves fewer and less complex decisions, and there are often opportunities to course-correct along the way. Further, during the accumulation phase, the entire process—enrollment, fund selection, savings rate, and escalation of the savings rate—is often automated, requiring fewer decisions for the employee. For example, Vanguard (2017) reported that nearly half of the plans they administer offer automatic enrollment, covering 61 percent of their participant population.

Generally speaking, accumulation portfolios for clients have different levels of equity and fixed income exposure as well as risk (Polansky and Sibears 2016), yet most of them operate within the generally accepted modern portfolio framework. There is little agreement among investment professionals about how best to decumulate assets, and few academic studies exist to guide investors and investment professionals through the decumulation phase.[1] Accordingly, without an agreed-upon decumulation methodology, investors may be exposed to greater variation in advisor approaches and strategies that may lack a sound basis. For example, one common maxim is the '4 percent rule,' which proposes that retirees withdraw 4 percent of their assets each year to avoid running out of money during retirement. Yet this is an overly simplistic rule that can result in asymmetric risks, leading to the serious problem of overspending in retirement, causing money to run out before death (Finke et al. 2013). Alternatively, it can result in underspending in retirement, leaving more assets at death than planned (Fellowes 2017). Other approaches include the use of annuities, bond ladders, interest-only withdrawals, longevity insurance, managed payout funds, or a combination of some or all of these.

Those facing the decumulation process may also fall prey to certain biases that negatively affect their financial decision-making. For example, overconfidence, loss aversion, mental accounting, the disposition effect, framing, anchoring (Byrne and Utkus 2013), choice overload (Iyengar and Lepper 2000), the certainty effect (Kahneman and Tversky 1979), emotions (Kircanski et al. 2018; Frydman and Camerer 2016; FINRA Foundation 2014), and impulsivity control (Knutson and Samanez-Larking 2014) all influence people's financial behavior. Additionally, some people cannot understand and use probabilities to make decisions, further impeding effective financial decision-making (Gigerenzer 2002).

For these reasons, some people seek financial advice where the level of service and personalization depends on their means, typically measured in assets. Wealthy retirees can afford to use traditional financial advisors who provide one-on-one personalized advice, financial plans, and tools to guide a client's investing and spending in retirement. Even here, however, some financial planners lack the technology and expertise to provide comprehensive advice on key decumulation decisions like Medicare or social security claiming, or they do not run simulations to evaluate how to optimize these and other decisions in concert with an investment plan. Retirees with fewer assets typically have fewer options, since lower balance accounts often are not cost-effective for traditional financial advisors. Yet our discussions with robo firms indicate that this clientele is potentially ripe for robo-advice platforms.

## Lessons from Industry Interviews

To delve further into the state of play in the robo-economy, we conducted interviews with more than a dozen representatives from digital investment advice providers, financial services companies, a data aggregation company, and members of an investor issues group organized by a leading consumer advocate. This last group consisted of investor advocates and securities industry representatives tasked with discussing important marketplace and policy issues in an off-the-record setting. We also interviewed a journalist who writes on retirement income issues. These interviews were conducted by phone, in person, and in writing, during the fourth quarter of 2017 and the first quarter of 2018. Where possible, we confirmed our findings with articles on or related to this topic.

Several questions guided our talks with robo-advisors, other industry participants and (with slight variation) consumer advocates: (1) How would you describe the state of robo-advisors and their decumulation strategies? (2) What business challenges do robos face related to decumulation? (3) Beyond robo-accumulation functionality, what other functionality do robos need to offer in order to provide advice on decumulation? (4) What additional information, beyond that which they collect for the accumulation phase of investing, do they need from the client in order to execute a decumulation strategy? (5) Is there agreement among robo-providers on the types of additional information they need to obtain from their clients for the decumulation phase? (6) Are there generally agreed upon approaches within the industry broadly for decumulating assets and, if so, do you see robos adopting these approaches for decumulating assets? (7) Do you see a 'pure robo' model as workable, or do the complexities of retirement planning require some level interaction with a human advisor? If the latter, are there key points where human intervention is needed? (8) What disclosure information should clients receive about the decumulation strategy that the robo provides? (9) What consideration, if any, are robo providers giving to cognitive decline experienced by clients using their decumulation services? (10) What role, if any, do you see human advisors playing in association with a robo provider's decumulation plan? (11) Are there other questions we should be asking/issues we should be looking into? Regarding the last question, no interviewees suggested additional areas or topics we should consider. Interviewees were told that no comments or insights would be attributed to them individually unless we obtained their permission, and that their organizations would be listed in the Acknowledgements section unless they did not want it listed. Interviewees had the opportunity to review a draft article and provide feedback prior to publication.

**The target market.** Most of the robo-advisors identified Millennials as a key target market, but they also indicated that they served a broader group including substantial Generation X and Baby Boomer customers, including some who were retired or close to retirement. Investors interested in using robos tended to have: (1) comfort using technology-based solutions with minimal or no human interaction; (2) insufficient funds for a traditional advised financial relationship; (3) lack of interest in and possible distrust of, traditional financial intermediaries; (4) a do-it-yourself attitude (i.e., they were interested in managing their investment process broadly, but not to the extent of constructing, managing, and rebalancing their portfolios); (5) confidence in passive, index-driven investment strategies possibly accompanied with a lack of confidence in the value of actively managed investment strategies and/or traditional financial advisors; and (6) a desire for a relatively simple, fully or substantially 'packaged' investing solution. A related factor was the desire for paying low management fees.

Mainstream robo-advice tends to be targeted at investors who do not engage in active trading nor are the interested in developing/implementing their own investment theses. Moreover, these investors tend to prefer a passive, index fund-based approach to investing, though some robos do target investors seeking more active management. Generally, robo providers expect that the investor will accept an 'off the rack' portfolio, and while investors may have some discretion to adjust their profiles to be placed in more or less aggressive portfolios, robo-firms anticipate that this is done infrequently. In addition, investors usually have limited or no choice in selecting the securities used to build their portfolios.

Some discussions cast investors' advice needs in binary terms: no advice/ full do-it-yourself all the time vs. fully advised all the time. Those with whom we spoke generally thought that investors' real-world needs were more nuanced. Some investment decisions are less complicated or less consequential, while others are more complex and may have far-reaching consequences, including some that cannot be easily adjusted. The former may lend themselves to simple, online solutions, while the latter may require more time and consultation with the investor, whether through online interaction and education or direct contact with a human advisor. Accordingly, robo business models are evolving to provide multiple levels of service at different price points, to help address these differing needs.

Some observers view robos as a democratizing force that can make high-quality financial advice available to a broad base of investors, many of whom lack sufficient assets to be attractive to many traditional brokerage and advisory firms. Cerulli and Associates (2017) reported 101 million US households have less than $250,000 in investible assets each, and 75 million of them have less than $50,000 in investible assets. Based on the feedback we received, robo-advisors appear well positioned to meet some of the needs of such investors. One caveat here is that investors with complicated financial situations, regardless of their level of investable assets, may require higher levels of advice.

**Industry evolution.** Robo advice is still a relatively new facet of the securities industry, and the players are evolving rapidly as they seek to gain a foothold in a highly competitive marketplace. Competition from new entrants, existing robos, and incumbent traditional financial firms is likely to drive continued innovation, while also amplifying forces that may drive both consolidation and fragmentation in the market. We anticipate that there will be innovation at each point along the existing advice value chain, and that some firms will add to the value chain by developing tools to support decumulation. Developments in the market for robo services may also be influenced by developments in the 'near robo' space, such as firms in adjacent financial services areas like broad financial planning. In this situation, the landscape of players is likely to become more complex, and the definition of what constitutes a robo will likely remain in flux.

**A changing robo landscape.** Most robos provide investment advice within the context of a client's single investment account, (i.e., the advice is limited to the account at the robo and does not factor in investments held elsewhere). Some firms are considering providing tools that take into account the totality of a client's investment accounts. In at least some cases, those firms offer the planning and advice service as a standalone service or through a Registered Investment Advisor (RIA).

While most robos we reviewed focus on general investment advice, some concentrate on a specific market niches or segments. Most notably for this article, one provides services specifically focused on the needs of individuals entering, or already in, retirement. Although not focused on decumulation, others did offer automated advice for 401(k) account holders.

In their early days, robo-advisors generally offered a service based on recommendations generated by the systems' algorithms and with limited opportunity for human interaction outside of tech support and account opening processes. As robo advice has developed, a number of firms now deliver tiered offerings where, for a higher fee, the firm can provide greater access to human advisors and more customized advice. As technology continues to advance, for example through the development of artificial intelligence techniques, robo-advisors may harness these advances to extend their service offerings. These advances may include functionality that would allow automated systems to handle the more complex situations individuals may face as they enter retirement.

## A View from the Industry

Next we identify contextual considerations or factors affecting the interactions between advisors and investors entering or in retirement.

**Context and considerations.** Moving from asset accumulation to asset decumulation marks a significant transition for both investors and advisors, and one that has major implications for the functionalities advisors may need to provide and the modes through which they deliver advice.

For investors, this change is typically characterized by increased uncertainty, the need to make point-in-time, highly consequential decisions, and limited or no experience upon which to draw to make these decisions.

During the accumulation stage of their lives, investors face some uncertainties (e.g., potential serious health problems or loss of employment), but uncertainty increases significantly as people enter retirement. Investors do not know, for example, how long they will live, what their health situation will be, how they will want to spend their time, and the financial demands they will face. Moreover, individuals have decades to 'learn by doing' in their investments with the opportunity to learn from mistakes, and in many cases to substantially correct those mistakes. Instead, investors need to make important financial decisions with limited or no previous experience facing these questions and little or no opportunity to correct mistakes.

As a consequence, the transition likely requires a substantial change in the ways investors interact with their advisors (robo, human, or hybrid), moving from a largely passive role, to active engagement with the advisor as the investor enters or moves through retirement. Key questions and issues include, for example, whether and when to purchase an annuity, or if an individual has a pension, whether to take a lump sum payment or an annuity, and when to start drawing social security (at retirement or a later date), among others.

From an advisory perspective, the informational needs to advise an individual on retirement financial planning increase significantly. Today, most robos advise on the assets they manage, and some robos can manage those assets within the context of an individual's broader portfolio, that is, assets the investor may hold elsewhere. Many interviewees noted that effective financial planning for retirement, however, requires a far broader view of the retiree's circumstances, to include not only a full view of the retiree's assets (e.g., potential social security and pension income) and liabilities (e.g., mortgage) but a number of other quantitative and qualitative factors, as well. For example, an advisor would benefit from understanding an individual's personal and family health history. If the retiree is married or has a partner, information about the partner's financial and health information would also be helpful. Finally, as noted above, individuals frequently do not know how they will spend their time during retirement, and how they spend their time typically changes with age.

There are some rules of thumb to guide decumulation, like the 4 percent rule, but these are not rooted in rigorous empirical analysis and most of the individuals we interviewed believe that the rule is inadequate. Instead, the firms we interviewed that did provide at least some level of service focused on approaches that reflected their own analysis and philosophical approach to decumulation. For example, some used low-risk, more liquid investments to provide a base level of income sufficient to meet a retiree's basic needs, and higher-risk investments to address optional desires such as travel or purchase of an additional house.

**Robo focus on decumulation.** While most of our discussions with robo-advisors reinforced the view that robos today focus on attracting investors and assets for the accumulation stage, aspects of some of these firms' product or service offerings are relevant to decumulation. For example, one firm offers an automatic withdrawal feature that investors can turn on and off. The firm also offers a more sophisticated approach to drawdowns that incorporates considerations related to required minimum distributions (RMDs), but this option requires an investor to use the firm's hybrid advisory service. Another firm noted that it has a heritage of working with 'do-it-yourself' oriented customers and offers them income-oriented portfolios and tools to project a sustainable withdrawal rate and track withdrawals against that rate. These tools are, however, best-suited for individuals with simple financial pictures. That firm also offers a hybrid robo service to address more complex questions, such as determining the sequencing of withdrawals from taxable and non-taxable accounts.

We also met with a company that focuses almost exclusively on decumulation. This firm offers three service tiers: free, self-service, and full-service. The self-service tier is essentially a robo for decumulation; that is, it offers clients a fully digital interaction, while the full-service tier combines both technology-based advice and access to a human advisor. The higher level service tiers have increasing account minimums and fee levels. This firm's decumulation-oriented services include account sequencing (i.e., advice on the order in which retirees should draw on their accounts), social security optimization, and health spending plans.

**Target market.** In an increasingly crowded market, some robo-advisors continue to pursue a broad range of potential investors, while some are taking a more targeted approach. The targeted approach may be reflected in marketing, as well as service or product offerings. At the broadest levels, robos are often characterized as a tool for Millennials; however, a number have a fairly broad age range of clients, including Generation X and Baby Boomer clients. At one firm, for example, 30 percent of clients are over 50.

Sometimes firms target specific markets based on demographic factors, investment objective, or investing styles. For example, one robo targets women, while some others invest only in securities that meet specific ethical or social interests such as Halal or socially responsible investing. Still other robos differentiate themselves through their investment style and/or product offerings. While many firms utilize passive investment strategies, others take a more active approach to their investment strategies or may offer a broader range of investments. For example, one firm engages in tactical asset allocation using ETFs, while another offers, among other things, a 'core-satellite' investing approach (offering ETFs and other mainstream securities products), along with access to bitcoin and venture capital investments, products not typically offered at other robos.

**How much human involvement does retirement planning require?** Many individuals we interviewed subscribed to the notion that the degree of human intervention required for decumulation is a function of two factors: (1) the complexity of the individual's financial situation; and (2) the degree of reassurance the individual may need around particular investment-related decisions. Some interviewees agreed that, currently, a purely robo-based service may be able to help address retirement planning for individuals with simple planning needs, such as only one or two accounts.

One respondent noted that robos are a bit like tax software: they can help people with a range of fairly standard financial situations, but investors will need to pay more for more sophisticated help, whether that comes in the form of more advanced software or access to a tax consultant. The good news is that robos do offer individuals with limited means access to financial planning options. Robos have made access to low-cost investment advice available to investors, and in many cases they have targeted investors in the earlier stages of their investing lives.

Once an individual starts having multiple accounts, perhaps special health needs, and/or a partner who needs to be factored into the retirement equation, the situation becomes more challenging for a pure-robo model based on current capabilities. Over time, however, advances in technology might enable a purely technology-based platform to address more complex situations.

One interviewee noted that a do-it-yourself approach could 'suffer from a GIGO (garbage in garbage out) problem.' This person went on to note that, 'There are not set-it-and-forget-it types of decumulation software, because retirement income plans must constantly adapt to changing financial and personal conditions, such as serious illness or the death of a spouse. Trying to be your own decumulation advisor has some of the same pitfalls as trying to be your own lawyer: You're likely to have a fool for a client. You'll be inexperienced, and you'll tend to discount or underestimate certain risks like health care costs risks and the cost of longevity risk. So there's a learning curve. Few people understand the spectrum of risk they will face in retirement. Most simply want an answer to the question, how much can I afford to spend?'

It is unclear whether a pure-robo could address investors' need for reassurance, especially around highly consequential or irreversible decisions, such as when to start drawing social security. In addition, as investors age, they may need more time, support, and assurance with their retirement income decisions. Conversely, individuals already inclined to a do-it-yourself approach might be comfortable with a purely technology-based solution. This may also be the case for individuals, such as Millennials, who will reach retirement age having used a variety of technology-based tools throughout their lives and who, when they retire, will likely have access to significantly more advanced tools available than currently exist. In addition, the more educated investors are about the decisions they will need to make and the factors to consider, the more comfortable they may feel making those decisions with input only from a robo platform. This may present an opportunity for firms to start educating investors about the decisions they will need to make well in advance of those decisions.

**Data and analytic requirements.** A purely technology-based platform will need to assimilate a broad range of quantitative and qualitative information to develop a sound, full-scope retirement financial plan. Factors include: the full range of an investor's assets and liabilities (e.g., bank accounts, 401(k)s, IRAs, pensions, mortgages and other debts), as well as those of the investor's spouse/partner, if relevant; an investor's plans or desires for activities in retirement, including how those plans may change as the retiree ages; an investor's health history as well as that of the spouse/partner; information about an investor's medical, long-term care and other insurance; and an investor's objectives regarding bequests.

The types of analyses a system would need to perform include: projecting the investor's lifespan; projecting health care expenses; budgeting for basic needs, health care and other desired goals, such as travel; assessing whether the investor is adequately funded to meet their projected basic needs, as well as other goals; assessing what measures, if any, to take if the investor is facing a shortfall (e.g., if assets are small relative to their retirement objectives and, most critically, relative to the retiree's basic needs); and determining when the investor should start drawing social security (which leaves aside the broader question of risks investors may face of not receiving some portion of their projected social security benefit due to policy or financial constraints on the system, if any). Also important is factoring in RMDs and tax planning; determining account withdrawal sequencing, that is, from which accounts withdrawals should be made; and performing ongoing assessments of both the investor's projected lifespan and withdrawal rate to determine whether the two are aligned, including with respect to any bequests the investor wishes to make.

**Competitive dynamics and the development of decumulation capabilities.** Interviewees generally grouped robo providers into two general classes, each following somewhat different imperatives and time horizons in developing their decumulation services. The first group was the start-up firms whose business model is built entirely around their robo or hybrid platform. These firms are focused on rapid asset accumulation, since this is essential to their long-term survival. (The economics of the robo business require scale to produce sufficient revenue for a firm to be viable.)

With respect to large incumbent players that offer robos, such players are seen as aiming to create a new channel to service existing low account balance clients in an economically viable manner, and attract new small accounts, including, potentially, the children and relatives of higher net worth clients, with the long-term goal of using both as a feeder to obtain higher margin, human-advised investors' assets under management. In some cases, these incumbent firms have developed their own platforms, while in others, they have acquired or white-labeled a third party's platform. One interviewee noted that these direct-to-consumer companies might be the best place to start looking for robo-like decumulation strategies because they have been serving do-it-yourself clients for decades.

For both types of firms, return on investment for decumulation capabilities was a key point of focus. While the potential market is large, a number of interviewees thought that developing a pure robo-based decumulation solution would be technologically and financially challenging, at least currently. Most interviewees thought that a hybrid approach would be necessary to serve investors effectively, at least in the near- to medium-term.

One interviewee commented, 'Companies are creating decumulation software for advisors, and advisors are creating decumulation software for themselves. Decumulation tools are at the stage where investment management software was several years ago—at the professional level. It's possible that some of the new decumulation software for advisors could eventually be streamlined enough and simple enough for a layperson to use.' If this development were to occur, it would, in some ways, mirror how robos developed capabilities previously available primarily to financial advisors and packaged that technology to make it directly accessible to consumers.

**Cognitive decline**. One significant aspect of aging is the increased incidence of cognitive decline, particularly as it relates to financial management. Interactions with a human advisor provide at least some opportunity for a firm to evaluate the competence of its clients, but that opportunity does not exist in an entirely online relationship. Most interviews agreed that this is a challenging problem for today's robos. The issue of cognitive decline is discussed in greater depth below.

**Investor advocates.** We spoke with investor advocates who noted that robos have significant potential to help consumers. Robos can democratize investing by offering investment and decumulation advice at a price point that most investors can afford. In addition, from a behavioral finance perspective, robos can help nudge investors to behave in ways that benefit them. For example, the online and mobile platforms that many robo-advisors offer is ideal for short and frequent communications to remind investors to update their information, check their spend rate, and monitor progress toward their goals.

The investor advocates also, however, raised important issues that investors should consider when considering a robo service. The first is that, even though robos may make advice affordable, consumers still need to ask about costs, as these vary significantly along with services offered. It is not necessarily true that a robo-advisor will always be a low-cost option. Second, one investor advocate noted that, by their nature, robo-advisors provide accumulation and decumulation advice investors based on a common methodology. Thus, if the robo-advisor makes a mistake, then the mistake will likely affect many investors. Stated by the investor advocate more succinctly, 'If robos get it wrong, they get it wrong for lots of people.' Of course, the opposite is true, as well. If robos get it right, they can successfully deliver low-cost advice to a large swath of investors. Either way, investors, robo-advisors, and regulators must consider this point as digital investment advice matures.

## Implications

**Investor considerations.** As older Americans shift from accumulating assets for retirement to decumulating assets in retirement, many will be looking for financial advice, regardless of the size and complexity of their asset base. In the accumulation phase, digital investment advice providers offer low-cost advice to investors both inside and outside employer-sponsored retirement plans, and they have an opportunity to do the same as people seek to generate income streams from these investments. There is surely a large market for investment advice for investors who have only a small pool of assets. Digital investment advice providers are filling this niche in the accumulation phase of retirement, and they hold the potential to fill this niche in the decumulation phase, as well.

As noted earlier, many firms offer hybrid advice models that provide different levels of interaction with a human advisor. This is a promising trend, because decumulating assets is complex and few digital investment advice platforms are advanced enough to handle complex decumulation scenarios without human intervention. Accordingly, the degree of customization that clients need (or simply feel more comfortable receiving) could point them toward a robo-advisor that also offers varying amounts of human interaction.

In addition, the need for financial advice during the decumulation phase is likely to be nonlinear, or 'lumpy.' That is, an investor may need more of it at different key points or events, but perhaps rarely between those events, and it would be those inflections where human interaction would be most likely, or most valuable, to take place. For instance, human interaction may be needed when initially establishing a retirement income strategy, and then again, when RMDs begin, a healthcare shock occurs, or a spouse dies. Having access to a human advisor at these critical junctures may be important for investors, though, according to several of our interviewees, there may come a day when technology advances enough to make a pure-robo model viable.

The nonlinear nature of retirement income needs, combined with the vagaries of the markets, make it very important for investors to monitor and perhaps amend their retirement income strategies throughout retirement. Thus, even with a pure or nearly-pure digital investment advice approach, investors may still need or want to engage with the robo to update it about material changes in their situations. This is similar to the accumulation phase, where even investors using target-date funds (i.e., investors not using a robo) wish to monitor their funds and risk tolerance, to be sure their investment goals still align with their fund's strategy.

**Age and cognitive decline.** As we age, our decision-making is likely to be impacted by cognitive decline (Spreng et al. 2016; Hammond et al. 2017). This is a concern for all financial service providers and investors, but it may be more problematic for investors using digital advice for decumulation. By the very nature of the service provided, digital investment advice clients may interact with their advice providers less frequently than investors paying for higher cost, in-person advice. This, coupled with the fact that some robo clients may never interact with human financial professionals, makes it harder for robo-advisors to identify cognitive decline. As such, investors using digital investment advice for decumulating their portfolios will need to carefully consider this issue.

One approach is for an investor to name a trusted contact whom an advisor can contact should the advisor be concerned about the client's pattern of financial actions. To encourage this practice, FINRA adopted amendments to FINRA Rule 4512 (Customer Account Information) in 2017, requiring firms to make reasonable efforts to obtain the names and contact information for trusted contact persons for each customer's account (see FINRA Regulatory Notice 17–11). This rule went into effect only recently (February 2018), and it is an important step in addressing the issue of investor cognitive decline in their later years.

Another important issue for investors to consider is the degree to which they wish to provide their advisor, whether human or robo, with a comprehensive view of their financial assets and liabilities, as opposed to simply an account-level view of assets. A more comprehensive understanding of a client's portfolio, and, if applicable, that of the client's partner, can help an advisor provide a more informed recommendations regarding how clients should decumulate their assets. Account aggregation can take three forms—the investor can actually move all their assets to one provider, inform their provider of all their holdings, or use an account aggregation tool, perhaps embedded within the robo-advisor's platform. The degree to which consumers are interested in account aggregation services is, as yet, unclear, given that the technology is fairly young. In addition, investors will need to weigh the perceived and actual risks of account aggregation, such as concerns about data security, privacy, and unauthorized access, with the benefits that data aggregation provides—namely, convenience and a comprehensive decumulation strategy (see also Rouse et al. 2019; CFPB 2017; FINRA 2018a).

**The role of education.** Much academic research shows that investor education is positively associated with effective financial decision-making (Lusardi and Mitchell 2014). The basics of investment risk, choosing an investment professional or firm, asset allocation, and the impact of fees on investment performance are all core building blocks of investor education, whether one is accumulating assets or drawing them down. But decumulation brings with it a different set of educational challenges than accumulation-oriented investor education.

During the accumulation stage, investor education typically focuses on issues like how to enroll (if not already automated) in a retirement plan, how much to save, and the benefits of diversification and compounding. Investors need additional information in the decumulation phase. For example, investors may need a refresher course on budgeting and debt management, basics that they may not have practiced for many years. In addition, as people evaluate robo providers, they will likely benefit from tips on questions to ask a robo firm prior to making a selection, including the level of human interaction a robo provides, and how a robo addresses issues such as cognitive decline, account aggregation, or privacy issues. Further, robo clients may need to hone their technical skills and upgrade their computer hardware/software, if they plan to utilize a digital investment advice provider (relying on computers at the public library is likely not an acceptable option for most).

Investors may also need assistance interpreting and utilizing the information that robo-advisors provide to their clients. One example pertains to the use of probabilities from Monte Carlo simulations, since some may not understand probabilities used when making financial decisions. Moreover, the manner in which this information is communicated can potentially affect investors' decisions. Gigerenzer (2002) has noted that using natural frequencies may be a better means of communicating risk than using probabilities—essentially changing the manner in which risks are framed. For example, a robo-advisor might communicate to a client that he or she has an 80 percent chance of meeting a retirement income goal, that is, not running out of money in retirement; alternatively, the advisor could communicate that eight out of ten investors in the same financial position will not run out of money in retirement. Research with physicians' understanding of risks to their patients suggests that the latter approach communicates risks more effectively than the former (Gigerenzer 1996; Hoffrage and Gigerenzer 1998).

Investors may also need to be educated about robo-advisors approaches to decumulation. As one interviewee put it, 'They all have tilts—some programs will lead clients toward the purchase of a fixed indexed annuity, for instance. Others will be tilted toward the 4 percent rule or the automatic de-risking of a portfolio as its market value declines, perhaps resulting in the automatic purchase of a single premium immediate annuity. It may be possible to have the client, in effect, choose the tilt by answering a series of non-technical questions about risk and risk capacity.'

A basic understanding of what strategy an advisor uses could help an investor make more informed decisions about which robo-advisor best meets his or her needs. This is similar to learning how target-date funds operate, the glide-path they employ, and whether they are 'to' or 'through' retirement, which can help investors accumulating assets choose the right target-date fund for their needs (FINRA 2018b, US SEC 2010). Investors should also be aware of the assumptions that go into their decumulation plan (e.g., which life tables a plan relies on). Similarly, something as straightforward as the assumed rate of return on equity investments can have a large impact on the retirement prospects of investors. For example, some investors use historical returns on equities despite market forecasts that future returns will be lower than historical returns (Horneff et al. 2018).

The channels through which this education will be delivered are as yet unknown, though most robo-advisors with whom we spoke recognized that they would need to bear some of the responsibility. Information to help investors navigate the decumulation phase may also be provided by regulators, employer, non-profit organizations, investor advocates, and the media. Sources of educational information are likely to grow, as Baby Boomers continue to retire and more people will need to generate sustainable retirement incomes.

## Conclusion

Assets under robo management have grown in recent years, with most robos catering to younger investors seeking to accumulate assets. Yet a few of these entities now provide decumulation services for their clients, and more intend to do so in the future.

This state of affairs offers both opportunities and challenges. Robo platforms offer promise in their ability to provide decumulation services to large numbers of investors, including those with relatively small accounts, at relatively low cost. As with automation and accumulation services, decumulation robo platforms also offer an opportunity to steer investors away from detrimental behaviors including overconfidence, loss aversion, mental accounting, framing, and more. In short, they take emotion out of decumulation. Consumers will also gain more choice, since even now there are differences in offered services, investments, decumulation strategies, assumptions, and costs.

We can expect continued innovation regarding how best to optimize retirement income while limiting risk. For instance, some robos are testing the practice of using more liquid and safer investments to provide a level of income sufficient to meet a retiree's basic needs, paired with higher-risk investments to cover discretionary expenses and to facilitate continued growth of the portfolio. The door is open to robo-specific studies focused on decumulation. Such research will help guide platform developers as they implement or modify their choice of decumulation models. Yet investors still face the challenge of having to select an appropriate advisor and remain engaged in the advice process, without having generally agreed-on benchmarks against which to assess the validity of a decumulation methodology or its historical effectiveness. Customers will also need to do their homework to understand what they receive for their money, what they own, and how their investments are managed.

It is also worth emphasizing that robos cannot solve the problem of financial illiteracy. Too many people still do not understand the basics of risk and reward, or how core investments such as bonds gain or lose value, much less more complicated concepts such as probability which figures in most robo simulations. Financial educators, including those who work for robo-advisors, face considerable challenges in explaining decumulation within a robo platform. Nevertheless, advances in robo capabilities may make financial education and financial capability less important, in the future.

## Acknowledgements

Many of the insights and perspectives reported here are based on interviews with over a dozen digital investment advice providers, investor advocates, and other experts. The authors thank the interviewees for sharing their time, insights, and expertise, and the following companies for providing subject matter experts: United Income, Betterment, E*Trade, Schwab, Retirement Income Journal, CFP Board, and the Consumer Federation of America's Investor Issues Dialog Group, three additional companies who chose to remain anonymous. They also thank Anna Rappaport, and several FINRA employees (Haime Workie, Sara Grohl, and Elena Schlickenmaier) for comments on early drafts of the chapter and the Board of the FINRA

Investor Education Foundation for the funding that made this chapter possible. While the authors are employees of FINRA and the FINRA Investor Education Foundation, the information and views expressed are those of the authors only. As such, the information contained within this document is for descriptive purposes only and has no regulatory implications.

## Note
1. See, however, Horneff et al. (2015).

## References
Ameriks, J. (2001). 'The Response of TIAA-CREF Participants to Software-Driven Asset Allocation Guidance,' TIAA-CREF Working Paper. New York, NY: TIAA Institute.

Agnew, J. (2006). 'Personalized Retirement Advice and Managed Accounts: Who Uses Them and How Does Advice Affect Behavior in 401(k) Plans?' Center for Retirement Research Working Paper No. 2006–9. Boston, MA: Boston College.

Bryne, A. and S. Utkus (2013). *Understanding How the Mind Can Help or Hinder Investment Decisions*. Valley Forge, PA: Vanguard Asset Management.

Cerulli and Associates (2017). *U.S. High-Net Worth and Ultra-High-Net-Worth Markets 2017: Emergent Product Trends for Sophisticated Investors*. Boston, MA. https://www.cerulli.com/vapi/public/getcerullifile?filecid=Cerulli-2017-US-High-Net-Worth-2017-Information-Packet (accessed March 1, 2019).

Consumer Financial Protection Bureau (CFPB) (2017). *Consumer-Authorized Financial Data Sharing and Aggregation: Stakeholder Insights That Inform the Consumer Protection Principles*. Washington, DC: CFPB. https://files.consumerfinance.gov/f/documents/cfpb_consumer-protection-principles_data-aggregation_stakeholder-insights.pdf (accessed March 1, 2019).

Deschenes, S. L. and B. Hammond (2019). 'Matching FinTech Advice to Participant Needs: Lessons and Challenges,' In J. Agnew and O. S. Mitchell (eds.), *The Disruptive Impact of FinTech on Retirement Systems*. Oxford, UK: Oxford University Press, pp. 172–89.

Fellowes, M. (2017). 'Living Too Frugally? Economic Sentiment & Spending Among Older Americans,' *United Income*. https://unitedincome.com/documents/papers/LivingTooFrugal.pdf (accessed March 1, 2019).

FINRA (2016). 'Report on Digital Investment Advice.' March: https://www.finra.org/sites/default/files/digital-investment-advice-report.pdf (accessed March 1, 2019).

FINRA (2018a). 'Know Before You Share: Be Mindful of Data Aggregation Risks.' *FINRA*. March 29. http://www.finra.org/investors/highlights/be-mindful-data-aggregation-risks (accessed March 1, 2019).

FINRA (2018b). 'Target-Date Funds—Find the Right Target for You.' http://www.finra.org/investors/target-date-funds-find-right-target-you (accessed March 1, 2019).

FINRA Foundation (2014). 'Thinking Money: The Psychology Behind our Best and Worst Financial Decisions,' Washington, D.C.: FINRA Investor Education Foundation.

Frydman, C. and C. Camerer (2016).'The Psychology and Neuroscience of Financial Decision Making,' *Trends in Cognitive Sciences*, 20(9): 661–75.

Finke, M., Pfau, W. and Blanchett, D. (2013). 'The 4 Percent Rule is Not Safe in a Low-Yield World.' *Journal of Financial Planning* 26(6): 46–55.

Gigerenzer, G. (1996). 'The Psychology of Good Judgement: Frequency Formats and Simple Algorithms,' *Medical Decision Making*, 16: 273–80.

Gigerenzer, G. (2002). *Calculated Risks*, New York, NY: Simon & Schuster.

Hammond, P. B., O. S. Mitchell, and S. P. Utkus, eds. (2017). *Financial Decision Making and Retirement Security in an Aging World*. Oxford: Oxford University Press.

Hoffrage, U. and G. Gigerenzer (1998). 'Using Natural Frequencies to Improve Diagnostic Inferences,' *Academic Medicine*, 73: 538–40.

Horneff, V., R. Maurer, and O. S. Mitchell (2018). 'How Low Returns Alter Optimal Life Cycle Saving, Investment, and Retirement Behavior.' In R. Clark, R. Maurer, and O. S. Mitchell, eds. *How Persistent Low Returns Will Shape Saving and Retirement*. Oxford: Oxford University Press. Forthcoming.

Horneff, V., R. Maurer, O. S. Mitchell, and R. Rogalla (2015). 'Optimal Life Cycle Portfolio Choice with Variable Annuities Offering Liquidity and Investment Downside Protection.' *Insurance: Mathematics and Economics*. 63: 91–107.

Iyengar, S. and M. Lepper (2000).'When Choice is Demotivating: Can One Desire Too Much of a Good Thing?' *Journal of Personality and Social Psychology*, 79(6): 995–1006.

Kahneman, D. and A. Tversky (1979).'Prospect Theory: An Analysis of Decision under Risk,' *Econometrica*, 47(2): 263–92.

Kieffer, C. and G. Mottola (2017). 'Understanding and Combating Investment Fraud,' in O. S. Mitchell, P. B. Hammond, and S. P. Utkus, eds., *Financial Decision Making and Retirement Security in an Aging World*. Oxford, UK: Oxford University Press, pp. 185–216.

Kircanski, K., N. Notthoff, M. DeLiema, G. Samanez-Larkin, D. Shadel, G. Mottola, L. Carstensen, and H. Gotlib (2018). 'Emotional Arousal Increases Susceptibility to Fraud in Older Adults and Younger Adults,' *Psychology and Aging*, 33(2): 325–37.

Knoll, M. (2011). 'Behavioral and Psychological Aspects of the Retirement Decision,' *Social Security Bulletin*, 71(4): 15–35.

Knutson, B. and G. Samanez-Larkin (2014). 'Individual Differences in Susceptibility to Investment Fraud.' Working Paper. Palo Alto, CA: Stanford University.

Lusardi, A. and O. S. Mitchell (2014). 'The Economic Importance of Financial Literacy: Theory and Evidence,' *Journal of Economic Literature*, 52(1), 5–44.

Polansky, S and D. Sibears (2016). *Report on Digital Investment Advice*. Washington, DC: FINRA.

Rouse, T., D. N. Levine, A. Itami, and B. Taylor (2019). 'Benefit Plan Cybersecurity Considerations.' In J. Agnew and O. S. Mitchell (eds.), *The Disruptive Impact of FinTech on Retirement Systems*. Oxford, UK: Oxford University Press, pp. 86–103.

Spreng, N., J. Karlawish, and D. Marson (2016). 'Cognitive, Social, and Neural Determinants of Diminished Decision-Making and Financial Exploitation Risk in

Ageing and Dementia: A Review and New Model,' *Journal of Elder Abuse & Neglect*, 28(4–5): 320–44.

US Securities and Exchange Commission (US SEC 2010). *Investor Bulletin: Target Date Retirement Funds*. Washington, DC: US SEC. https://www.sec.gov/investor/alerts/tdf.htm (accessed March 1, 2019).

Vanguard (2017). *How America Saves 2017: Vanguard 2016 Defined Contribution Plan Data*. Valley Forge, PA: Vanguard. https://pressroom.vanguard.com/nonindexed/How-America-Saves-2017.pdf (accessed March 1, 2019)

# Chapter 9

# Behavioral Finance, Decumulation, and the Regulatory Strategy for Robo-Advice

*Tom Baker and Benedict Dellaert*

This chapter surveys the decumulation services offered by investment robo-advisors as a case study with which to examine regulatory and market structure issues raised by automated financial advice. Based on this case study, we reach two provisional conclusions. First, the principles-based regulatory approach of the Investment Advisers Act of 1940 appears adequate and sufficiently flexible to address the new issues raised by automation, at least for now. Second, there is a pressing need to develop new mechanisms for encouraging investment robo-advisors (and financial advisors generally) to provide high quality decumulation services to their customers, because neither of the two prevailing compensation approaches—assets under management and commissions—provides sufficient incentive at present, and consumers are poorly equipped to evaluate the quality of decumulation services on their own.

After introducing investment robo-advisors, we provide a short introduction to decumulation, describing some of the uncertainties involved in identifying optimal decumulation strategies and sketching a few of the 'rules of thumb' that financial advisors have developed in this area in the face of this uncertainty. Next we describe behavioral effects that could inhibit consumers from following an optimal decumulation strategy, concluding that, left to their own devices, consumers are likely to make sub-optimal decumulation decisions. Then we describe some potentially useful automated decumulation services that are available on the market and present the results of a survey assessing whether those services are offered by investment robo-advisors. Finally, we discuss market structures that may inhibit financial advisors from implementing optimal decumulation strategies for their clients and explore whether there are regulatory strategies that could encourage financial advisors to provide better decumulation services. Two promising strategies are (1) adopting a record-keeping requirement for robo-advisors that is conceptually similar to the 'black box' requirement for commercial airlines, and (2) developing a set of robo-advice 'do's and don'ts' and related input/output tests to confirm that these requirements are met.

## Investment Robo-Advisors

We define a 'robo-advisor' as an automated service that ranks or matches consumers to financial products on a personalized basis. In the popular press and the financial planning community, the term 'robo-advisor' is most often used to refer to automated investment services that assemble and manage an investment portfolio for consumers. The technology, organizational structure, marketing, and many other aspects of investment robo-advising present a common set of public policy issues across the financial services sector (Baker and Dellaert 2018). In the present chapter, we focus on investment robo-advisors, but some of the conclusions we draw also have application in the insurance and banking contexts.

The intellectual history of investment robo-advice begins with modern portfolio theory (Lam 2016), which provided a mathematically based and empirically tested method for constructing and maintaining a passive investment portfolio on an automated basis. The resulting automated tools could create portfolios, rebalance and otherwise modify them, and (for taxable accounts) engage in tax loss harvesting. The modern asset management industry makes these tools available to consumers in a variety of ways. In the robo context, media attention has focused on the fully automated, consumer-facing systems pioneered by companies like Betterment and Wealthfront, and on the 'hybrid robos' offered by established asset managers like Vanguard and Schwab (the latter of which provides investors with access to human financial advisors in addition to direct access to automated services). Nevertheless, traditional registered investment advisors also use automated tools to construct and maintain portfolios for their clients on a behind-the-scenes basis (FINRA 2016; SEC 2017a). Additionally, the increasingly-popular target date funds (TDFs) typically are 'funds of funds' that use an algorithmic approach to portfolio management that could also be considered an investment robo-advisor. Whether accessed directly or indirectly, these robo-advisors have the potential to provide quality investment services at a lower cost than traditional financial advising services (Lam 2016; Baker and Dellaert 2018).

## Accumulation and Decumulation

Modern portfolio theory and passive investing strategies have become increasingly important to the asset *accumulation* phase of life-cycle investing, ever since the historic shift to defined contribution (DC) retirement plans in the United States and elsewhere (Zelinsky 2012; Baker and Simon 2002). This shift to passive investing did not occur overnight, but it is now widespread in financial markets. Eventually, the shift may produce opportunities for active investing that will slow, and then halt, the increase in the share of assets under management in passive funds. But even then, finance theory and empirical research on market performance and investing behavior will continue to play a significant role in helping individuals manage the investment risk aspects of their DC retirement plans. One among many reasons is that theory and research produce the investment strategies programmed into investment robo-advisors.[1]

Finance theory and empirical research have had less of an impact in helping individuals manage longevity risk or in managing other aspects of the *decumulation* phase of life-cycle investing. Although retirement research has contributed significantly to our understanding of the 'annuity puzzle' (Benartzi et al. 2011; Yaari 1965), these and other insights have not yet influenced decumulation advice comparable with the influence of finance theory and research on accumulation. For example, despite repeated demonstrations of the theoretical benefits of annuitization, only a very small share (under 9 percent) of private US retirement assets are in annuity reserves (Salisbury and Nenkov 2016).

This lack of influence may be attributable to the fact that researchers have begun focusing on the decumulation phase of the life-cycle only relatively recently (e.g. Mitchell and Moore 1997). Prior to the shift from defined benefit to DC retirement plans, decumulation (or the avoidance thereof) was largely of concern to the wealthy and, thus, of primary interest to the wealth management industry, but not to retirement researchers or the social welfare policy community. In the absence of authoritative guidance from the research community, financial planning professionals have yet to reach as much consensus regarding decumulation strategies that they have reached regarding accumulation strategies.

Providing decumulation advice involves guiding clients through numerous complex decisions including:

(1) Whether client assets should be annuitized and, if so, in what forms and when;
(2) Assessing the potential exposures to uncertain, unavoidable costs such as health care expenses, and the risk management strategies that exist to address them;
(3) How much money can be withdrawn from the available assets each year without unduly exposing people to the risk of outliving their assets; and
(4) The order in which money should be withdrawn from different categories of accounts.

Making the wrong decision can have dire consequences: causing clients to draw down their portfolio too quickly, under-consuming when their preference would be to spend, or losing money by choosing a poor annuity or Medicare insurance product. People can also purse a tax-inefficient withdrawal strategy. Broadly speaking, these decisions are complicated because they depend on uncertain future states of the world, they consist of many different components that are difficult to understand, and the clients making these decisions have heterogeneous needs and preferences.

In the face of such uncertainty, financial planners have developed some rules of thumb about decumulation. The most famous is the 'Bengen 4 Percent Rule,' which stated that retirees who withdrew 4 percent of their portfolios annually (adjusting for inflation) would not outlive their wealth (Bengen 1994) (Bengen later revised his rule, suggesting that retirees could withdraw 4.5 of their portfolio if the withdrawals were tax-free and 4.1 percent if the withdrawals were taxed; Scott et al. 2009). An alternative to the 4 percent rule is a family of actuarial methods of spending advice which incorporate the client's life expectancy and adjust spending amounts each year based on assets remaining in the portfolio.

The 4 percent rule has been criticized for several reasons. Some advisors argue that retiree spending usually follows a 'smile curve' pattern, where retirees spend more early on in retirement, less halfway through, and then more again late in life. Also, retirees often face spending shocks—for example from a hospitalization or other significant health care event—when they will need to withdraw an unusual amount to cover costs. As a result, some financial advisors consider it imprudent to recommend a spending plan based around relatively constant spending. Financial advisors also complain that the Bengen rule can be too conservative, leading clients to chronically underconsume (e.g. JP Morgan 2014). Other financial advisors contend that the Bengen rule is too aggressive in a long term, low interest environment (Blanchett et al. 2013).

Another 'rule of thumb' in decumulation is the retirement withdrawal sequence. Consider this excerpt from the Fidelity (2018: n.p.) website:

A straightforward strategy is to withdraw money from your retirement and investment accounts in the following order:

Required minimum distributions (RMDs), from traditional IRA, 401(k), 403(b), or 457 and Roth 401(k), 403(b), or 457 retirement accounts;

Taxable accounts, such as brokerage accounts;

Tax-deferred traditional IRA and 401(k), 403(b), or 457 retirement accounts;

Tax-exempt Roth IRA and 401(k).

Why in this order? First, it ensures that you take any RMDs if you're older than 70½. (Roth IRAs don't have RMDs while the original owner is alive.) If you don't take the full RMD, in most cases you'll pay a penalty of half the amount you failed to withdraw.

While some financial advisors recommend such a strategy, it may not be optimal for everyone, especially for people whose top income tax bracket changes over the course of their retirement (Cook et al. 2015).

These rules of thumb and debates about their reliability suggest three important things about the development and dissemination of optimal decumulation strategies. First, there remains significant work to be done to develop theoretically sound and empirically tested decumulation strategies. Second, as even these simple rules of thumb demonstrate, decumulation decisions involve calculation-heavy, future-oriented decisions that people are not very good at making, but that algorithms can do quite well, provided of course that there is an optimal decumulation strategy to follow. Third, recent advances in optimal life-cycle portfolios (e.g., Horneff et al. 2009, 2015; Hubener et al. 2015; Chai et al. 2011) have yet to be incorporated in much of the prevailing decumulation advice provided to consumers.

## Behavioral Effects and Retirement Decumulation

An optimal decumulation model would maximize utility over the life-cycle (Chen et al. 2017; Chai et al. 2011). Yet maximizing lifetime utility is a hard problem to solve: it not only imposes large cognitive demands, but it also requires people to make decisions that are subject to behavioral effects that could lead to suboptimal decisions. In this section, we review various behavioral effects that can impact individuals' decisions regarding capital decumulation. To do so, we follow a broad classification of these effects into three domains that reflect different aspects of individuals' decision-making processes.

First, individuals draw on their knowledge of their situations, their larger economic and social environments, and the alternatives that are available to compose a *mental representation* of the decumulation decision that they face (Johnson-Laird 1983). These mental representations are likely to be incomplete or inaccurate due to high cognitive costs that are involved in mentally representing many different components (Gershman et al. 2015), or because of emotional reactions to thinking about the decision, for example because it involves contemplating death. As a result, individuals do not fully and accurately anticipate the future (Huffman et al. 2017). These biases in mental representations are the first domain of behavioral effect.

Second, individuals must process information about the choice alternatives that are available to *evaluate* those alternatives. In particular, people must make judgments about the attractiveness of each alternative based on how well it matches their preferences (Lancaster 1966). This process is unlikely to reflect the fully rational process underlying the normative model (e.g., Tversky and Kahneman 1992), among other reasons because individuals may have incorrect perceptions of the values of alternatives (e.g., they may overweigh certain probabilities), or they may have non-normative preferences (e.g., they may be strongly loss averse) (Dimmock et al. 2016). These evaluation-based biases constitute the second domain of behavioral effects.

Third, individuals need to come to a decision by applying a *decision rule* that allows them to compare and decide among alternatives (Payne et al. 1993). These rules are unlikely to reflect the fully rational process underlying the normative model, among other reasons because individuals can be confused by the complexity or the sheer number of the alternatives that they face (Chernev et al. 2015). The use of such non-normative decision rules or heuristics constitutes a third domain of behavioral effects.

In the remainder of this section, we review specific examples in each of these domains of possible behavioral effects to set up our subsequent discussion of how automated advice can help individuals counter these effects to make more optimal decumulation decisions. Note that while we distinguish these three behavioral effect domains conceptually, they overlap in practice. For example, the strength of the *evaluation* of a feature of an alternative may influence whether this feature and alternatives are activated in a *mental representation* and how the feature and alternatives are captured in a *decision rule*.

**Mental representation effects.** One important way in which mental representations affect decisions is by making it easier or harder for individuals to access relevant knowledge. For example, the availability heuristic refers to the fact that individuals tend to confuse how easily they can recall an event with the likelihood of the event occurring (Schwarz et al. 1991). Because of these and other heuristics, mental representations are almost certainly incomplete, biasing the decisions that individuals make using these representations (Hegarty and Just 1993).

Differential mental representation of the components that affect decisions can also generate behavioral effects. Recent research on construal level theory is an excellent example of this mechanism (Liberman and Trope 2008). For example, individuals may cognitively represent events and alternatives that are further away in time (or some other dimension such as space) differently than those that are close. These findings have implications for retirement related decision-making as many decisions span considerable periods of time (e.g., Van Schie et al. 2015; Gottlieb and Mitchell 2015).

Goals represent a third aspect of mental representations that can affect individuals decumulation decisions (Austin and Vancouver 1996). Depending on the goals that are activated in an individual's mind, his evaluation of alternatives and choice between alternatives may differ. For example, individuals who mainly think about the health consequences of aging may assess their decumulation and other retirement alternatives differently from individuals who mainly think about the fun and enjoyment that they can get out of retirement. This may influence for example the investment, savings, and insurance decisions that they make, such that individuals who are more focused on potential health consequences may spend more on health insurance and saving for health care support, while individuals who are more focused on enjoyment may spend more on travel and regular housing.

**Evaluation effects.** In the evaluation domain, the best known behavioral effects relate to the evaluation of risky alternatives (Tversky and Kahneman 1992). Individuals often exhibit biased perceptions of probabilities (e.g., probability weighting) and biased preferences for alternatives (e.g., loss aversion), and they prefer not to choose alternatives when they lack information about the risks involved, or when they are not knowledgeable about a specific domain (ambiguity aversion; see Fox and Tversky 1995; Borghans et al. 2009).

Anticipated regret is another important example of behavioral effects in the evaluation of alternatives. Research shows that regret avoidance can impact individuals' evaluations, for example by making inaction more attractive than action, guiding behavior towards deviation from a normative decision model (Zeelenberg and Pieters 2007). In retirement decisions, individuals may fear experiencing more regret when the self-chosen option turns out to be sub-optimal (Bodie and Prast 2012; Muermann et al. 2006).

Finally, individuals may exhibit non-normative inter-temporal discounting (trade-offs between the present and the future). For example, people may too quickly discount future events compared to a normative discounting model, known as hyberbolic discounting (Laibson 1997). In particular, in the context of retirement, individuals may discount future returns at a higher rate than economic models would prescribe (Brown et al. 2017a). This may lead them to commit less of their current income to long term savings for retirement.

**Decision rule effects.** Another behavioral decision rule that can lead to potentially suboptimal retirement decisions is acceptance of a default. Default effects are often observed in the retirement investment domain: for instance, Choi et al. (2003) showed that 56–87 percent of employees participated in a 401k plan because of automatic enrolment, and these employees tended to stick with the default contribution rate. Beshears et al. (2009) showed that when a company changed its default retirement savings rate for new employees from 3 to 6 percent, the participation rate did not change, despite the doubling of the default rate.

In addition, decision rules may differ depending on the number of alternatives that an individual faces. Research has also shown that more choice is not always better in terms of promoting individuals' active decision making. Sethi-Iyengar et al. (2004) illustrate that more individuals participate in a pension plan when fewer choices were offered. More generally, individuals may avoid making complex decisions (Agnew and Szykman 2011; Brown et al. 2017b). When analyzing the savings contribution rate and the asset allocation of a retirement savings portfolio, research has shown that many individuals do not reallocate their investment funds throughout their working lives (Beshears et al. 2009).

## What do Robo-Advisors Say About Decumulation?

Next we identify automated decumulation services available on the market and report the results of our survey of investment robo-advisors that provided these automated services. We included in our survey the two independent consumer-facing investment robo-advisors with the largest amount of assets under management (Wealthfront and Betterment), two investment company direct-to-consumer robo-advisors with the largest amount of assets under management (Vanguard Personal Advisor Services and Schwab Intelligent Portfolios), two consumer-facing investment robo-advisors with a target market of older Americans (United Income and True Link), and two companies that provide automated decumulation tools for advisors (BlackRock's iRetire and Income Discovery). We included the latter companies because most general-purpose investment robo-advisors do not currently provide comparable automated decumulation services; thus, we had to look elsewhere to gain insight into the kinds of decumulation robo-advice available in the market.

Several automated decumulation services are available at present:

(1) Services that adjust the allocation of retirement assets as the expected lifespan of the individual declines or milestones (such as stopping work) are reached. This service is embedded in target date funds, is presently offered by most of the consumer-facing robo advisors we surveyed, and could easily be offered by the others;

(2) Services that assist individuals in making annuitization decisions. This service appears to be presently available on an automated basis only in decision support tools marketed to advisors;

(3) Services that help individuals optimize their social security claiming decisions. This service is available in several consumer-facing investment robo-advisors and in one of the support tools marketed to advisors. We consider this to be a decumulation service because the timing of the social security claiming decision can have a significant impact on the lifetime value of social security retirement benefits

and, thus, on the amount of money available to an individual for consumption in any given year;

(4) Services that help individuals optimize their Medicare plan selections and predict their out-of-pocket medical expenses. This service is available on private health insurance exchanges offered by health benefit companies such as Aon Hewitt and Willis Towers Watson and (a less sophisticated version) at Medicare.gov. We consider this to be a decumulation service because of the impact that healthcare expenses can have on financial security (Hoffman and Jackson 2013), the significant differences in the benefits available under different Medicare plans (which can have a financial impact that exceeds the lifetime value of making the wrong social security claiming decision), and the high level of difficulty involved in choosing among plans without expert assistance (Handel and Kolstad 2016). Two of the consumer-facing investment robo advisors have such tools in production, and two others implicitly recognize the importance of such tools by offering human advice about Medicare choices.

(5) Services that help individuals with multiple retirement accounts determine which to draw from and when. This service is available from certain robo-advisors and in advisor facing decision support tools.

(6) Services that help individuals calculate the amount of money they can safely withdraw from savings to use for consumption on an ongoing basis. This service is also available from certain robo-advisors and in advisor facing decision support tools.

At the time of our survey, we found no investment robo-advisor offering all these services. None of the consumer-facing robo-advisors surveyed offered Medicare decision support tools, and none offered annuitization decision support tools, although several of the robo-advisors employed human advisors who could provide advice about annuities and Medicare plans.

Some companies have developed software services embedding most or all of these tools, but most sell the services to human financial advisors. Accordingly, it appears that a well-equipped traditional financial advisor can today provide more complete decumulation services than can a robo-advisor. The larger investment companies with robo-advisor services do offer all or most of these decumulation services, but the fact that they do so in many cases through humans providing general advice calls the quality of that advice into question, at least in relation to computationally difficult topics like selecting the right Medicare plan and making the right annuitization decision.

We should be clear that we are not criticizing the consumer-facing robo-advisors for business decisions about which automated services to offer. For example, Wealthfront focuses entirely on Millennials who do not yet need

TABLE 9.1 Survey of decumulation features of leading investment robo-advisors

| Firm | Business model | Side payments | Human assist | Auto reallocate with age? | Retirement income tool? | Annuity support? | Soc. sec. tool? | Medicare tool? |
|---|---|---|---|---|---|---|---|---|
| United income | Indep. B2C Senior focus | None | Robo or hybrid | Yes | Yes | Human advisor; tool in production | Yes | Human advisor; tool in production |
| True Link | Indep. B2C Senior focus | Annuity commissions | Pure hybrid | Yes | Yes | Human advisor | No | No |
| Betterment | Indep. B2C | None | Robo or hybrid | Yes | Yes | Human advisor | Yes | Human advisor |
| Wealthfront | Indep. B2C millennial focus | Fees from related fund (can opt out) | Pure robo | No | No | No | No | No |
| Vanguard | FundCo B2C | Fees from related funds & annuity commissions | Pure hybrid | Yes | Yes | Human advisor | Yes | Human advisor; tool in production |
| Schwab | FundCo B2C | Fees from related funds & annuity commissions | Pure hybrid | No | Yes | Human advisor | Human advisor | Human advisor |
| BlackRock iRetire | FundCo B2B2C | Fees from related funds | Adviser tool | Advisor dependent | Yes | Yes | No | No |
| Income Discovery | SAAS B2B & B2B2C | None | Adviser tool | Yes | Yes | Yes | Yes | No |

Source: Authors' calculations.

decumulation services; we have no basis for second-guessing other firms' decisions about what to automate and when. United Income and True Link would seem to be the best candidates to offer all these services because of their focus on the senior market, but they are new companies and are still growing. (We note that United Income has most of the automated tools in operation and has the two missing ones in production.)

In our survey, we coded the robo-advisors according to their characteristics within the following categories: business model, whether they receive side payments, human assistance, whether asset allocation changes automatically with age, and whether they offer the following decumulation services: a retirement income calculator, a social security decision tool, and a Medicare decision tool (see appendix for description of these characteristics and the coding). The results appear in Table 9.1.

## Robo-Advice Market Structure and Regulatory Issues

As our survey makes clear, robo-advisors have only recently begun to address decumulation. None of the market leaders surveyed offered the full range of automated decumulation services needed by someone depending primarily on a DC retirement plan to fund retirement consumption. We expect that expert knowledge about decumulation will increase significantly over the next decade, and that the quality of, and confidence in, expert decumulation advice will rise. Because the advice will involve the kinds of calculations, rankings, and predictions that can be automated and incorporated into robo-advice services, robo-advisors are likely to play an important role in disseminating that advice.

It is worth considering whether there are market structures offering the potential to inhibit the development and dissemination of unbiased, high-quality decumulation robo advice. If so, we also ask whether the existing regulatory frameworks are adequate to address these market structures.

Robo-advisors present a contemporary example of the trilateral dilemma in financial regulation first generalized by Jackson (2009). Like other financial advisors, robo-advisors present a principal-agent problem, namely the problem of agents whose interests are not fully aligned with the principals that retain them. Robo-advice presents a *trilateral* principal-agent problem because there are three categories of parties involved in the robo-advice relationship: the client seeking the advice, the entity providing the advice, and the companies providing the financial products whose purchase is affected by the advice.

Ideally, robo-advice would be fully aligned with consumers' interests and would aim to overcome the various behavioral decision-making challenges that they face. Two of the main ways that robo-advisors can do this are: (1) using algorithms to solve complex optimization problems that consumers cannot easily solve on their own; and (2) providing choice architectures and online interfaces that help consumers develop a better understanding of their situations and make better decisions about complex decumulation products and strategies (Baker and Dellaert 2018; Philippon 2019).

These two types of support have the potential to help consumers avoid the behavioral limitations due to the behavioral domains identified above. In the mental representation domain, a robo-advisor could consider all available options in the market, taking into account all key attributes of those options and tailor the outcome to the individual's circumstances. Robo-advisors could also provide consumers with empirically validated projections of likely future developments in the financial markets and in their own lives (e.g., life span and medical expenses). In the evaluations domain, robo-advisors can allow consumers to systematically weight the attributes of the options that they face, and robo-advisors can be designed to allow consumers to choose their own weighting. A robo-advisor can also offer digital environments that help consumers better understand the options, including future scenarios to allow more informed trade-offs between different attributes. Finally, in the decision rule domain, robo-advisors can offer balanced decision rules that include all attributes of the different options and that rank these options in order of predicted attractiveness to the consumer. This would facilitate a decision-making process that focused the consumers' attention on the most important options and attributes, helping them make better use of their cognitive capacities (Dellaert et al. 2018).

Because decumulation decisions are so difficult for people to make and evaluate on their own, however, there is a concern that robo-advisors (like their human counterparts) could selectively adapt the emerging expert advice on decumulation to increase their compensation at the expense of their clients. In that regard, financial product companies may be motivated to persuade advisors to be a less-than-fully faithful to their clients. Financial product companies understand the financial product domain much better than the advisors' clients. They also understand the behavioral effects described above better than those clients, so they can design their products to exploit those effects. Moreover, because financial product companies are repeat players with advisors, they can monitor their advisors more effectively than can the advisors' clients, and they have greater ability to adjust the terms of their contracts with the advisors in response to this feedback.

Even if robo-advisors steadfastly refuse to be influenced by financial product companies, there is still no guarantee that their interests will be fully aligned with those of their customers. A more strategic, short-term profit-oriented type of robo-advisor could exploit the behavioral effects to influence consumer decision making in a direction that is in the interest of the advisor, but not of the consumer. For instance, in the mental representation domain, a robo-advisor might restrict consumer access to available options in the market by only surveying a strategic subset of options that are most profitable for the firm. The advice could also focus on a certain subset of attributes of these options that guide consumers towards more profitable options (e.g., by focusing on attributes correlated with higher profit margins), or provide projections of future scenarios that highlight these attributes. In the evaluation domain, a robo-advisor could selectively apply weightings to the evaluations of attributes that guide consumers towards more profitable options. A robo-advisor could also apply behavioral strategies such as framing and selective highlighting that make consumers more sensitive to profitable options for the firm. Finally, in the decision rule domain, a robo-advisor could apply selective decision rules or strategic defaults making it more burdensome for consumers to select their most valuable options.

We are by no means making the claim that robo-advisors in the market are currently applying these behavioral techniques, merely that there is ample opportunity to do so and, based on experience in other markets, reason for concern that some market actors will do so. For example, when Jackson (2009) surveyed a wide range of financial products and services from real estate sales to financial institutions' sale of customer data to third parties, he reported that, in every financial product market considered, advisors were receiving side payments from financial product companies that had led (at least some of) the advisors to act contrary to their clients' interests. Not surprisingly, lawmakers had intervened in all these markets except one to try to align the advisors' interests more fully with those of their clients, following a modal regulatory strategy that combined fiduciary and transparency obligations.[2]

Jackson (2009: 107–8) also raised concerns—which we share—about whether these obligations were sufficient to protect consumers, saying:

> In contexts where the underlying problems arise—that is, where market forces are not sufficient to protect consumers—one wonders whether the mere imposition of fiduciary obligations, which typically call upon the recipients of side payments to assess their reasonableness in light of numerous factors, is likely to be effective. . . . One could raise similar concerns about generalized disclosure regarding the existence of payments to consumers. It is hard to argue how vaguely worded disclosure can assist most consumers.

This is the same regulatory strategy—disclosure plus fiduciary obligations— that is the primary regulatory strategy today for investment robo-advisors. Consumer-facing investment robo-advisors are subject to SEC registration, supervision, and enforcement procedures under the Investment Advisers' Act (SEC 2017a).[3] The Act imposes certain fiduciary and transparency obligations, often referred to in shorthand as 'suitability' and 'disclosure' obligations, and it authorizes the SEC to examine advisors to determine whether they are meeting those obligations. Although investment robo-advisors that sell their services to other financial advisors are not subject to this oversight directly, the SEC (2017a) can evaluate these 'B2B' robo-advisors when examining their financial advisor customers (see also Mottola et al. 2019 and Klass and Perelman 2019), as can FINRA (2016) when examining the broker-dealers that it regulates.

In this short chapter, we cannot fully consider whether this principles-based regulatory strategy makes sense for all financial advisors, as this is a larger question affecting much more than robo-advising. Instead, we focus on how the known limits of this strategy interact with two special features of the financial advice we are examining here: the automated nature of robo-advice and the decumulation context.

**Automation.** The automated nature of robo-advice has several potential consequences for a regulatory strategy that employs fiduciary and transparency obligations. First, the automated nature of the advice has the potential to make the content of, and potential biases in, the advice more transparent to regulators, both ex ante and ex post.[4] This should be the case even with hybrid systems (i.e., when there is a human who interacts with the client), provided that those systems record both the automated advice and the subsequent action, thereby permitting examination of the reasons for systematic variations between advice and action (in order to check whether the human is introducing a bias—e.g., in favor of high commissions—not present in the automated part of the system). This provides reason to be optimistic that the growth of robo-advisors will increase the ability of existing disclosure and suitability requirements to mitigate the trilateral dilemma of financial advisors (Schwarcz and Siegelman 2015), provided of course that regulators develop the expertise needed to examine robo advice (Baker and Dellaert 2018; Philippon 2019).

Second, because the disclosures that consumer-facing robo-advisors make to consumers are also automated, they should be subject to collection, tracking, and comparison by third parties better-equipped than individual consumers to evaluate and compare them. This second difference also provides reason for optimism about improvements in transparency based on existing disclosure obligations. Of course, if robo-advisors were to make side payments to such third parties, this market development could simply relocate the trilateral dilemma rather than mitigate it. For this reason, it will be important to consider whether the receipt of such side payments is consistent with existing fiduciary obligations and, if so, whether those obligations should be modified to regulate or even prohibit such payments.

Third, unless the robo-advisors themselves win the competition to become consumers' primary financial platforms, the winners of that competition will receive recurring data feeds from robo-advisors and will be able to monitor, compare, and report the robo-advisors' fidelity to their customers. These platforms will also be subject to their own trilateral dilemma, as all the financial platforms of which we are aware are either owned by, or receive side payments from, financial product companies. Accordingly, as with the more limited third-party advice platforms just discussed, this market development may simply relocate the robo-advisor trilateral dilemma. Thus, it will be important for regulators to monitor developments in the financial platform market and to consider whether they have the authority they need to examine the business practices of the entities that are likely to succeed and, if so, whether their existing statutory authority provides them with the tools needed to protect consumers facing this trilateral dilemma.

Fourth, because of the 'weapons of math destruction' problem—for example, the problem of widely used models that turn out to have unanticipated flaws—there are reasons to be wary of safe harbors and other prescriptive alternatives to fiduciary obligations in the context of automated advice (O'Neil 2016). Especially because of the market concentration potential of robo-advice, there is a significant risk that a prescriptive approach to robo-advice could lead to convergence on a single model that could have negative effects as robo-advice scales. For this reason, as we have argued elsewhere, regulators should consider relying on competitions (and competitions of competitions) to enhance the quality of robo-advice, rather than prescription (Baker and Dellaert 2018).

**Decumulation.** Decumulation services present different incentives for financial advisors than asset accumulation services. The practice of paying fees that are based on assets under management (AUM) is generally understood to align the incentives of financial advisors and their clients in the accumulation phase. Although the AUM fee structure gives advisors an incentive to recommend excessive savings, most of the behavioral effects discussed earlier lead individuals to save less than would be optimal, making it unlikely that investment advisors' clients in fact generally save too much. Indeed, as Barr et al. (2009) have argued, the market for saving products is an example of a market in which the compensation incentives may reduce the negative impacts of behavioral effects.

Decumulation services present a more difficult alignment problem. As our survey suggests, there is demand for decumulation services and some financial advisors provide those services, if only to stand out in the market for financial advice. Unfortunately, none of the existing models for financial advisor compensation are well-calibrated to the quality of decumulation services.

On the one hand, AUM-based compensation partially aligns the interests of financial advisors with their clients' interests in not outliving their assets.

On the other hand, AUM-based compensation does not provide an incentive to recommend annuity products (because they reduce AUM), nor does it provide any obvious incentives for other decumulation services, except as needed to satisfy consumer demand in the advisors' target market. Commission-based compensation provides an incentive to offer annuities and Medicare plans, but that incentive is not well tailored to quality. One suggestive illustration of the lack of demand for quality can be seen in the Medicare insurance market, in which, based on our scan of that market, we conclude that the only advisors that are using available high-quality advice tools are those whose clients are large employers that are transitioning retirees from a traditional retirement health plan to a private exchange and who demand high quality decision support for their retirees. (In that regard it is worth noting that we learned from our survey that Vanguard is developing its Medicare tools in cooperation with Mercer, which is one such advisor (Thornton 2018)). Because individuals are poorly equipped to evaluate the quality of decumulation services, the market does not appear to provide incentives to develop high quality decumulation services. Moreover, because decumulation presents some difficult modeling challenges that have not yet been well-implemented in real-world models, there remains significant uncertainty about which decumulation strategies are best for which consumers. These challenges include questions that are purely technical, such as the potential role of loans in addressing large unexpected expenses, or the special role of the home as a largely illiquid asset that is not purely financial in nature.

These challenges also involve questions that present a challenging combination of normative and behavioral considerations that may be hard to elicit from retirees and may be highly heterogeneous, such as bequest motives and the ability of individuals to adapt to changed circumstances (which would affect the weighting of downside outcomes in a predictive model). The resulting uncertainty presents opportunities for robo-advisors (or financial advisors choosing among robo-advisors) to take their own interests into account in how they resolve that uncertainty in their models, for example by recommending (or not recommending) the purchase of annuities, or certain kinds of annuities, if doing so increased the compensation (or decreased the compensation) of the advisor.

As with automated investment advice more generally, the principles-based approach of the Investment Advisers Act provides the SEC with authority to examine advisors' decumulation tools and perhaps even to raise questions about why advisors are not making use of such tools, and FINRA appears to have similar authority in the broker dealer domain (SEC 2017a; FINRA 2016). The SEC's examination priorities now include 'electronic investment advice,' and examinations 'focus on registrants' compliance programs, marketing, formulation of investment recommendations, data protection, and disclosures relating to conflicts of interest' (SEC 2017b at 2). FINRA appears similarly to have concluded that its existing authority is sufficient for this purpose. The FINRA Report on Digital Investment Advice identifies 'practices that we believe firms should consider and tailor to their business model' without the need for 'any new legal requirements' or change to 'any existing broker-dealer regulatory obligations' (FINRA 2016 at 1).

Thus, in our view, the difficult challenge in moving forward along the regulatory trajectory for robo-advice does not lie in obtaining the legal authority to consider these questions (see also Klass and Perelman 2019). Indeed, on the regulatory front, we are encouraged by Polansky et al. (2019)). Although these authors are of course presenting their personal views and not those of FINRA, their investigation of digital investment advice and decumulation demonstrates that this important topic could easily be put on the financial regulatory agenda. Instead, the pressing decumulation challenge lies in research and development, so that there can be the kind of reliable 'best practices' regarding decumulation that FINRA referred to in its 2016 Report.

## Conclusion

The decumulation stage of the life-cycle presents difficult theoretical and behavioral challenges. The theoretical challenges lie in developing optimal decumulation strategies given real-world tax, transfer, insurance, medical care, and other institutional rules. The behavioral challenges lie, first, in recognizing the behavioral effects that could prevent consumers from following these strategies and that could be exploited by firms and, second, in developing strategies to address these behavioral effects. Robo-advice, whether provided direct-to-consumer or indirectly through human advisors, has great potential in this regard, and our market survey demonstrates that decumulation tools have begun to emerge. Moreover, recent SEC and FINRA attention to digital investment advice indicates that financial services regulators have both the authority and the willingness to examine these emerging tools.

Accordingly, we conclude this chapter with two concrete observations for regulatory consideration. First, regulators could adopt a requirement that Advisers and Broker Dealers only use automated tools that incorporate the robo-advisor equivalent of the 'black box' that commercial airplanes carry to record what happens on the plane and, thus, create and maintain a record that will permit after-the-fact evaluation of any recommendation. Second, regulators should begin the process of developing a list of simple requirements—do's and don'ts—for robo-advice, and for developing tests to determine whether those requirements are followed. The inputs would be standard (but changing and secret) individual scenarios that could be used to test whether the outputs vary in a manner consistent with the requirements and to compare different advisor tools.

The first approach would facilitate after-the-fact evaluation of failures, just like black boxes on airplanes. Given the early stage of the development of the technology and the significant risks from adopting a highly prescriptive ex ante regulatory approach, there is a need for an ex post liability approach. A record-keeping requirement would facilitate that approach. Like airline black boxes, comparable record-keeping practices are unlikely to be implemented across the robo-advice market on a voluntary basis, because of the potential liability risks such records could create for individual firms. Thus, a black-box mandate represents a solution to a collective action problem. This record-keeping requirement is important because firms update their algorithms, models, and data sources over time. Thus, absent a requirement to keep a record of exactly how a given recommendation was made, it may be impossible for it to be determined after the fact.

Our second approach is a concrete example of the 'regulatory trajectory' referred to in prior work (Baker and Dellaert 2018). Although it would be a mistake to tightly prescribe the data sources and algorithms that robo-advice must use (among other reasons because of the weapons of math destruction problem discussed above), the efforts that the SEC and FINRA are under-taking to study automated advice are certain to produce actionable do's and don'ts. One benefit of automated advice is that it can be tested in a way that human advice cannot. While getting from here to there is obviously not a simple task, policymakers should at the very least consider developing simple input/output tests that their examiners can use to determine whether those do's and don'ts are being followed.

## Appendix: Characteristics Used to Code Robo-advisor Attributes

**Business model.** Categories are: independent consumer-facing investment advisor (indep. B2C); fund company consumer-facing investment advisor (FundCo B2C); fund company advisor tool (FundCo B2B2C); and inde-pendent advisor tool (SAAS B2B).

**Side payments.** Here we report what we could discern about whether the advisor received payments from parties other than their customers that could provide an incentive to bias the services. Categories are: none; fees from related funds that are included in the asset allocation; and commis-sions from annuities.

**Human assistance.** Categories are: Pure robo (no human assistance offered as an option); Pure hybrid (human assistance always included at no extra charge); Robo/hybrid (option to purchase human assistance); and Adviser tool (automated tool licensed to human advisors for their use with clients).

**Automatic reallocation.** Here we report whether the asset allocation changes automatically as individuals age or reach milestones (such as no longer working). Categories are: yes, no, and advisor dependent. The latter category is for the advisor tools, which supplement whatever asset allocation method the advisor is using.

**Retirement income calculator.** Categories are: yes or no. A 'yes' means the service has an automated decision tool that recommends a retirement paycheck or similar personalized spending recommendation, based on all assets and income sources that the individual discloses.

**Annuity support.** Categories are: yes, no, human advisor. A 'yes' means that the service includes annuitization options in the automated retirement income calculator. A 'human adviser' means that human advisors who work for the service can provide advice about annuitization.

**Social security tool.** Categories are: yes or no. A 'yes' means that the service offers a tool that helps individuals decide when to claim and includes social security income in any retirement income tool.

**Medicare tool.** Categories are: no, human adviser, and under development. A 'human advisor' means that human advisors who work for the service can provide general advice about Medicare plans. 'Under development' means that the robo advisor informed us that they are working on an automated decision tool that is similar to that presently offered through the Aon Hewitt and Willis Towers Watson retirement health insurance exchanges.

## Notes

1. Of note, the Department of Labor Rule regarding the use of investment robo-advisors in the employee benefits context requires the robo-advisor to use 'generally accepted investment theories that take into account the historic risks and returns of different asset classes over defined periods of time.' Investment advice - participants and beneficiaries, 29 CFR 2550.408g-1(4), https://www.law.cornell.edu/cfr/text/29/2550.408g-1 (accessed March 2, 2019).
2. The one exception at the time was university financial aid offices' relationships with private lenders, and that relationship is no longer an exception. (Barr et al. 2017)
3. State securities regulators have primary responsibility for regulating robo-advisors with less than $100 million assets. Because of the economies of scale in robo-advising, we focus on federal regulation in this chapter.

4. Aspects of robo-advice that are based on machine learning models may be less transparent because of the interpretability problems that accompany such models. We set those problems aside here for two reasons. First, our understanding is that the current generation of investment robo-advisors uses intelligible models. Second, this interpretability problem is a more general one that is receiving significant attention elsewhere (Selbst and Barocas 2018).

# References

Agnew, Julie R. and Lisa R. Szykman (2011). 'Annuities, Financial Literacy and Information Overload' In *Financial Literacy: Implications for Retirement Security and the Financial Marketplace* (eds.) Olivia S. Mitchell and Annamaria Lusardi, 260–97. Oxford, UK: Oxford University Press.

Austin, J. T. and J. B. Vancouver (1996). 'Goal Constructs in Psychology: Structure, Process, and Content.' *Psychol Bull* 120(3): 338–75.

Baker, T. and B. Dellaert (2018). 'Regulating Robo Advice across the Financial Services Industry.' *Iowa L. Rev.* 103: 713.

Baker, T. and J. Simon (2002). *Embracing Risk: The Changing Culture of Insurance and Responsibility.* Chicago, IL: University of Chicago Press.

Barr, M. S., H. E. Jackson, and M. E. Tahyar (2017). *Financial Regulation: Law and Policy.* St. Paul: Foundation Press.

Barr, M., S. Mullainathan, and E. Shafir (2009). 'The Case for Behaviorally Informed Regulation,' in D. Moss and J. Cisternino, eds., *New Perspectives on Regulation.* Cambridge, MA: pp. 25–61.

Benartzi, S., A. Previtero, and R. H. Thaler (2011). 'Annuitization Puzzles,' *Journal of Economic Perspectives*, 25(4): 143–64.

Bengen, W. P. (1994). 'Determining Withdrawal Rates Using Historical Data.' *Journal of Financial Planning* 7, 4 (October): 171–80.

Beshears, J., J. Choi, D. Laibson, and B. Madrian (2009). 'The Importance of Default Options for Retirement Saving Outcomes: Evidence from the United States,' in J. R. Brown, J. B. Liebman and D. A. Wise eds., *Social Security Policy in a Changing Environment.* Chicago, IL: University of Chicago Press, pp. 167–95.

Blanchett, D. M., M. Finke, and W. D. Pfau (2013). 'Low Bond Yields and Safe Portfolio Withdrawal Rates,' *The Journal of Wealth Management*, 16(2): 55.

Bodie, Z. and H. Prast (2012). 'Rational Pensions for Irrational People, Behavioral Science Lessons for the Netherlands,' in L. Bovenbyrg eds., *The Future of Multi-Pillar Pensions.* Cambridge, UK: Cambridge University Press, pp. 299–29.

Borghans, L., J. Heckman, B. Golsteyn, and H. Meijers (2009). 'Gender Differences in Risk Aversion and Ambiguity Aversion,' *Journal of the European Economic Association*, 7(2–3): 649–58.

Brown, J. R., A. Kapteyn, E. F. P. Luttmer, and O. S. Mitchell (2017a). 'Cognitive Constraints on Valuing Annuities,' *Journal of the European Economic Association* 15(2): 429–62.

Brown, J. R., A. Kapteyn, E. F. P. Luttmer, O. S. Mitchell, and Anya Samek (2017b). 'Behavioral Impediments to Valuing Annuities: Evidence on the Effects of

Complexity and Choice Bracketing.' NBER Working Paper No. 24101. http://www.nber.org/papers/w24101 (accessed March 2, 2019).

Chai, J., W. Horneff, R. Maurer, and O. S. Mitchell. (2011). 'Optimal Portfolio Choice over the Life Cycle with Flexible Work, Endogenous Retirement, and Lifetime Payouts.' *Review of Finance.* 15(4): 875–907.

Chen, A., S. Haberman, and S. Thomas (2017). 'Optimal Decumulation Strategies during Retirement with Deferred Annuities.' https://ssrn.com/abstract=2911959 (accessed March 2, 2019).

Chernev, A., U. Böckenholt, and J. Goodman (2015). 'Choice Overload: A Conceptual Review and Meta-Analysis.' *Journal of Consumer Psychology,* 25(2): 333–58.

Choi, J. J., D. Laibson, B. C. Madrian, and A. Metrick (2003). 'Optimal Defaults.' *American Economic Review,* 93(2): 180–5.

Cook, K. A., W. Myer, and W. Reichenstein (2015). 'Tax-Efficient Withdrawal Strategies.' *Financial Analysts Journal,* 71(2): 16–28.

Dellaert, B. G. C., T. Baker, and E. J. Johnson (2017). *Partitioning Sorted Sets: Overcoming Choice Overload while Maintaining Decision Quality.* Columbia Business School Research Paper No. 18(2).

Dimmock, S. G., R. Kouwenberg, O. S. Mitchell and K. Peijnenburg (2016). 'Ambiguity Attitudes and Economic Behavior: Results from a US Household Survey.' *Journal of Financial Economics.* 119(3): 559–77.

Fidelity (2018). '4 Tax-Efficient Strategies in Retirement,' *Fidelity Viewpoints.* March 5. https://www.fidelity.com/viewpoints/retirement/tax-savvy-withdrawals (accessed March 2, 2019).

Financial Industry Regulatory Authority (FINRA) (2016). *Report on Digital Investment Advice.* FINRA Report. Washington, DC.

Fisch, J. E., M. Labouré, and J. A. Turner (2019). 'The Emergence of the Robo-advisor' in J. Agnew and O. S. Mitchell, eds., *The Disruptive Impact of FinTech on Retirement Systems.* Oxford, UK: Oxford University Press, pp. 18–37.

Fox, C. R. and A. Tversky (1995). 'Ambiguity Aversion and Comparative Ignorance.' *The Quarterly Journal of Economics,* 110(3): 585–603.

Gershman, S. J., E. J. Horvitz, and J. B. Tenenbaum (2015). 'Computational Rationality: A Converging Paradigm for Intelligence in Brains, Minds, and Machines.' *Science,* 349(6245): 273–8.

Gottlieb, D. and O. S. Mitchell (2015). 'Narrow Framing and Long-Term Care Insurance.' NBER WP 21048. *R&R.*

Handel, B. R. and J. T. Kolstad (2015). 'Health Insurance for "Humans": Information Frictions, Plan Choice, and Consumer Welfare.' *American Economic Review* 105(8): 2449–2500.

Hegarty, M., and M. A. Just (1993). 'Constructing Mental Models of Machines from Text and Diagrams.' *Journal of Memory and Language,* 32: 717–42.

Hoffman, A. and H. Jackson (2013). 'Retiree Out-of-Pocket Healthcare Spending: A Study of Consumer Expectations and Policy Implications,' *American Journal of Law & Medicine,* 39: 62–133.

Horneff, V., R. Maurer, O. S. Mitchell, and R. Rogalla. (2015). 'Optimal Life Cycle Portfolio Choice with Variable Annuities Offering Liquidity and Investment Downside Protection,' *Insurance: Mathematics and Economics,* 63: 91–107.

Horneff, W., R. Maurer, O. S. Mitchell, and M. Stamos (2009). 'Asset Allocation and Location over the Life Cycle with Survival-Contingent Payouts,' *Journal of Banking and Finance*, 33(9): 1688–99.

Hubener, A., R. Maurer, and O. S. Mitchell. (2015). 'How Family Status and Social Security Claiming Options Shape Optimal Life—Portfolios.' *Review of Financial Studies*, 29(1): 937–78.

Huffman, D., O. S. Mitchell, and R. Maurer (2017). 'Time Discounting and Economic Decision-making among the Elderly.' *Journal of the Economics of Ageing*. https://doi.org/10.1016/j.jeoa.2017.05.001 (accessed March 2, 2019).

Jackson, H. (2009). 'The Trilateral Dilemma in Financial Regulation,' in A. Lusardi eds., *Overcoming the Saving Slump: How to Increase the Effectiveness of Financial Education and Saving Programs*. University of Chicago Press, pp. 82–116.

J.P. Morgan Asset Management (2014). 'Breaking the 4% Rule.' https://am.jpmorgan.com/blob-gim/1383280103367/83456/RI-DYNAMIC.pdf?segment=AMERICAS_US_ADV&locale= en_US (accessed March 2, 2019).

Johnson-Laird, P. N. (1983). *Mental Models*. Cambridge, MA: Harvard University Press.

Laibson, D. (1997). 'Golden Eggs and Hyperbolic Discounting.' *The Quarterly Journal of Economics*, 112(2), 443–78.

Lam, Jonathan (2016). 'Robo-Advisers: A Portfolio Management Perspective.' Yale Department of Economics Senior Essay.

Klass, J. and E. L. Perelman (2019). '*The Transformation of Investment Advice: Digital Investment Advisers as Fiduciaries*' in J. Agnew and O. S. Mitchell, eds., *The Disruptive Impact of FinTech on Retirement Systems*. Oxford, UK: Oxford University Press, pp. 38–58.

Lancaster, K. J. (1966). 'A New Approach to Consumer Theory.' *Journal of Political Economy*, 74 (2): 132–57.

Liberman, N., and Y. Trope (2008). 'The Psychology of Transcending the Here and Now.' *Science*, 322(5905): 1201–5.

Mitchell, O. S. and J. Moore (1997). 'Projected Retirement Wealth and Savings Adequacy in the Health and Retirement Study.' NBER Working Paper No. 6240.

Muermann, A., O. S. Mitchell, and J. Volkman. (2006). 'Regret, Portfolio Choice, and Guarantees in Defined Contribution Schemes.' *Insurance: Mathematics and Economics*. 39: 219–29.

O'Neil, C. (2016). *Weapons of Math Destruction: How Big Data Increases Inequality and Threatens Democracy*. New York, NY: Crown Publishers.

Payne, J. W., J. R. Bettman, and E. J. Johnson (1993). *The Adaptive Decision Maker*. New York, NY: Cambridge University Press.

Philippon, T. (2019). 'The FinTech Opportunity' in J. Agnew and O. S. Mitchell (eds.), *The Disruptive Impact of FinTech on Retirement Systems*. Oxford, UK: Oxford University Press, pp. 190–217.

Polansky, S., P. Chandler, and G. R. Mottola (2019). 'The Big Spend Down: Digital Investment Advice and Decumulation' in J. Agnew and O. S. Mitchell (eds.), *The Disruptive Impact of FinTech on Retirement Systems*. Oxford, UK: Oxford University Press, pp. 129–48.

Salisbury, L. C. and G. Y. Nenkov (2016). 'Solving the Annuity Puzzle: The Role of Mortality Salience in Retirement Savings and Decumulation Decisions,' *Journal of Consumer Psychology*, 26(3): 417–25.

Schwarcz, D. and P. Siegelman (2015). 'Insurance Agents in the 21st Century: The Problem of Biased Advice' in D. Schwarcz and P. Siegelman, (eds.), *Handbook on the Economics of Insurance Law*. Cheltenham, UK: Edward Elgar Publishing, pp. 36–70.

Schwarz, N., H. Bless, F. Strack, G. Klumpp, H. Rittenauer-Schatka, and A. Simons (1991). 'Ease of Retrieval as Information: Another Look at the Availability Heuristic.' *Journal of Personality and Social Psychology*, 61(2): 195–202.

Scott, J. S., W. F. Sharpe, and J. G. Watson (2009). 'The 4% Rule – At What Price?' *Journal of Investment Management*, 7(3): 31–48.

Securities and Exchange Commission (SEC), Division of Investment Management (2017a). *Robo Advisers Guidance Update*. No. 2017–2. https://www.sec.gov/investment/im-guidance-2017-02.pdf (accessed March 2, 2019).

Securities and Exchange Commission (SEC), Office of Compliance Inspections and Examinations (2017b). 'Examination Priorities for 2017.' https://www.sec.gov/about/offices/ocie/national-examination-program-priorities-2017.pdf (accessed March 2, 2019).

Selbst, A. D. and S. Barocas (2018). 'The Intuitive Appeal of Explainable Machines.' *Fordham Law Review*, forthcoming.

Sethi-Iyengar, S., G. Huberman, and W. Jiang (2004). 'How Much Choice Is Too Much? Contributions to 401 (k) Retirement Plans.' *Pension Design and Structure: New Lessons from Behavioral Finance*, 83: 84–7.

Thornton, Nick (2018). 'Vanguard, Mercer Roll Out New Healthcare Cost Model. *Benefits Pro*, June 20, 2018. https://www.mercer.us/our-thinking/healthcare/new-model-for-estimating-healthcare-costs-in-retirement.html (accessed March 2, 2019).

Tversky, A., and D. Kahneman (1992). 'Advances in Prospect Theory: Cumulative Representation of Uncertainty.' *Journal of Risk and Uncertainty*, 5(4): 297–323.

van Schie, R. J., B. G. Dellaert, and B. Donkers (2015). 'Promoting Later Planned Retirement: Construal Level Intervention Impact Reverses with Age.' *Journal of Economic Psychology*, 50: 124–31.

Yaari, M. E. (1965). 'Uncertain Lifetime, Life Insurance, and the Theory of the Consumer,' *The Review of Economic Studies*, 32(2), 137–50.

Zeelenberg, M. and R. Pieters (2007). 'A Theory of Regret Regulation 1.0.' *Journal of Consumer Psychology*, 17(1): 3–18.

Zelinsky, E. (2012). *The Origins of the Ownership Society: How the Defined Contribution Paradigm Changed America*. New York, NY: Oxford University Press.

# Chapter 10

# Matching FinTech Advice to Participant Needs: Lessons and Challenges

*Stephen L. Deschenes and P. Brett Hammond*

The provision of goods and services online is growing rapidly across a wide range of industries, including financial services. In financial services, online innovation has often focused on transforming the back and middle offices, assisting investment management (the front office) in order to realize economies of scale and/or networking effects. By contrast, now we are seeing the application of increased computing power, internet bandwidth, and cloud capacity to customer acquisition, service, education, and advice. In this vein, online financial robo-advice has garnered significant public attention and sizable venture capital funding based on the promise that, through digitization, advice offerings can deliver a quality experience to individual investors at lower cost, thereby disrupting the financial industry.

While robo-advice is arguably in its early days, some lessons and continuing challenges are already emerging, shaped by several identifiable forces that we consider from the perspective of both the investor and the advice provider. This chapter takes both perspectives by reviewing the goals and objectives of robo-advice, the evolving business models, and available evidence on the demographics of robo-advice, the advice 'models,' and investor behavior. We conclude that, on the customer side, robos are being used not only by affluent Millennial investors, but also by others who want fast, mobile, and easy access to their finances. On the business side, early proponents promised to upend or disrupt the financial advice industry. Yet in practice, robo-advice is used by both traditional and startup providers to replace entirely traditional 'human touch' advice delivery models, but also to reach new customers and serve current ones. Moreover, providing advice is not enough: to be successful, firms must also sell advice-driven investments fulfilled by passive exchange-traded funds (ETFs) and mutual funds.

For both investors and providers, the overall effect is to lower prices of individualized advice as well as to enable providers to offer and users to select from price and customization points on the advice spectrum. Consequently, advice is coming in various flavors including 'pure' robo-advice, hybrid robo-advice supplemented by a 'human touch,' traditional face-to-face advising (sometimes supplemented by online tools), and advice embodied in low-cost products such as target date and other allocation funds.

It is too early to say which are strong or weak trends, and robo-advice models differ in terms of their underlying algorithms, the resulting advice offered, and ease of access. In rising markets, these differences may not be as discernable as they will be during a market downturn. We conclude by considering where the advice experience might be going, including what will happen during an industry shakeout. We also consider the potential for further evolution of investment offerings to include actively managed funds able to better manage market swings. Clearly robo-advice offers numerous promises, yet little evidence is available so far on the actual effects of using advice, such as changes in asset allocation and long-term effects on financial security.

## Understanding the Robo-advice Experience

Many might think the robo-advice experience would be shaped entirely by the nature, quality, and presentation of information provided to investors via an automated tool. Accordingly, one could focus on the technical algorithms behind online advice, the details of the advice offered, and the look and feel of the interface. Yet in practice, the robo-experience is also powerfully shaped by the complexity of the financial problems that this advice is meant to address. This includes the prescriptiveness of the advice system, individual investor characteristics including goals, objectives, and behaviors, and the availability and suitability of different investment options. In turn, these are structured by the goals and organizational arrangements of advice provider firms.

As noted by Fisch et al. (2019), robo-advice tends to cover pre-tax and after-tax asset allocation and fund selection through time, as well as saving and spending; less often does it include estate and tax plans. As such, robo-advice stands at one end of a customization and regulatory oversight continuum. Financial education is at the other end, where firms and advisors provide information about the benefits of saving, investing, and asset allocation without reference to individuals' circumstances (see Figure 10.1).

**Customization and complexity.** *Guidance* tends to offer clients saving targets and broad asset allocation recommendations, but it generally does not recommend specific securities or investment products. By contrast, *advice* goes beyond education and guidance to cover specific recommendations for financial products suitable for individuals. As such, advice implies that the advisor has gathered necessary and sufficient information about

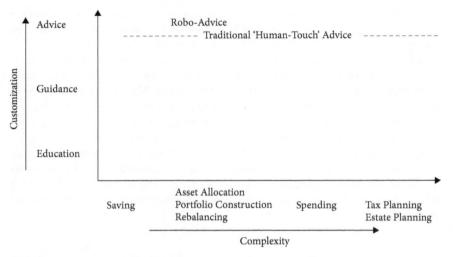

**Figure 10.1** Customization and complexity in the advice space

*Note*: Currently, robo-advice offerings largely focus on asset allocation, fund selection, and rebalancing.

*Source*: Author's analysis.

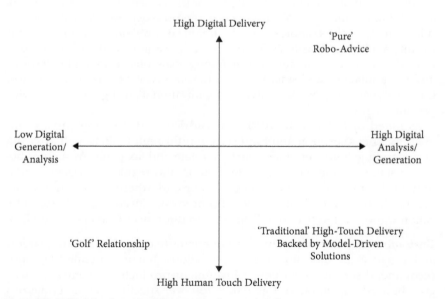

**Figure 10.2** Digitization of advice generation and delivery

*Source*: Authors' analysis.

TABLE 10.1 Types of robo-advice and firms in the US marketplace

| Type | Description | Level of discretion | Clients | Examples |
|---|---|---|---|---|
| Guidance | Portfolio assessment which determines a recommended allocation | Nondiscretionary, nonadvisory | All clients | E*Trade's Online Advisor |
| Financial planning | One time full review of portfolios which determines potential to meet financial goals. Makes recommendations on savings rates, withdrawal rates, optimized allocation, and investments for meeting goals. | Nondiscretionary, advisory | Complimentary for clients meeting asset threshold. Available for fee to other clients | Vanguard's financial planning group |
| Managed accounts | Provider determines appropriate allocation and investments and provides ongoing portfolio management. | Usually discretionary, advisory | Clients pay asset-based fee. Account minimums vary, start as low as $20K. | Fidelity's Portfolio Advisory Service® |
| Private client | Provider determines appropriate allocation and investments and provides ongoing portfolio management. Client receives other services as necessary such as tax, estate, and financial planning. | Discretionary, advisory | Clients pay an asset-based fee, minimums usually around $500K. | Schwab's Private Client |
| RIA referral | Provider refers a client seeking advice to an local RIA who custodies assets with the direct provider. | N/A | Clients with more complex financial needs | TD Ameritrades' AdvisorDirect™ |

*Note*: RIA refers to Registered Investment Advisor.

*Source*: Analysis based on authors' survey of advisor offerings.

the client and evaluated it to determine the suitability of investment recommendations.[1] Left for interpretation are the practical definitions of sufficient and suitable investment recommendations.

From an investor's perspective, the overall objective is to save, invest, and spend to meet his or her goals. From the advice provider's perspective, the objective is to adequately serve the investor, to meet fiduciary responsibilities, and to gather and/or retain assets. While the investor's and the provider's objectives are not identical, both the investor and the provider are interested in efficiency, balancing the costs of information gathering, evaluation, and advice delivery against the benefits of potential increases in lifetime consumption.

Theoretical research shows that when portfolio and/or financial advice is adopted early in consumers' lives, the certainty-equivalent consumption generated for clients can rise by 1.1 percent per year over the entire lifetime (Kim et al. 2016), and by 23 percent during retirement (Blanchett and Kaplan 2013). Although those studies do not distinguish between traditional and robo-advice, they are particularly applicable to robo-advice since they apply robo-like systematic and rules-based approaches to financial behavior. As such, robo-advisors claim to offer some or most of the customization a financial advisor can provide, while they do it systematically and precisely via software algorithms that are documentable, replicable, and repeatable, and potentially at lower cost. What sets robos apart is their potential through digitization, automation, and ease of use, to systematize advice offering and lower its cost for current investors and new consumers (see Figure 10.2).

Many different organizational arrangements are associated with robo-advisors. In some cases, stand-alone robo-advisors offer advice online. In other cases, full-service financial services firms use automated asset allocation advice as one of many tools to assist financial advisors in working one-on-one with investors to construct and manage portfolios and make other financial planning decisions (see Table 10.1).

## Evolution, Not Revolution

The automated or digitized features of robo-advice did not spring forth fully formed. Thus robo-advice started in 2008 with Betterment followed by Wealthfront, and in the early days the focus was on rebalancing across target date funds (Scott-Briggs 2016). In turn, this process was inspired by Mint, an online checking account aggregator, later sold to Intuit (Future Advisor 2015). Nevertheless, this Silicon Valley-centric view gives insufficient attention to the earlier antecedents of robo-advice such as Mpower and Financial Engines, which were startups offering services to employers and their employees. For example, Financial Engines, Ibbotson, and other independent robo-advisors provided pre-tax asset allocation and savings advice through defined contribution (DC) plans, when employers sought to offer employees financial advice but were legally required to do so via an independent provider.

Adoption and takeup of such advice was initially disappointing, both in terms of numbers of individuals and amounts of revenue. Subsequently, Ibbotson was sold to Morningstar, and both Financial Engines and Morningstar offered to manage the assets on which they gave advice. As of 2018, Financial Engines had nearly one million advised and managed accounts inside employer plans at nearly 150 Fortune 500 firms, with a growing number of customers through the Wells Fargo-managed 401k platform (Toonkel and Randall 2015).

More recently, Financial Engines moved into managed income for 401k accounts and IRA rollovers. This advice plus asset management business model, pre- and/or post-tax, has now become the industry standard, for standalone firms and financial services conglomerates. In addition, traditional financial firms such as Fidelity, Vanguard, and TIAA also began to offer online advice as a way of retaining assets and gathering more through additional services.

## The Robo-advice Process

Robo-advice processes and models differ not only in terms of what they cover, but also by the intensity of human involvement. Many investors learn about robo-advisors via online, radio, or television advertising; word of mouth; an employer pension plan; or, in some cases, a financial advisor's recommendation. One or more of these would prompt a visit to the robo-advisor's website. Overall, the advice process involves initial awareness, assessment, modeling, results and recommendations and follow-up. Each of these steps may be conducted exclusively online, or via telephone or face-to-face interactions with a human advisor.

**Assessment.** Investment advice is often provided based on a web-based questionnaire used to assess the investor's goals, financial circumstances, and personal characteristics. As with other aspects of robo-advice, the purpose and quality of questionnaires varies across the industry. Such assessments are used to gauge investors' risk perceptions and risk tolerance, as well as risk capacity. These are usually summarized in a risk tolerance score or label, such as 'conservative,' 'moderately conservative,' 'moderate,' 'moderately aggressive,' or 'aggressive.' At a financial firm where an investor already has a relationship, some financial and personal information may be transported over from the investor's current accounts.

Some question this approach to measuring risk tolerance and risk perception-related responses since behavioral research has shown that people often behave in what appears to be non-rational ways. Examples in the literature include asymmetric risk aversion (prospect theory), anchoring, and the 'house money' effect (where 20 percent loss after a 20 percent gain is perceived differently from a 20 percent loss after a previous 20 percent loss). Additional behavioral factors include 'dual self' theory, where actual behavior differs from self-predicted behavior.

Nevertheless, the psychology literature lends support for the use of validated questionnaires. For instance, questions designed to assess loss aversion and the self-assessed risk of previous financial decisions are believed reliable when explaining variations in people's portfolio allocations and investment decisions (Guillemette et al. 2012). Moreover, clients' risk self-assessments and validated questionnaires have been shown to better determine risk tolerance than financial advisors' assessments (Roszkowski and Grable 2005; Elsayed and Martin 1998). On the other hand, risk questionnaires rarely are psychometrically tested for validity or reliability, and many use poorly constructed questions, conflate risk tolerance versus risk capacity, and cannot identify highly risk-averse investors (Kitces 2016). Handling poor financial literacy is also difficult.

As an alternative to assessing an individual's risk characteristics, a different approach assigns risk to each of an investor's goals so that, for example, all investors saving for college would have a similar risk metric which differs from the risk metric assigned to saving for retirement or paying rent. Different goals can also be assigned relative importance weights, as implemented by Veritat and WealthBench (Weinrich 2012). While this tactic requires individuals to identify, schedule, and rank their financial goals, it does avoid the potential pitfalls of individual risk tolerance assessments.

**Asset allocation and fund selection calculators.** Robo-advisors employ formal models to create investment and savings advice, many of which share a foundation in modern portfolio theory (MPT). Inputs to these models include investor risk aversion, age, current assets, and other information along with the provider's estimates of expected asset returns, volatilities, and correlations. Model capabilities range from fairly simple, offering advice on overall asset allocation and fund packages, to comprehensive, also recommending insurance, trusts, wills, and other financial planning products and services.

Not surprisingly, robo-advisor asset allocation and fund selection models generate different results depending on statistical assumptions about capital market processes. Analytic approaches use historical returns and volatilities, estimated expected inputs, and Bayesian approaches, all of which generate different predictions. They also can use different measurement periods as well as re-estimation and historical sampling frequencies. Unlike the mutual fund industry where fund benchmarks are required and ubiquitous, the advice industry has not yet established standards on capital market assumptions, measurement periods, or 'what to solve for.' Additionally, models and inputs are rarely made public, making it impossible to compare methodologies and approaches. And, of course, historical evidence can mislead, as during the financial crisis when traditionally uncorrelated securities became highly correlated.

**Advice delivery.** In practice, a variety of robo-advice delivery systems has emerged. Some providers, such as Acorns, enable new customers to download an app to a mobile phone, input basic information, get an allocation and fund selection recommendation, transfer funds from a personal bank account, and be up and running within ten minutes. Others work closely with advisors at independent firms or financial services conglomerates; in this case, advisors specialize in communications including the initial conversation, advice delivery, portfolio implementation, and additional follow-ups. An automated system takes care of receiving investor data inputs and producing recommendations, which in turn are conveyed by the advisor. Some firms such as Vanguard offer different levels of 'human touch' at different price points.

**Investor receptivity.** Based on industry surveys of higher net worth households (over $100,000 in investable assets), it appears that many customers deem it important to have access to their portfolio information at all times (Cerulli Associates 2017). No matter what the channel (bank, wirehouse, financial advisor, direct investment provider, retirement plan provider) or size of assets, 20–30 percent of those investors used online tools and calculators, and 30–55 percent viewed their accounts or traded via online tools. Even for those who did not currently use robo-advisors, 20–45 percent of those under age 40 were 'somewhat likely' or 'very likely' to use a robo-advisor, with older and wealthier investors much less unlikely to do so.

Interestingly, when prompted, some 80 percent of those surveyed reported not having heard of most robo-advice providers, the exceptions being Vanguard and Charles Schwab. Of the 13 most prominent robo-providers, only 2–5 percent of respondents indicated that they used their robo-services (Cerulli Associates 2017). Those who did cited ease of use and cost as the main reasons for doing so. Among investors unlikely to use a digital advice provider, nearly 60 percent preferred human interaction to technology, and as many as 40 percent of those under age 40 said the same.

Though only a small percentage of the investor population has actually adopted robo-advice to date, it appears that Millennials and younger cohorts are more receptive than their predecessors. Among younger investors, robo-advice is most used by those with higher income and net worth, people who are online facile, and investors willing to take more risk (Cohen 2018; Cerulli 2017). Interestingly, investors using robo-advice did so using new assets rather than transferring assets away from current managers (Cerulli 2017). In other words, robo-advice at present is being used for incremental savings, tempering the likely growth of the sector.

## Investor Behavior and Impact

Of ultimate interest is how robo-advice will shape investors' consumption, retirement incomes, and overall well-being. As noted above, theoretical studies predict improvements in these, but real-world evidence is sparse. Early research by Warshawsky and Ameriks (2000), Bodie (2003), Kotlifoff (2006), Dowd et al. (2008), and Turner (2010) evaluated the advice provided, and these studies found significant shortcomings. These included the fact that too little financial information was gathered, risk tolerance assumptions were not well-grounded, overall net worth was not examined, asset allocation models and advice were too simplistic, and the client interfaces were often confusing.

More recently, comparisons of robo-offerings have become popular and can be found on a variety of financial websites (e.g., Investor Junkie, Investopedia, Kiplinger, Motley Fool, and more). Still, while most compare features and ease of use, few examine results or impacts. A more systematic examination of advice was offered by Aon Hewitt Financial Engines (2014) which studied 14 large DC plans offering three types of 'help' or advice. The topics covered included target-date funds, managed accounts, and online advice based on data from 2006 to 2012. During that period, online or robo-advice was used by only 5.4 percent of all plan participants, compared to 17 percent for target date plans (TDF) and 12 percent for managed accounts, while the rest (a little less than 65 per cent) were self-directed.[2] Target-date fund usage was driven primarily by an automatic enrollment ('opt-out') feature in some plans, while managed account and robo-advice usage was entirely 'opt-in.'

Regarding returns, plan participants opting for any kind of 'help' or advice between 2006 and 2012 achieved over 3 percent better net annual returns compared to participants not opting for help. Those using a combination of TDFs and self-directed investing did better than fully self-directed participants by about 90 bps/year, but they did significantly worse than participants receiving any form of help or advice (by about 2 percent per year). Notably, the return differences between participants using different types of help or advice were negligible.

Prior research has confirmed that most influential contributor to long-term financial security is the individual's contribution rate, followed by the length of the contribution period (Hammond and Richards 2010). There-fore, it is useful to note that the Aon Hewitt Financial Engines (2014) study found that online advisees had the highest contribution rates of any group, 9 percent on average, versus 4.4 percent for TDF participants, 7.5 percent for managed account participants, and 6.6 percent for self-directed partici-pants. While managed account participants were older than online advice users, online advice users had significantly higher average account balances than other plan participants.

Though hardly definitive, this evidence suggests that advice—including robo-advice—has been associated with better outcomes, at least in the short-to-medium time frame. While we cannot know whether advice seekers would have done better in the absence of advice than non-advice seekers, it is safe to conclude that advice, including robo-advice is not harmful and may be helpful.

In a related chapter (Fisch et al. 2019), the authors survey in some detail the nature of these models and the quality of the actual advice offered by robo-advisors. That study noted that, while an individual investor would receive the same advice with repeated visits to a single provider's website, he or she could be provided with different advice from different providers due to different ways of assessing risk tolerance and financial circumstances, the underlying model, and the model's inputs. Some models have been validated by the experience of their recommended portfolios through a full business cycle, while others have yet to experience a full cycle. It is also important to note that many studies suffer from self-selection or the ten-dency for people who use advisors (versus those who do not) to be more likely to take steps that positively affect their wealth and lifetime consump-tion, regardless of what the advisor recommends.

Research by Marsden et al. (2011) that controlled for self-selection showed that some types of activities increased when working with a financial advisor (e.g., goal setting, calculating retirement needs, portfo-lio diversification), yet there were no significant effects on saving rates and short-term asset values. Other evidence comes from comparing advisors with brokers, as the latter are not required to act in clients' best interest. In an experiment (Guillemette and Jurgensen 2017) and also in a comparative study (Martin and Finke 2012), advice from a certified financial planner resulted in higher investor account balances than did broker advice. A comparative study by Chalmers and Reuter (2012) concluded that invest-ment outcomes associated with broker advice were considerably worse than from self-directed portfolios and target date funds. Work by Hoechle et al. (2018) that accounted for self-selection found that bank customers who followed bank advisor recommendations did worse than had they followed a broad stock benchmark. Yet on the whole, these studies did not focus on robo-advisors.

## An Ongoing Case Study

An interesting ongoing analysis sponsored by Condor Capital (2018) is focusing on the effects of robo-advice by establishing both taxable and tax-deferred accounts at 20 prominent robo-advisors, some standalone while others form part of a broader financial services firm.[3] The taxable accounts established used an investor profile appropriate to a long-term investor with a moderate risk tolerance, while the tax-deferred account used the profile of a long-term investor with a high risk tolerance. In analyzing the findings, it is important to keep in mind that this analysis is limited by the short time frame (two years or fewer) and the effects of many unknown variables including the specific funds used to build portfolios, and when the providers changed asset allocations.

Several outcomes from the Condor Capital report on taxable account experience are worth highlighting; findings and relative comparisons were roughly similar for tax-deferred accounts. First, robo-advisor fees vary across firms and within firms by size of assets. In some cases, they also differ by whether the account holder uses only the digital platform or supplements it with a human advisor. As seen in Table 10.2, robo-only taxable account fees vary from zero bps (per year) on the account assets, to about 90 bps, with most fees in the 25–30 bps range. Minimum investment amounts also vary, from none to $100,000.

Presumably, low fee and low minimum robo-offerings are cross-subsidized by investment management and other charges. When 'premium' or 'selective' service is offered (i.e., the ability to work with a human advisor), fees are 15–25 bps higher over digital-only service, for totals in the 40–50 bps range. This may be compared to managed accounts, where fees are typically at least twice that. Note that for many premium robo offerings, account minimums are higher as well.

Second, we compare outcomes regarding asset allocation and fund selection. The classic rule-of-thumb for a medium-risk tolerant, long-term investor is a 60/40 portfolio (60 percent equities and 40 percent bonds, with an expected annual volatility of about 10 percent). In Table 10.3, we see that 11 of the 20 robo-advisor equity allocations were within 2 percentage points of the classic allocation (60 percent) for a similar investor profile.
Overall, allocations ranged from 56 to 71 percent equity and from 22 to 41 percent fixed income, with between 0 and 15 percent in 'miscellaneous' investments and cash. Within equities, the allocation to domestic equities (versus international equities) ranged from 45 to 75 percent.

It is worth noting that many robo-advisors are active allocators and manage their portfolios dynamically or even tactically, both in terms of the equity/fixed income split and the domestic equity/international equity split. For example, while Betterment did not change its allocations during the last two

TABLE 10.2 Taxable account fees and investment minimums for 20 robo-advisors

| Advisor | Fees | Account Minimums |
|---|---|---|
| Acorns | $1/mo <$5K; 25 bps/yr >$5K | None |
| Ally Financial | 30 bps/yr | $2,500 |
| Betterment | 25 bps/yr digital only; 40 bps 'Plus' (unlimited chat, 1 call/yr w/advisor); 50 bps 'Premium' (unlimited calls and chat); no fee if assets > $2M | None digital only; $100K 'Plus' and 'Premium' |
| Ellevest | 25 bps digital only; 50 bps 'Premium' (access to live advisor) | None digital only; $50K premium |
| E*Trade (ETFs) | 30 bps/yr | $5,000 |
| Fidelity Go | 35 bps/yr | $5,000 |
| FutureAdvisor | 50 bps/yr | $10,000 |
| Hedgeable | 75 bps/yr <$50K; decreasing to 30 bps/yr to $1M and above | None |
| Merrill Edge | 45 bps/yr | $5,000 |
| Personal Capital | 89 bps/yr <$1M; decreasing above $1M | $100,000 |
| Schwab | No fee digital only; 28 bps/yr for access to live advisor | $5,000 |
| SigFig | No fee <$10K; 25 bps/yr >$10K | $2,000 |
| SoFi | No fee <$10K; 25 bps/yr >$10K; no fee if client has a SoFi loan | $100 |
| TD Ameritrade | 30 bps/yr 'Essential'; higher fee tiering depending on asset size and portfolio 'Selective' | $5,000 'Essential'; $25,000 'Selective' |
| TIAA | 30 bps/yr | $5,000 |
| Vanguard | 30 bps yr <$5M; decreasing above $5M | $50,000 |
| WealthFront | No fee <$10K; 25 bps/yr >$10K | $500 |
| WealthSimple | 50 bps/yr <$100K; 40 bps/yr >$100K | None |
| WiseBanyan | No fee | None |
| Zack's Advantage | 50 bps/yr <$100K; 35 bps/yr >$100K | $5,000 |

*Source*: Derived from Condor Capital (2018).

years, TD Ameritrade raised its equity allocation from 65 to 71 percent and lowered its domestic equity allocation from 65 to 60 percent. For the funds in the Condor Capital study (2018), we see that robo-advisors generally used index funds, particularly on the equity side. Unsurprisingly, then, the equity allocations all showed similar large-cap blend behavior, with a pronounced tilt toward large-cap stocks and a slight tilt toward growth stocks. Fixed income holdings were more diverse across providers, with some favoring municipal bonds, treasury inflation protected securities (TIPS), and Treasuries, while others tilted toward emerging markets; still others were closer to 'neutral.' Nearly all of the fixed income allocations were neutral to negative on corporate, high-yield, and mortgage-backed securities.

Table 10.3 Taxable account asset allocations and equity splits for 20 robo-advisors

| Advisor | Allocation % | | | | | | | | Equity split % | | | |
| | 2017 | | | | 2018 | | | | 2017 | | 2018 | |
| | Equities | Fixed Income | Misc | Cash | Equities | Fixed Income | Misc | Cash | Domestic | International | Domestic | International |
|---|---|---|---|---|---|---|---|---|---|---|---|---|
| Acorns | 62 | 38 | 0 | 0 | 62 | 38 | 0 | 0 | **84** | **16** | 75 | 25 |
| Ally Financial | 59 | 38 | 2 | 1 | 61 | 37 | 0 | 3 | 69 | 31 | 59 | 41 |
| Betterment | 65 | 35 | 0 | 0 | 65 | 35 | 0 | 0 | **49** | **51** | **49** | **51** |
| Ellevest | 62 | 36 | 0 | 2 | 56 | **41** | 0 | 2 | 71 | 29 | 63 | 73 |
| E*Trade (ETFs) | 60 | 39 | 0 | 1 | 61 | 36 | 0 | 2 | 75 | 25 | 76 | 24 |
| Fidelity Go | 61 | 39 | 0 | 0 | 60 | 40 | 0 | 1 | 71 | 29 | 70 | 30 |
| FutureAdvisor | 59 | **41** | 8 | 0 | 59 | 39 | 0 | 1 | 49 | 51 | 45 | 55 |
| Hedgeable | **56** | 34 | 8 | 2 | 59 | 32 | **8** | 2 | **79** | **21** | **79** | **21** |
| Merrill Edge | 60 | 39 | 0 | 1 | 60 | 36 | 0 | 4 | 66 | 34 | 64 | 36 |
| Personal Capital | **68** | 25 | 5 | 2 | **71** | 24 | 4 | **11** | 70 | 30 | 69 | 31 |
| Schwab | 62 | **23** | 5 | **10** | 64 | **22** | 4 | **11** | 51 | 49 | 51 | 49 |
| SigFig | 61 | 37 | 0 | 2 | 63 | 35 | 0 | 2 | 59 | 41 | 60 | 40 |
| SoFi | 60 | 40 | 0 | 0 | 60 | 40 | 0 | 0 | 67 | 33 | 66 | 34 |
| TD Ameritrade | 65 | 33 | 0 | 2 | 71 | 28 | 0 | 2 | 65 | 35 | 60 | 40 |
| TIAA | 61 | 37 | 0 | 3 | 62 | 36 | 0 | 2 | 61 | 29 | 71 | 29 |
| Vanguard | 59 | **41** | 0 | 0 | 62 | 38 | 0 | 0 | 61 | 29 | 60 | 40 |
| WealthFront | 58 | **41** | 0 | 1 | 63 | 35 | 0 | 2 | 69 | 31 | 70 | 30 |
| WealthSimple | 62 | 38 | 0 | 0 | 62 | 38 | 0 | 0 | 66 | 34 | 66 | 34 |
| WiseBanyan | 65 | 35 | 0 | 0 | 65 | 35 | 0 | 0 | 62 | 38 | 63 | 37 |
| Zack's Advantage | 58 | 32 | 0 | 9 | **58** | 32 | 0 | 9 | 72 | 38 | 72 | 28 |

Source: Derived from Condor Capital (2018).

Third, we compare the investment performance for a moderately risk tolerant investor in Figures 10.3 and 10.4. For the seven providers with two-year results, total returns varied from 21 to 27 percent (10–13% on an annualized basis). For these same providers, Sharpe Ratios were impressive, ranging from 1.5 (Acorns) to 2.2 (Schwab)%. Of course, these results are indicative of recent robust equity markets. A better test of what robo-advisors can deliver will come during market downturns, as may be gleaned from a glance at the upside and downside capture ratios of the accounts having two-year histories. Figure 10.5 shows that the providers with better downside capture ratios (i.e., capture less of any market decline) are to the left, and those with better upside capture (i.e., capture more of any market increase) are higher, so providers that are up and to the left have better upside/downside capture ratios.

Two providers (Vanguard and Betterment) appear right at the center, both of which had identical 65/35 asset allocations that did not change over the two years. Interestingly, Schwab had a nearly identical allocation to equities (64%), but a lower allocation to fixed income and a signifi-cant allocation to cash (10–11%), which presumably provided downside protection while preserving equity exposure. On the other end, while Acorns had a slightly lower equity allocation (62%), it had the highest allocation to domestic equities of any provider; the recent outperformance

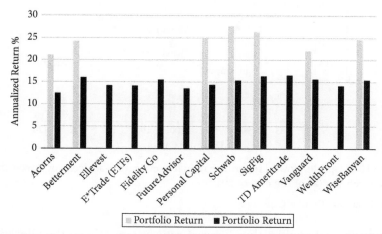

**Figure 10.3** Taxable account portfolio and asset returns (%) for 20 robo-advisors 'moderate risk' investor

*Note*: Condor Capital and Backend Benchmarking report that they established accounts at 20 robo-advisors, 7 at the beginning of 2016 and an additional 14 at the beginning of 2017.

*Source*: Data from Condor Capital (2018).

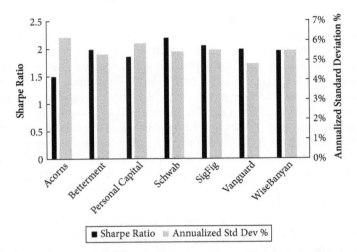

**Figure 10.4** Taxable account annualized risk/return statistics for seven robo-advisors with two years of returns (as of the end of 2017)

*Source*: Data from Condor Capital (2018).

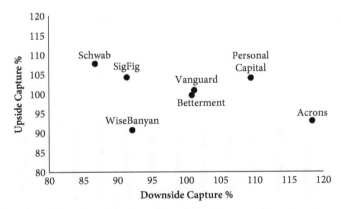

**Figure 10.5** Upside/downside capture ratio for seven robo-advice providers with two years of returns (as of the end of 2017)

*Source*: Data from Condor Capital (2018).

of international equities thus lowered returns and limited the allocation's downside protection.

In the years to come, the Condor Capital project will generate a longer-term view of the impact and characteristics of robo-advice offerings. Only then can we draw firmer conclusions about the long-term impact of robo-advice on investor wellbeing.

## Conclusions

To date, robo-advice has been concentrated among younger and more affluent investors, so changes in usage may be gradual and cohort-driven. These investors seem drawn to robo-advice by its ease of access and usage, compared to the time, number of forms, signatures, and face-to-face meetings required in most traditional advice and investment offerings. There is also promising early evidence that investors who used online advice save more and improve returns compared to investors who did not.

While robo-advice is apparently not producing a major disruption in the types of firms offering advice, the industry is changing. There is a proliferation of standalone robo-advice firms where the early firms moved from charging for advice without direct asset management, to charging for advice embedded along with managed accounts. Moreover, traditional investment firms and advisors are buying startup robo-advice firms, licensing technology, and creating new tiered advice models. These traditional firms are also adopting so-called 'cyborg solutions'—part-human, part-computer, in the way face-to-face banking with tellers evolved to include on-line banking as an option. As with other services, firms are likely to use robo-advice to attract and retain customers attracted to its ease of use along with their assets.

The next big test will be a market downturn. Some standalone startups have already survived at least one major market shakeout (for instance, Financial Engines and others established before the global financial crisis). We can expect that differences in allocations and advice delivery will be made evident in the next shakeout.

Nevertheless, more remains to be learned about how robo-advice content and models, as well as industry organization and delivery, affect behavior. A related question is whether robo-advice obviates the need for improved financial literacy. And crucially, although beyond the scope of the present chapter, legal and regulatory concerns are raised by advice generally and robo-advice in particular. Some of these are addressed elsewhere in this volume by Baker and Delleart (2019), Fisch et al. (2019), and Polansky et al. (2019).

## Notes

1. Financial education, guidance, and advice all have specific regulatory definitions. For example, a discussion of what financial advice covers in the UK is reported in HM Treasury (2017).
2. To count, a participant had to have at least 95 percent of her assets in the TDF.
3. Sponsored and reported by Condor Capital, this ongoing study is being conducted by Backend Benchmarking. Not that some prominent firms were not included in this study, most notably Financial Engines, which is one of the oldest and most successful robo-advisors.

# References

Aon Hewitt Financial Engines (2014). *Help in Defined Contribution Plans: 2006 Through 2012,* May. https://corp.financialengines.com/employers/FinancialEngines-2014-Help-Report.pdf (accessed March 2, 2019).

Baker, T. and B. Dellaert (2019). 'Behavioral Finance, Decumulation and Robo-Advice.' In J. Agnew and O. S. Mitchell (eds.), *The Disruptive Impact of FinTech on Retirement Systems.* Oxford, UK: Oxford University Press, pp. 149–71.

Blanchett, D. and P. Kaplan (2013). 'Alpha, Beta, and Now...Gamma,' *Journal of Retirement,* 1(2), Fall: 29–45.

Bodie, Z. (2003). 'An Analysis of Investment Advice to Retirement Plan Participants.' In O. S. Mitchell and K. Smetters eds., *The Pension Challenge: Risk Transfers and Retirement Income Security.* Oxford, UK: Oxford University Press, pp. 19–32.

Cerulli Associates (2017). 'Chapter 6: Digital Preferences' in *The Cerulli Report: U.S. Retail Investor Products and Platforms 2017: Retooling for the Modern Investor.* Boston, MA: Cerulli Associates, pp. 92–105.

Chalmers, J. and J. Reuter (2012). *What is the Impact of Financial Advisors on Retirement Portfolio Choices and Outcomes?* May 21. https://ssrn.com/abstract=2078536 (accessed March 2, 2019).

Cohen, L. (2018). 'ETFs and Mutual Fund Households,' Strategic Business Insights, *CFD's MacroMonitor,* March.

Condor Capital (2018). 'Bringing Transparency to Robo Investing,' *The Robo Report, 6th ed., 4th Quarter 2017.* Martinsville, NJ: Condor Capital.

Dowd, B., A. Atherly, and R. Town (2008). 'Planning for Retirement? Web Calculators Weak on Health Care Costs.' AARP Public Policy Institute Working Paper. Washington, DC: AARP Public Policy Institute.

Elsayed, H. and J. Martin (1998). 'Survey of Financial Risk Tolerance.' *Australian Technical Brief, Chandler and Macleod Consultants.*

Fisch, J. E., M. Labouré, and J. A. Turner (2019). 'The Emergence of the Robo-adviser' in J. Agnew and O. S. Mitchell (eds.), *The Disruptive Impact of FinTech on Retirement Systems.* Oxford, UK: Oxford University Press, pp. 13–37.

Future Advisor (2015). *A History of Robo-advisors.* April 8. San Francisco, CA: FutureAdvisor.

Guillemette, M., M. S. Finke, and J. Gilliam (2012). 'Risk Tolerance Questions to Best Determine Client Portfolio Allocation Preferences.' *Journal of Financial Planning,* 25(5): 36–44.

Guillemette, M. and J. B. Jurgenson (2017). 'The Impact of Financial Advice Certification on Investment Choices.' *Journal of Financial Counseling and Planning.* 28(1): 129–39.

Hammond, P. B. and D. P. Richardson (2010). 'Retirement Saving Adequacy and Individual Investment Risk Management Using the Asset/Salary Ratio,' in O. S. Mitchell and R. Clark (eds.), *Reorienting Retirement Risk Management.* New York: Oxford University Press, pp. 13–35.

HM Treasury (2017). 'Annex A: Revised Text for Article 53 of the Regulated Activities Order'. *Amending the Definition of Financial Advice: Consultation.* 27 February. https://www.gov.uk/government/consultations/amending-the-definition-of-financial-

advice-consultation/amending-the-definition-of-financial-advice-consultation#
annex-a-revised-text-for-article-53-of-the-regulated-activities-order (accessed March 2,
2019).

Hoechle, D., S. Ruenzi, N. Schaub, and M. Schmid (2018). 'Financial Advice and
Bank Profits.' *The Review of Financial Studies* (31)11: 4447–92.

Kim, H., R. Maurer, and O. S. Mitchell. (2016). 'Time is Money: Rational Life Cycle
Inertia and the Delegation of Investment Management.' *Journal of Financial Economics.* 121(2): 231–448.

Kitces, M. (2016). 'The Sorry State of Risk Tolerance Questionnaires for Financial
Advisors.' Kitces.com, *Nerd's Eye View.* September 14: https://www.kitces.com/
blog/risk-tolerance-questionnaire-and-risk-profiling-problems-for-financial-advisors-
planplus-study/ (accessed March 2, 2019).

Kotlikoff, L. J. (2006). *Is Conventional Financial Planning Good for Your Financial Health?*
Boston, MA: Boston University. https://www.kotlikoff.net/sites/default/files/Is%
20Conventional%20Financial%20Planning%20Good%20for%20Your%20Financial
%20Health_0.pdf (accessed March 2, 2019).

Marsden, M., C. D. Zick, and R. N. Mayer (2011). 'The Value of Seeking Financial
Advice.' *Journal of Family and Economic Issues,* 32(4): 625–43.

Martin, T. and M. S. Finke (2012). *Planning for Retirement.* https://ssrn.com/abstract=
2195138 (accessed March 2, 2019).

Polansky, S., P. Chandler, and G. Mottola (2019). 'Digital Investment Advice and
Decumulation.' In J. Agnew and O. S. Mitchell (eds.), *The Disruptive Impact of
FinTech on Retirement Systems.* Oxford, UK: Oxford University Press, pp. 129–48.

Roszkowski, M. J. and J. Grable (2005). 'Estimating Risk Tolerance: The Degree of
Accuracy and the Paramorphic Representations of the Estimate,' *Journal of Financial Counseling and Planning,* 16(2): 29–47.

Scott-Briggs, A. (2016). 'What is a Robo-advisor, Origin and History?' *Techbullion.*
November 24. https://www.techbullion.com/robo-advisor-origin-history/ (accessed
March 2, 2019).

Toonkel, J. and D. Randall (2015). 'Original Robo-adviser Financial Engines Seeks
Life Beyond 401(k)s.' Reuters, *Retirement News.* May 25. https://www.reuters.com/
article/us-financialengines-future-insight/original-robo-adviser-financial-engines-
seeks-life-beyond-401s-idUSKBN0OC0BE20150527 (accessed March 2, 2019).

Turner, J. (2010). 'Rating Retirement Advice: A Critical Assessment of Retirement
Planning Software.' Pension Research Council Working Paper No. 2010-03. Philadelphia, PA: Pension Research Council.

Warshawsky, M. and J. Ameriks (2000). 'How Prepared Are Americans for Retirement?' in O. S. Mitchell, P. B. Hammond, and A. Rappaport, eds., *Forecasting Retirement Needs and Retirement Wealth.* Philadelphia, PA: University of Pennsylvania
Press, pp. 33–67.

Weinrich, G. (2012). 'Wharton Professor Gives Advisory Model Radical Makeover.'
*Think Advisor.* February 27. https://www.thinkadvisor.com/2012/02/27/wharton-
professor-gives-advisory-model-radical-mak/ (accessed March 2, 2019).

# Chapter 11

# The FinTech Opportunity

*Thomas Philippon*

This chapter studies the FinTech movement in the context of the long run evolution of the finance industry and its regulations. The 2007–09 financial crisis triggered new regulatory initiatives and accelerated existing ones. I argue that the current framework has been useful, but it has run its course and is unlikely to deliver significant welfare gains in the future. If regulators want to go further, they will need to consider alternative approaches to involve FinTech.

FinTech covers digital innovations and technology-enabled business model innovations in the financial sector. Such innovations can disrupt existing industry structures and blur industry boundaries, facilitate strategic disintermediation, revolutionize how existing firms create and deliver products and services, provide new gateways for entrepreneurship, democratize access to financial services, but also create significant privacy, regulatory and law-enforcement challenges. Examples of innovations that are central to FinTech today include cryptocurrencies and the blockchain, new digital advisory and trading systems, artificial intelligence and machine learning, peer-to-peer lending, equity crowdfunding, and mobile payment systems.

The starting point of my analysis is that the current financial system is rather inefficient. To show this, I update Philippon (2015) with post-crisis US data and I show that the unit cost of financial intermediation has declined only marginally since the crisis. The evidence outside the US is remarkably similar (Bazot 2017). Recent research also suggests that many advanced economies have reached a point where 'more finance' is not helpful.[1] Significant welfare gains from improvement in financial services are technologically feasible but unlikely to happen without entry of new firms.

Next I review recent regulatory efforts and challenges. The financial regulations enacted after 2009 are not as far reaching as the ones implemented after the Great Depression, but the evidence suggests that these efforts have made the financial sector safer.[2] A defining feature of the current approach, however, is that it focuses almost exclusively on incumbents. This approach is unlikely to deliver much further improvement because of ubiquitous ratchet effects in leverage, size, and interconnectedness, preferential tax treatments, and oligopoly rents. These distortions are embedded in the current financial system to such an extent that the political and coordination costs of removing them have become prohibitive.

An alternative approach to financial regulation isbased on the idea that encouraging entry and shaping the development of new systems might be the best way to solve the remaining challenges in financial regulation. With respect to incumbents, this alternative approach would be a form of containment: its goal would be to consolidate existing efforts, and prevent future regulatory arbitrage, but not to impose top-down structural changes. The new approach would focus on entrants and take advantage of the ongoing development of FinTech firms. The main idea is to achieve bottom-up structural change by encouraging, for instance, firms that provide transaction services without leverage, and trading systems that are cheap, transparent and open-access. I conclude by sketching out some guiding principles for this new approach.

## Inefficiency of the Existing System

The unit cost of financial intermediation in the US has stayed at around 2 percent for the past 130 years (Philippon 2015); Bazot (2017) finds similar unit costs in other major countries (Germany, UK, France). Improvements in information technologies have not been passed through to the end users of financial services. This section offers an update of this work, with two goals in mind. First, measurement is difficult and statistical agencies have recently made some significant data revisions to financial accounts. We need to know if these revisions affect the main insights of the original paper. A second reason for updating the series is that the data in Philippon (2015) predate the financial crisis, so it is of interest to know how the unit cost of intermediation has evolved since then. I then discuss recent trend in labor compensation and employment. Finally, I discuss the evidence on the link between finance and growth.

**Financial expenses and intermediated assets.** To organize the discussion I use a simple model economy consisting of households, a non-financial business sector, and a financial intermediation sector. The details of the model are in the Appendix. The income share of finance, shown in Figure 11.1, is defined as[3]

$$\frac{y_t^f}{y_t} = \frac{\text{Value Added of Finance Industry}}{\text{GDP}}.$$

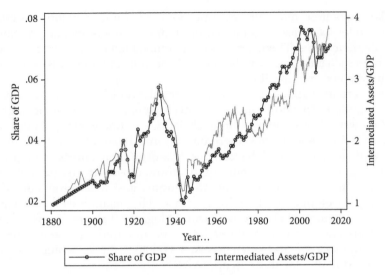

**Figure 11.1** Finance income and intermediated assets

*Note*: Both series are expressed as a share of GDP. Finance income is the domestic income of the finance and insurance industries, i.e., aggregate income minus net exports. Intermediated assets include debt and equity issued by non financial firms, household debt, and various assets providing liquidity services. Data range for intermediated assets is 1886–2012.

*Source*: Philippon (2015).

The model assumes that financial services are produced under constant returns to scale. The income of the finance industry $y_t^f$ is then given by

$$y_t^f = \psi_{c,t} b_{c,t} + \psi_{m,t} m_t + \psi_{k,t} k_t, \qquad (11.1)$$

where $b_{c,t}$ is consumer credit, $m_t$ are assets providing liquidity services, and $k_t$ is the value of intermediated corporate assets. The parameters $\psi_{i,t}$' s are the unit cost of intermediation, pinned down by the intermediation technology. The model therefore says that the income of the finance industry is proportional to the quantity of intermediated assets, properly defined. The model predicts no income effect (i.e., no tendency for the finance income share to grow with per-capita GDP). This does not mean that the finance income share should be constant, since the ratio of assets to GDP can change. But it says that the income share does not grow mechanically with total factor productivity. This is consistent with the historical evidence.[4]

Measuring intermediated assets is complicated because these assets are heterogeneous. As far as corporate finance is concerned, the model is fundamentally a user cost model. Improvements in corporate finance (a decrease in $\psi_k$) lower the user cost of capital and increase the capital stock, which, from a theoretical perspective, should include all intangible investments and should be measured at market value. A significant part of the growth of the finance industry over the past 30 years is linked to household credit. The model provides a simple way to model household finance. The model also incorporates liquidity services provided by specific liabilities (deposits, checking accounts, some form of repurchase agreements) issued by financial intermediaries. One can always write the RHS of (11.1) as $\psi_{c,t}\left(b_{c,t} + \frac{\psi_{m,t}}{\psi_{c,t}} m_t + \frac{\psi_{k,t}}{\psi_{c,t}} k_t\right)$. Philippon (2015) finds that the ratios $\frac{\psi_{m,t}}{\psi_{c,t}}$ and $\frac{\psi_{k,t}}{\psi_{c,t}}$ are close to one.[5] As a result one can define intermediated assets as:

$$q_t \equiv b_{c,t} + m_t + k_t \tag{11.2}$$

The principle is to measure the instruments on the balance sheets of non-financial users, households, and non-financial firms. This is the correct way to do the accounting, rather than looking at the balance sheet of financial intermediaries. After aggregating the various types of credit, equity issuances, and liquid assets into one measure, I obtain the quantity of financial assets intermediated by the financial sector for the non-financial sector, displayed in Figure 11.1.

**Unit cost and quality adjustments.** I can then divide the income of the finance industry by the quantity of intermediated assets to obtain a measure of the unit cost:

$$\psi_t \equiv \frac{y_t^f}{q_t} \tag{11.3}$$

Figure 11.2 shows that this unit cost is around 2 percent and relatively stable over time. In other words, I estimate that it costs two cents per year to create and maintain one dollar of intermediated financial asset. Equivalently, the annual rate of return of savers is on average two percentage points below the funding cost of borrowers. The updated series are similar to the ones in the original paper. The unit costs for other countries are estimated by Bazot (2017) who finds convergence to US levels.

The raw measure of Figure 11.2, however, does not take into account changes in the characteristics of borrowers. These changes require quality adjustments to the raw measure of intermediated assets. For instance, corporate finance involves issuing commercial paper for blue chip companies as well as raising equity for high-technology start-ups. The monitoring requirements per dollar intermediated are clearly different in these two activities. Similarly, with household finance, it is more expensive to lend to poor households than to wealthy ones, and relatively poor households have gained access to credit in recent years.[6] Measurement problems arise when the mix of high- and low-quality borrowers changes over time.

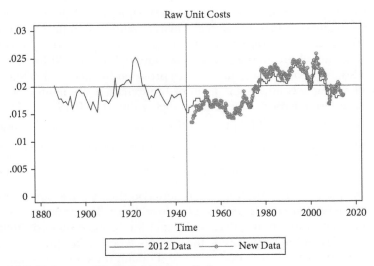

**Figure 11.2** Unit cost of financial intermediation

*Notes*: The raw measure is the ratio of finance income to intermediated assets, displayed in Figure 11.1. The 2012 data are from Philippon (2015), while the new data were accessed May 2016. Data range is 1886–2015.

*Source*: Philippon (2015) with updated data.

I then perform a quality adjustment to the intermediated assets series, following Philippon (2015). Figure 11.3 shows the quality-adjusted unit cost series. It is lower than the unadjusted series by construction, since quality adjusted assets are (weakly) larger than raw intermediated assets. The gap between the two series grows when there is entry of new firms, and/or when there is credit expansion at the extensive margin (i.e., new borrowers). Even with the adjusted series, however, we see no significant decrease in the unit cost of intermediation over time.

Finance has benefited more than other industries from improvements in information technologies. But unlike in retail trade, for instance, these improvements have not been passed on as lower costs to the end users of financial services. Asset management services are still expensive. Banks generate large spreads on deposits (Drechsler et al. 2017). Finance could and should be much cheaper. In that respect, the puzzle is not that FinTech is happening now. The puzzle is why it did not happen earlier.

**Wages and employment.** The relative wage in the finance industry is defined as

$$relw = \frac{\bar{w}_t^{fin}}{\bar{w}_t^{all}} \tag{11.4}$$

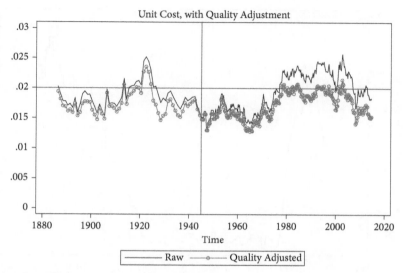

**Figure 11.3** Unit cost and quality adjustment

*Notes*: The quality adjusted measure takes into account changes in firms' and households' characteristics. Data range is 1886–2015.

*Source*: Philippon (2015).

where $\bar{w}$; is the average wage (total compensation divided by total number of employees). This measure does not control for changes in the composition of the labor force within a sector (see Philippon and Reshef (2012) for micro evidence on this issue). Figure 11.4 updates previous findings. One can clearly see the high wages of the 1920s, the drop following the Great Depression and WWII, and then a period of remarkably stability from 1945 to 1980. After 1980, the relative wage starts increasing again, in part because low skill jobs are automated (ATMs) and in part because the finance industry hires more brains.

There was some relative wage moderation following the 2007/2009 crisis, but it was clearly limited. The labor share in finance has increased a bit relative to the rest of the private sector (i.e., the profit share has fallen a bit more in finance), suggesting some moderation in the future, but the changes are not large.

Figure 11.5 compares the employment dynamics in finance and other industries over the past 25 years. It is quite striking to see that the financial crisis did not initially hit the finance industry more than the rest of the economy. The main difference is the weaker recovery of employment in finance from 2010 onward. Overall, finance has shrunk somewhat after the crisis but nowhere near as much as after the Great Depression.

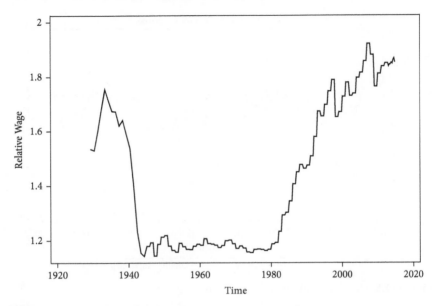

**Figure 11.4** Evolution of relative wage in finance vs. all industries

*Notes*: Wage in finance divided by average wage in all industries.

*Source*: Philippon and Reshef (2012), updated.

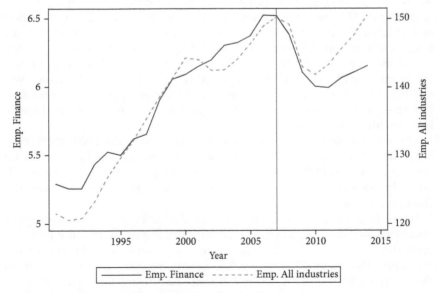

**Figure 11.5** Employment in finance vs. all industries

*Notes*: Employment is measured in millions of jobs.

*Source*: Philippon and Reshef (2012), updated.

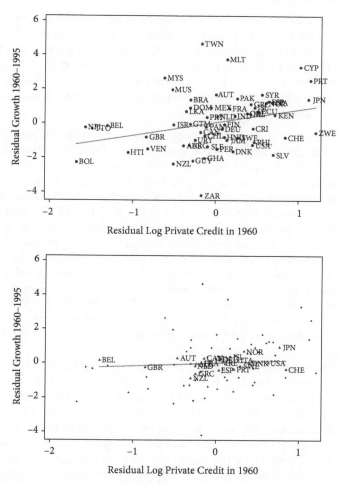

**Figure 11.6** Credit and growth, all vs. OECD countries

*Source*: Beck et al. (2011) dataset. Available at http://www.worldbank.org/en/publication/gfdr/data/financial-structure-database (accessed March 25, 2019).

**Finance and growth.** There is a large literature studying the links between finance and growth. Levine (2005) provides an authoritative survey, and Levine (2014) a recent discussion. One main finding is displayed in the left panel of Figure 11.6. Countries with deeper credit markets in 1960 (measured as credit outstanding over GDP) grew faster between 1960 and 1995.

It is also important to emphasize that the link between finance and (long-term) growth is not a mechanical consequence of credit expansion. As Levine (2005) emphasized, the primary driver of the finance–growth nexus is the allocation of capital. Better financial systems provide a better allocation of capital, not necessarily more overall credit, as noted by Favara (2009) and Cechetti and Kharroubi (2012), who argued that the relation between credit and growth is not monotonic.[7] One way to quickly see this is to examine the same data for only the OECD countries. Among OECD countries the link between credit and growth is not significant, as can be seen in the right panel of Figure 11.6.

**Summary.** Finance is important for growth, in particular for the allocation of capital, but much of the recent growth of the finance industry had little to do with efficient capital allocation. Financial services remain expensive and financial innovations have not delivered significant benefits to consumers. The point is not that finance does not innovate: It does, yet these innovations have not improved the overall efficiency of the system. This is not a great theoretical puzzle: we know that innovations can be motivated by rent seeking and business stealing, in which case the private and social returns to innovation are fundamentally different. The race for speed is an obvious example: there is a large difference between foreknowledge and discovery in terms of *social* welfare, even though the two activities can generate the same *private* returns (Hirshleifer 1971). This tension between private and social returns exists in most industries, but economists tend to think that entry and competition limit the severity of the resulting inefficiencies.

Lack of entry and competition, however, has been an endemic problem in finance in recent decades. Berger et al. (1999) review the evidence on consolidation during the 1990s. The number of US banks and banking organizations fell by almost 30 percent between 1988 and 1997, and the share of total nationwide assets held by the largest eight banking organizations rose from 22.3 percent to 35.5 percent. Several hundred mergers and acquisitions (M&As) occurred each year, including mega-mergers between institutions with assets over $1 billion.[8] The main motivations for consolidation were market power and diversification. Berger et al. (1999) found little evidence of cost efficiency improvement, which is consistent with Figure 11.5 and 11.3. De Young et al. (2009) showed that consolidation continued during the 2000s. They argued that there was growing evidence that consolidation is partly motivated by the desire to obtain too-big-to-fail status, and that M&As have a negative impact on certain types of borrowers, depositors, and other external stakeholders.

It is also important to keep in mind that the welfare implications of financial efficiency are significant. In order to calculate welfare, we use a simple model presented in the appendix. Figure 11.7 plots the welfare of agents in the economy as a function of the unit cost of intermediation. Welfare is measured in equivalent consumption units and normalized to

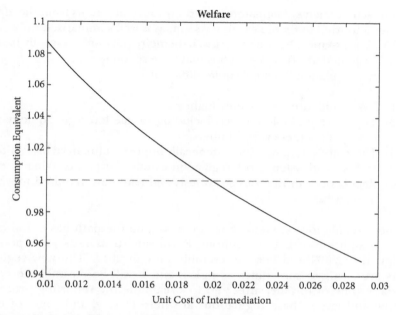

**Figure 11.7** Welfare and the unit cost of intermediation

*Notes*: The welfare calculations are constructed using the model in the appendix. Welfare is calculated as the amount of consumption agents would be willing to give up to reduce the unit cost of intermediation.

one in the benchmark case of a unit cost of 2 percent. I have found that agents in the economy would be willing to pay 8.7 percent of consumption to bring the unit cost of intermediation down to 1 percent.

If one steps back, it is difficult not to see finance as an industry with excessive rents and poor overall efficiency. The puzzle is why this has persisted for so long. There are several plausible explanations for this: zero-sum games in trading activities, inefficient regulations, barriers to entry, increasing returns to size, etc.[9] I will not attempt to disentangle all these explanations. The important point for my argument is simpler: there is (much) room for improvement. In the next section, I will argue that the current regulatory approach is unlikely to bring these improvements.

## A Perspective on Current Regulations

Rather than providing a comprehensive overview of recent financial regulations, instead I make the case that the focus on incumbents inherent in current regulations increases political economy and coordination costs.

**Recent achievements.** Regulators have drawn several lessons from the 2008 disaster and tried to fix the existing system, as is well summarized in Ingves (2015). For instance, before the crisis, banking regulation was mostly based on risk-weighted assets (RWA) ratios that were set quite low.

Today's regulation is actually quite different:

(1) RWA ratios are significantly higher;
(2) There are multiple metrics, including simple leverage, liquidity ratios, and counter-cyclical buffers;
(3) There are surcharges for Systemically important financial institutions (SIFIs), and systemic risk regulation extends beyond banking; and
(4) Regulators run rigorous stress tests and banks are required to write living wills.

These regulations are a work in progress, and the path has not always been straightforward. For example, European stress tests were poorly designed in 2009 and became credible only in 2014. The new regulations are costly to sometimes complex, and it will be desirable to consolidate some of the measures and to streamline the reporting process. But by and large, these regulations are here to stay, and some of the complexity is by design. As Ingves (2015) argues, multiple metrics make it harder for banks to game the system. Using several measures of risk is also useful because different measures have different advantages and drawbacks. For instance, RWA is better than simple leverage if we think about arbitrage across asset classes at a point in time. On the other hand, simple leverage is more counter-cyclical, as shown by Brei and Gambacorta (2016).

This regulatory tightening, although not as ambitious as after the Great Depression, has achieved several important goals. Capital requirements have increased without adverse effects on funding costs (Cecchetti and Schoenholtz 2014). For instance, EBA (2015) reports that the 'common equity tier 1' (CET1) ratio of banks in the European Union increased by 1.7 percent between December 2013 and June 2015, with a 1.9 percent increase in capital and about 0.1 percent increase in RWA. The banking industry has become less risky, at least in developed economies.[10] Nevertheless, some important goals remain elusive.

**The leverage controversy.** The most important regulatory debate following the 2007–09 crisis revolves around the appropriate level of capital requirement for banks. Admati et al. (2011) argued for high capital ratios and debunked several misleading claims about the supposed cost of such requirements. In the end, capital ratios have been raised significantly, but not to the extent advocated by these authors. The bank leverage debate illustrates an important pitfall of the current approach to financial regulation. Almost everyone agrees that bank leverage was too high before the crisis, but agreeing on a new target capital ratio has proved more difficult. Countries have conflicting objectives, lobbies are powerful, and, perhaps most importantly, we do not know what the 'right' ratio is because there are several tradeoffs to consider. If the world had only commercial banks and one global regulator, we would be able to estimate an optimal capital ratio, and it would probably be rather high, for the reasons explained in Admati and Hellwig (2013). But this is not our world. Regulators do not always cooperate, jurisdictions compete and undermine each other, and we worry about pushing activities away from the regulated banking sector. Regulatory arbitrage is omnipresent and regulators are highly uncertain about when and how it could happen. Finding the second-best (or third-best) optimal ratio then becomes a daunting task. The information and coordination requirements of the current regulatory approach are prohibitive. I will argue in the final section of the chapter that another approach might be preferred.

<u>Leverage is difficult to measure</u>. Regulating leverage is also particularly difficult because there are many ways for banks to take risks without increasing their 'measured' leverage. One example is the use of derivatives. Figure 11.8, from Cecchetti and Schoenholtz (2016), shows the impact of

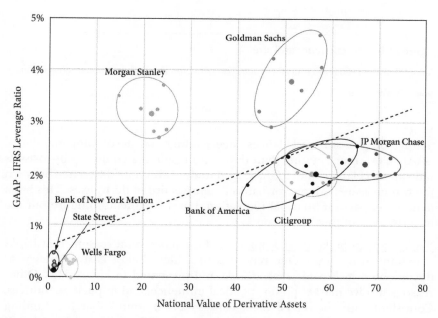

**Figure 11.8** Differences in leverage accounting and derivatives

*Notes*: Vertical axis is leverage (equity divided by assets) as measured by the GAAS minus leverage as measured by the IFRS.

*Source*: Cecchetti and Schoenholtz (2016), Leverage and Risk: http://www.moneyandbanking. com (accessed March 3, 2019).

Normalized Efficiency Ratio

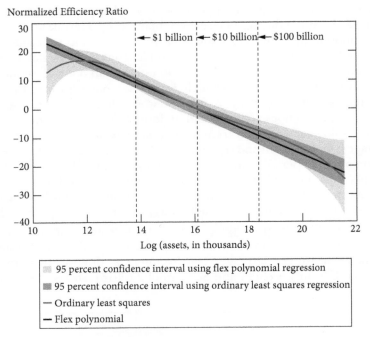

**Figure 11.9** Cost efficiency and size

*Notes*: Efficiency ratio is non-interest expense over (net interest income + non-interest income).

*Source*: Kovner et al. (2014).

netting on the size of balances sheets under two accounting standards. GAAP allows more netting than IFRS. As a result, the equity equity-to-assets ratio appears larger under GAAP than under IFRS. The difference between the two measures is large for banks that are active in derivatives. This has a material impact on financial regulation, but it is difficult to figure out the true riskiness of these positions.

<u>Banks want to be large and opaque.</u> There are several reasons that banks may want to be large. One reason is to achieve better cost efficiency, as documented in Kovner et al. (2014) and presented in Figure 11.9. Other reasons involve market power, political influence, and implicit guarantees. Consistent with the TBTF idea, Santos (2014) found that the funding advantage enjoyed by the largest banks was significantly larger than that of the largest non-banks and non-financial corporations. As banks grow, they take on more leverage and they become more opaque. Cetorelli et al. (2014) considered the implications of increasing complexity for supervision and resolution. Finally, implicit guarantees are not only a function of a

bank's individual size. Kelly et al. (2016) found evidence of collective government guarantees for the financial sector.

**G-SIFIs versus narrow banks.** A formidable challenge for financial regulation is to provide credible resolution mechanisms for global systemically important financial institutions (G-SIFIs). There are two fundamental difficulties. One comes from the sheer size and complexity of these organizations and the impossibility to forecast what would happen during a crisis. A second issue is that there is little scope for learning and testing various mechanisms because G-SIFIs do not usually fail for idiosyncratic reasons. Living wills, total loss-absorbing capacity (TLAC) requirements, are necessary, but in all likelihood they will not be properly battle-tested before a crisis actually happens.

This has led several observers to argue for some form of 'narrow banking.' As Pennacchi (2012) explained, a narrow bank is a financial firm that invests in assets with little nominal risk and issues demandable liabilities. Depending on how restrictive one's definition is, narrow banking can range from money market funds investing exclusively in Treasury Bills to commercial banks which are restricted to back all their deposits with money market instruments but can hold many other assets.[11] Pennacchi (2012: 8) also noted that 'recommendations for narrow banking appear most frequently following major financial crises.' The crisis of 2008 was no exception. Chamley et al. (2012) explained how limited-purpose banking could work, and Cochrane (2014) proposed reforms to make the financial system 'run-proof.'

These are certainly powerful arguments in favor of narrow banking, but there are also several counterarguments. The theoretical case is not as clear-cut as some proponents argue. Wallace (1996) showed that narrow banking negates liquidity risk sharing, in the sense that, in a Diamond and Dybvig (1983) setup, any allocation under narrow banking can be achieved under autarky. Another critique of the narrow banking proposal is that the joint provision of demand deposits and loan commitments allows banks to diversify the use of liquidity Kashyap et al. (2002). Pennachi (2012), however, argued that this synergy might in fact be a consequence of the insurance provided by the Federal Deposit Insurance Corporation (FDIC).

Another major issue is that narrow banking would require powerful regulators to implement a radical transformation of existing firms, and it would also create incentives to move maturity transformation outside the regulated system. Of course, the fact that an idea would be difficult to implement should not prevent us from studying its merits. As Zingales (2015: 1355) argued, 'when we engage in policy work we try to be relevant,' and this can be a problem because it is easy to discredit good ideas by labelling them politically unrealistic. Nevertheless, it does prompt reason to thinking about different ways to reach the same goal.

**Why a new strategy is needed.** There is an apparent contradiction between the widely shared diagnostic of the problems and the disagreements about how to address them. Essentially everyone agrees that leverage (especially short-term leverage), opacity, and complexity were significant contributors to the financial crisis of 2007–09. It seems also clear that many large financial firms still enjoy too big to fail (TBTF) subsidies and oligopolistic rents. Yet, as I have argued earlier, our tools and our understanding of how to use them are limited; the problem is not so much that we do not know where we would like to go, but that we do not know which path to follow.

Two factors are at the source of these difficulties. The first is the complexity and depth of the distortions embedded in the current system: the tax treatment of interest expenses, too-big-to-fail subsidies, oligopoly rents, and much of the plumbing of the global financial system. These distortions are protected by powerful incumbents who benefit directly and indirectly from them (Rajan and Zingales 2003; Admati and Hellwig 2013). The bottom line is that transforming incumbent financial firms into safe and efficient providers of financial services is an uphill battle. At best, it will be long and costly, and worst, it will simply not happen.

The second concern is that it is genuinely difficult to design good regulations. When we think about systemic risk, for instance, there is always a tension between regulating by entity and regulating by function. Regulating by function is intellectually appealing, but it is technically challenging and requires cooperation among many parties. By contrast, regulating by entity is simpler but designating non-bank G-SIFIs creates legal challenges, as seen recently in the case of MetLife. Tightening regulations is not only difficult; it can also be counter-productive. The most obvious risk is that of shifting activities outside the regulated banking system. Another risk is to make compliance costs prohibitive for would-be entrants. Finally, and most importantly, no one knows what a safe and efficient financial system should look like. All we know is that the current one is expensive, risky, and dominated by too-big-to-fail companies. Many proposals for wide-ranging structural change would require unrealistic amounts of foresight by regulators.

The current regulatory approach, then, has reached its limits because of political economy and coordination costs. If we could design the rules from scratch, we would write them quite differently from what they are today. We do not have this luxury for the legacy systems, but we surely could for the new ones. My point is that it is a lot easier to create and maintain a simple and transparent system, than it is to transform a complex and opaque system into a simple and transparent one.

## The FinTech Opportunity

Above I argued that the current approach to financial regulation mostly impose changes on existing firms. This section asks if the same regulatory goals could be achieved via a different approach, focused on new financial firms and systems. The alternative approach creates new challenges, but I argue that it is likely to benefit from the FinTech movement. This section is therefore not a survey of current trends in FinTech. Instead, I highlight instances where there is a tension between private incentives to innovate and broad regulatory objectives.

**Some specific features of FinTech.** The FinTech movement shares some features with all other movements of disruptive innovations, but it also has some features that are specific to the finance industry. As in other industries, FinTech startups propose disruptive innovations for the provision of specific services. The key advantages of incumbents are their customer base, their ability to forecast the evolution of the industry, and their knowledge of existing regulations. The key advantage of startups is that they are not held back by existing systems and are willing to make risky choices. In banking, for instance, successive mergers have left many large banks with layers of legacy technologies that are, at best, partly integrated (Kumar 2016). FinTech startups, by contrast, have a chance to build the right systems from the start. Moreover, they share a culture of efficient operational design that many incumbents lack.

A feature more specific to the finance industry is the degree to which incumbents rely on financial leverage. As argued earlier, leverage is embedded in many financial contracts and subsidized by several current regulations. This gives the illusion that leverage is everywhere needed to operate an efficient financial system. Conceptually, one can think of leverage today as partly a feature and partly a bug. It is a feature, for instance, when it is needed to provide incentives, as in Diamond and Rajan (2001). It is a bug when it comes from bad design or regulatory arbitrage (as in fixed face value money market funds), or when it corresponds to an old feature that could be replaced by better technology (as in some payment systems discussed below). The issue, of course, is that it is difficult to distinguish the leverage-bug from the leverage-feature. FinTech startups can therefore help for two reasons. First, they will show how far technology can go in providing low-leverage solutions. Second, they are themselves funded with much more equity than existing financial sector firms.

**An alternative approach to financial regulation.** Financial stability and access to financial services are often stated as two important goals of financial regulation. My goal is to explore whether an alternative approach to regulation can make progress toward these goals, specifically in many areas of finance, as discussed by Yermack (2015) in the case of corporate governance. There is no reason to think, however, that these innovations will automatically enhance stability or even access to services. If regulators want FinTech to reduce the risks created by TBTF firms and high leverage, they must adapt the regulatory framework. This section discusses the challenges they are likely to face.

Challenge 1: Entry and level-playing field. FinTech's interests are not naturally aligned with regulators' long term goals. That is, FinTech firms will enter where they think they can make a profit, but there are many regions of the financial system where incumbents are entrenched and entry is difficult. An example of a highly concentrated market is custody and securities settlement. In theory, the blockchain technology could improve market efficiency, but if there is no entry, this could simply increase incumbents' rents. For instance, a restricted blockchain could be used by incumbents to stifle innovation. As successful firms grow large, they seek to alter the political system to their advantage and increase the cost of entry. The beneficiaries are open, competitive system often work to close the system and stifle competition (Rajan and Zingales 2003).

This highlights the complex issue of biased competition between entrants and incumbents. Ensuring a level playing field is a traditional goal of regulation Darrolles (2016) discusses this idea in the context of FinTech and argues, from a microeconomic perspective, that regulators should indeed ensure a level playing field. This line of argument, however, does not readily apply to many of the distortions that plague the finance industry. For instance, what does a level playing field mean when incumbents are too-big-to-fail? Or when they rely excessively on short-term leverage? The level playing field argument applies when entrants are supposed to do the same things as incumbents, only better and/or cheaper. But if the goal is to change some structural features of the industry, then a strict application of the level-playing-field principle could be a hindrance.

The level-playing field argument also sheds new light on some old debates such as over capital requirements. In the past, incumbents have optimized their use of implicit and explicit public subsidies and barriers to entry, and it is costly to undo these distortions one by one.[12] Regulators can, however, prevent an erosion of the standards agreed upon after the crisis, and given the various subsidies and advantages of debt, one can see capital requirements as a way to reduce barriers to entry and foster a level-playing field. The substantial increase in bank capital that has occurred since the crisis does not appear to have shifted activity from banks to shadow banks (Cecchetti and Schoenholtz 2014).

Challenge 2: Leverage and history-dependence. Payment systems have been an early target of FinTech firms, as noted by Rysman and Schuh (2016) who review the literature on consumer payments and discuss three recent innovations: mobile payments, real-time payments, and digital currencies. Mobile payments are already popular in Asia and parts of Africa, and faster systems are often encouraged by central banks. These innovations are likely to improve retail transactions, but they are unlikely to fundamentally change the payment system. In particular, they are unlikely to decrease its reliance on short-term claims that are subject to runs.

We are used to thinking that many financial services (payment among others) require accounts with fixed nominal values: the best examples are retail deposits and checking accounts. This has been true for over 300 years of banking history, but today's technologies open new possibilities. We can assess the value of many financial assets in real time, and we can settle payments (almost) instantly. Many transactions could therefore be cleared using floating value accounts.[13] Suppose buyer $B$ and seller $S$ agree on a price $p$ in units of currency. $B$ and $S$ can both verify with their smartphones the value $v$ of a financial security (say a bond index fund). $B$ can transfer $p/v$ units of the security to $S$ to settle the transaction. $S$ does not need to keep the proceeds in the bond fund. $S$ could immediately turn them into currency or shares of a treasury bill fund. The point here is that new systems would not need to rely on (fixed nominal value) deposits like the old system did. Deposit-like contracts create liquidity risk, and macro-financial stability would be enhanced if more transactions could be settled without them. This was not technologically feasible a few years ago, but today it is, although there are non-technological impediments, most notably with accounting and taxes. Interestingly, in the field of credit, we see that innovative players such as Square propose loan contracts with repayments indexed on sales, instead of fixed coupons.

Another important point here is history-dependence. Regulations are likely to be more effective if they are put in place early, when the industry is young. A counter-factual history of the money market mutual fund industry can be used to motivate this idea. Suppose that regulators had decided in the 1970s that, as a matter of principle, all mutual funds should use a floating Net Asset Value. Such regulation would have been relatively straightforward to implement when the industry was small, and it would have guided market evolution and encouraged innovations consistent with the basic principle. Now it is significantly more difficult to change regulation when the industry has several trillion of dollars under management. A challenge for regulators is then to be forward-looking when dealing with FinTech. Effective regulation requires them to identify some basic features they would like FinTech to have in 30 years, and mandate them now.

Challenge 3: Consumer protection. FinTech is likely to create new issues of consumer protection, illustrated by example with robo-advisors for portfolio management. An important issue for the industry is when and how investors will 'trust' robots (Dhar 2016). Robo-advising will certainly create new legal and operational issues, and it is likely to be a headache for consumer protection agencies, as discussed in Baker and Dellaert (2019).

Yet if the goal is to protect consumers, robo-advising does not need to be perfect: it only needs to be better than the current system. As well, it is important to keep in mind just how bad the track record of human advisors has been. First, at an aggregate level, fees have not declined because, as standard product became cheaper, customers were pushed into higher fee products (Greenwood and Scharfstein 2013). Second, conflicts of interest have been pervasive in the industry. For instance, Bergstresser et al. (2009) found that broker-sold mutual funds delivered lower risk-adjusted returns, even before subtracting distribution costs. Chalmers and Reuter (2012) showed that broker client portfolios earned significantly lower risk-adjusted returns that matched portfolios based on target-date funds, but they offered similar levels of risk. Broker clients allocated more dollars to higher fee funds and participants tended to perform *better* when they did not have access to brokers. Mullainathan et al. (2012) documented that advisers failed to de-bias their clients and often reinforced biases that were not their interest. Advisers encouraged returns-chasing behavior and pushed for actively managed funds with higher fees, even if a client started with a well-diversified, low-fee portfolio. Foà et al. (2015) found that banks were able to affect customers' mortgage choices not only by pricing but also through and advice channel. Egan et al. (2016) showed that misconduct was concentrated in firms with retail customers and in counties with low education, elderly populations, and high incomes. They also documented that the labor market penalties for misconduct were small.

So robo-advisors will have issues, but there is so much room for improvement that it should be easy for them to do better than human advisors, on average. One can also make the case that a software program should be easier to monitor than a human being. For instance, if the robo-advisor contained a line of code that says: 'if age>70 & education<High School, then propose fund X,' and X happens to be a high-fee actively managed fund, then the meaning of the advice is clear. Any equivalent advice a human advisor could give would certainly be much more ambiguous. Humans are good at maintaining plausible deniability, and in the case of financial advising, that's a serious problem.

## Conclusion

The goal of financial regulation is to foster stability and access to services. Accordingly, regulators should consider policies that promote low-leverage technologies and the entry of new firms. This approach applied to FinTech, can complement the current, incumbent-focused approach. It does not require regulators to forecast which technology will succeed or which services should be unbundled (i.e., what the 'finance-Uber' or 'finance-Airbnb' would look like). It also does not require regulators to force top-down structural changes onto powerful incumbents.

# Appendix: A Simple Model of Financial Intermediation Accounting

In this Appendix I sketch a model, based on Philippon (2015), that can be used for financial intermediation accounting. The model economy consists of households, a non-financial business sector, and a financial intermediation sector. Long-term growth is driven by labor-augmenting technological progress $A_t = (1 + \gamma)A_{t-1}$. In the benchmark model borrowers are homogenous, which allows a simple characterization of equilibrium intermediation.

I consider a setup with two types of households: some households are infinitely lived, the others belong to an overlapping generations structure. Households in the model do not lend directly to one another. They lend to intermediaries, and intermediaries lend to firms and to other households.

## Technology and Preferences

<u>Long-lived households.</u> Long-lived households (index $l$) are pure savers. They own the capital stock and have no labor endowment. Liquidity services are modeled as money in the utility function. The households choose consumption $C$ and holdings of liquid assets $M$ to maximize:

$$E \sum_{t \geq 0} \beta^t u(C_t, M_t).$$

I specify the utility function as $u(C_t, M_t) = \frac{(C_t M_t^v)^{1-\rho} - 1}{1-\rho}$. As argued by Lucas (2000), these homothetic preferences are consistent with the absence of trend in the ratio of real balances to income in US data, and the constant relative risk aversion form is consistent with balanced growth. Let $r$ be the interest rate received by savers. The budget constraint becomes:

$$S_t + C_t + \psi_{m,t} M_t \leq (1 + r_t) S_{t-1},$$

where $\psi_m$ is the price of liquidity services, and $S$ are total savings. The Euler equation of long lived households $u_C(t) = \beta E_t[(1 + r_{t+1}) u_C(t+1)]$ can then be written as:

$$M_{l,t}^{v(1-\rho)} C_{l,t}^{-\rho} = \beta E_t[(1 + r_{(t+1)}) M_{l,t+1}^{v(1-\rho)} C_{l,t+1}^{-\rho}].$$

The liquidity demand equation $u_M(t) = \psi_{m,t} u_C(t).$ is simply:

$$\psi_{m,t} M_{l,t} = v C_{l,t}.$$

<u>Overlapping generations.</u> The other households live for two periods and are part of on overlapping generation structure. The young (index 1) have a labor endowment $\eta_1$ and the old (index 2) have a labor endowment $\eta_2$. We normalize the labor supply to one: $\eta_1 + \eta_2 = 1$. The lifetime utility of a young household is $u(C_{1,t} M_{1,t}) + \beta_u(C_{2,t+1}, M_{2,t+1})$. I consider the case where they want to borrow when they are young (i.e., $\eta_1$ is small enough). In the first period, its budget constraint is $C_{1,t} + \psi_{m,t} M_{1,t} = \eta_1 W_{1,t} + (1 - \psi_{c,t}) B_t^c$. The screening and monitoring cost is $\psi_{c,t}$ per unit of borrowing. In the second period, the household consumes $C_{2,t+1} + \psi_{m,t+1} M_{2,t+1} = \eta_2 W_{t+1} - (1 + r_{t+1}) B_t^c$. The Euler equation for OLG households is:

$$(1 - \psi_{c,t}) M_{1,t}^{v(1-\rho)} C_{1,t}^{-\rho} = \beta E_t [(1 + r_{t+1}) M_{2,t+1}^{v(1-\rho)} C_{2,t+1}^{-\rho}].$$

Their liquidity demand is identical to the one of long-lived households.

<u>Non-financial business.</u> Non-financial output is produced under constant returns technology, and for simplicity I assume that the production function is Cobb-Douglass:10

$$F(A_t n_t, K_t) = (A_t n_t)^a K_t^{1-a}.$$

The capital stock $K_t$ depreciates at rate $\delta$, is owned by the households, and must be intermediated. Let $\psi_{k,t}$ be the unit price of corporate financial intermediation. Non-financial firms therefore solve the following program: $max_{n,K} F(A_t n, K) - (r_t + \delta + \psi_{k,t}) K - W_t n$. Capital demand equates the marginal product of capital to its user cost:

$$(1 - a) \left( \frac{A_t n_t}{K_t}, \right)^a = r_t + \delta + \psi_{k,t}.$$

Similarly, labor demand equates the marginal product of labor to the real wage:

$$a \left( \frac{A_t n_t}{K_t}, \right)^{a-1} = \frac{W_t}{A_t}.$$

<u>Financial intermediation.</u> Philippon (2012) discusses in details the implications of various production functions for financial services. When financial intermediaries explicitly hire capital and labor there is a feedback from intermediation demand onto the real wage. This issue is not central here, and I therefore assume that financial services are produced from final goods with constant marginal costs. The income of financial intermediaries is then:

$$Y_t^f = \psi_{c,t} B_{c,t} + \psi_{m,t} M_t + \psi_{k,t} K_t,$$

where $B_{c,t}$, $M_t$ and $K_t$ have been described above.

**Equilibrium comparative statics.** An *equilibrium* in this economy is a sequence for the various prices and quantities listed above such that households choose optimal levels of credit and liquidity, financial and non-financial firms maximize profits, and the labor and capital markets clear. This implies $-n_t = 1$ and

$$S_t = K_{t+1} + B_t^c.$$

Let us now characterize an equilibrium with constant productivity growth in the non-financial sector $(\gamma)$ and constant efficiency of intermediation $(\psi)$. On the balanced growth path, $M$ grows at the same rate as $C$. The Euler equation for long-lived households becomes $1 = \beta E_t[(1 + r_{t+1})(\frac{C_{t+1}}{C_t})^{v(1-\rho)-\rho}]$, so the equilibrium interest rate is simply pinned down by:

$$\beta(1 + r) = (1 + \gamma)^\theta,$$

where $\theta \equiv \rho - v(1 - \rho)$. Let lower-case letters denote de-trended variables, i.e. variables scaled by the current level of technology: for capital $k \equiv \frac{K_t}{A_t}$, for consumption of agent $ic_i \equiv \frac{C_{i,t}}{A_t}$, and for the productivity adjusted wage $w \equiv W_t/A_t$. Since $n = 1$ in equilibrium, Equation (11.2) becomes:

$$k^a = \frac{1 - a}{r + \delta + \psi_k}.$$

Non-financial GDP is $y = k^{1-a}$, and the real wage is:

$$w = ak^{1-a} = ay.$$

Given the interest rate in (11.4), the Euler equation of short-lived households is simply:

$$c_1 = (1 - \psi_c)^{\frac{1}{\theta}} c_2.$$

If $\psi_c$ is 0, we have perfect consumption smoothing: $c_1 = c_2$ (remember these are de-trended consumptions). In addition, all agents have the same money demand $\psi_m m_i = vc_i$. The budget constraints are therefore $(1 + v)c_1 = n_1 w + (1 - \psi_c)b$ and $(1 + v)c_2 = n_2 w - \frac{1+r}{1+\gamma} b$. We can then use the Euler equations and budget constraints to compute the borrowing of young households:

$$\frac{b_c}{w} = \frac{(1 - \psi_c)^{\frac{1}{\theta}} n_2 - n_1}{1 - \psi_c + (1 - \psi_c)^{\frac{1}{\theta}} \frac{1+r}{1+\gamma}}.$$

Borrowing costs act as a tax on future labor income. If $\psi_c$ is too high, no borrowing takes place and the consumer credit market collapses. Household borrowing increases with the difference between current and future income, captured by $\eta_1 - \eta_2$. Liquidity demand is:

$$m = \frac{vc}{\psi_m}.$$

and aggregate consumption is:

$$c = \frac{1}{1+v}\left(w - \psi_c b_c + (r-\gamma)k\right).$$

The comparative statics are straightforward. The ratios are constant along a balanced growth path with constant intermediation technology, constant demographics, and constant firms' characteristics. Improvements in corporate finance increase $y, w, k/y, c/y$ and m/y, but leave $b^c/y$ constant. Improvements in household finance increase $b^c/y$, c/y and m/y, but do not affect $k$. Increases in the demand for intermediation increase the finance income share $\emptyset$ while supply shifts have an ambiguous impact.

The utility flow at time $t$ is $u(c, m) = \frac{(cm^v)^{1-\rho}}{1-\rho}$ and since $m = \frac{vc}{\psi_m}$, we have:

$$u(c, m) = \frac{\left(\frac{v}{\psi_m}\right)^{v(1-\rho)} c^{(1+v)(1-\rho)} - 1}{1-\rho}.$$

Imagine $A = 1$ for simplicity. Then welfare for a particular generation is:

$$W = u(c_1, m_1) + \beta_u(c_2, m_2) + \frac{\omega}{1-\beta} u(c_1, m_1)$$

$$= \frac{\left(\frac{v}{\psi_m}\right)^{v(1-\rho)}}{1-\rho}\left(c_1^{1-\theta} + \beta c_2^{1-\theta} + \omega\frac{c_l^{1-\theta}}{1-\beta}\right) - \frac{1}{1-\rho},$$

where $\omega$ is the Pareto weight on the long-lived agents.

## Notes

1. See Favara (2009), Cecchetti and Kharroubi (2012), Shin (2012) among others.
2. For instance, capital requirements are significantly higher, but funding costs have not increased (Cecchetti 2015). Of course, higher capital ratios could be desirable (Admati et al. 2013).
3. Philippon (2015) discusses various issues of measurement. Conceptually, the best measure is value added, which is the sum of profits and wages. Whenever possible, I therefore use the GDP share of the finance industry, i.e., the nominal value added of the finance industry divided by the nominal GDP of the US economy. One issue, however, is that before 1945 profits are not always properly measured and value added is not available. As an alternative measure I then use the labor compensation share of the finance industry, i.e., the compensation of all employees of the finance industry divided by the compensation of all employees in the US economy. Philippon (2015) also explains the robustness of the main findings to large changes in government spending (because of wars), the rise of services (finance as a share of services displays a similar pattern to the one presented here), globalization (netting out imports and exports of financial services).

4. The fact that the finance share of GDP is the same in 1925 and in 1980 makes is already clear that there is no mechanical relationship between GDP per capita and the finance income share. Similarly, Bickenbach et al. (2009) show that the income share of finance has remained remarkably constant in Germany over the past 30 years. More precisely, using KLEMS for Europe (see O'Mahony and Timmer (2009)) one can see that the finance share in Germany was 4.3 percent in 1980, 4.68 percent in 1990, 4.19 percent in 2000, and 4.47 percent in 2006.

5. This is true most of the time, but not when quality adjustments are too large. Philippon (2015) provides calibrated quality adjustments for the US financial system.

6. Using the Survey of Consumer Finances, Moore and Palumbo (2010) document that between 1989 and 2007 the fraction of households with positive debt balances increases from 72 percent to 77 percent. This increase is concentrated at the bottom of the income distribution. For households in the 0-40 percentiles of income, the fraction with some debt outstanding goes from 53 percent to 61 percent between 1989 and 2007. In the mortgage market, Mayer and Pence (2008) show that subprime originations account for 15 percent to 20 percent of all HMDA originations in 2005.

7. It is also related to the issue of credit booms. Schularick and Taylor (2012) document the risk involved in rapid credit expansions. This is not to say that all credit booms are bad. Dell'Ariccia et al. (2016) find only one-third of credit booms end in a financial crisis, while many booms are associated with financial reform and economic growth.

8. Banking M&As were part of a large wave. Nine of the ten largest M&As in US history in any industry occurred during 1998 (Moore and Siems 1998). Of these M&As, four occurred in banking (Citicorp-Travelers, BankAmerica-NationsBank, Banc One-First Chicago and Norwest-Wells Fargo).

9. Greenwood and Scharfstein (2013) provide an illuminating study of the growth of modern finance in the US. They show that two activities account for most of this growth over the past 30 years: asset management and the provision of household credit. For asset management, they uncover an important stylized fact: individual fees have typically declined but the allocation of assets has shifted toward high fee managers in such a way that the average fee per dollar of assets under management has remained roughly constant. In Glode et al. (2010), an 'arms race' can occur as agents try to protect themselves from opportunistic behavior by (over)-investing in financial expertise. In Bolton et al. (2016), cream skimming in one market lowers assets quality in the other market and allows financial firms to extract excessive rents. In Pagnotta and Philippon (2018) there can be excessive investment in trading speed because speed allows trading venues to differentiate and charge higher prices. Gennaioli et al. (2014) propose an alternative interpretation for the relatively high cost of financial intermediation. In their model, trusted intermediaries increase the risk tolerance of investors, allowing them to earn higher returns. Because trust is a scarce resource, improvements in information technology do not necessarily lead to a lower unit cost.

10. See for instance the real time value of the Systemic Risk Measure of Acharya et al. (2017) at http://vlab.stern.nyu.edu (accessed March 3, 2019).
11. Narrow banking has deep historical roots. The evidence suggests that, prior to the twentieth century, British and American banks lent mostly short term. Early American banks did not offer long-term loans. According to Bodenhorn (2000), banks made short-term loans that early manufacturing firms used to finance inventories and pay rents and wages. According to Summers (1975: 1), 'the practice of guaranteeing future credit availability has existed since the beginning of banking in the United States,' but 'it has only been since the mid-1960's that the topic of commercial bank loan commitment policies has become an explicit issue in banking circles.'
12. In addition, as Barker and Wurgler (2015) argue, leverage can be rewarded by institutional investors who like to lever up but who are precluded by charter or regulation.
13. This possibility was recognized by Samuelson (1947: 123) 'in a world involving no transaction friction and no uncertainty . . . securities themselves would circulate as money and be acceptable in transactions . . .' and discussed in Tobin (1958). I thank Kim Schoenholtz for these references.

# References

Acharya, V. V., L. H. Pedersen, T. Philippon, and M. Richardson (2017). 'Measuring Systemic Risk.' *The Review of Financial Studies*, 30(1): 2–47.

Admati, A. R., P. M. DeMarzo, M. Hellwig, and P. Pfleiderer (2013). 'Fallacies, Irrelevant Facts, and Myths in the Discussion of Capital Regulation: Why Bank Equity is not Socially Expensive.' Working Paper No. 2065. Stanford, CA: Stanford University.

Admati, A. R. and M. Hellwig (2013). *The Bankers' New Clothes*. Princeton, NJ: Princeton University Press.

Baker, T., and B. Dellaert (2019). 'Decumulation and the Regulatory Strategy for Robo Advice' in J. Agnew and O. S. Mitchell (eds.), *The Disruptive Impact of FinTech on Retirement Systems*. Oxford, UK: Oxford University Press, pp. 149–71.

Barker, M. and J. Wurgler (2015). 'Do Strict Capital Requirements Raise the Cost of Capital? Bank Regulation, Capital Structure, and the Low Risk Anomaly.' *American Economic Review Papers and Proceedings*, 105(5): 315–20.

Bazot, G. (2017). 'Financial Consumption and the Cost of Finance: Measuring Financial Efficiency in Europe (1950–2007),' *Journal of the European Economic Association*, 16(1): 123–60.

Beck, T., A. Demirguc-Kunt, and R. Levine (2011). 'The Financial Structure Database' in L. Lusinyan ed., *Financial Structure and Economic Growth: A Cross-Country Comparison of Banks Markets, and Development*. Cambridge, MA: MIT Press, pp. 17–80.

Berger, A., R. Demsetz, and P. E. Strahan (1999). 'The Consolidation of the Financial Services Industry: Causes, Consequences, and Implications for the Future.' *Journal of Banking and Finance*, 23: 135–94.

Bergstresser, D., J. Chalmers, and P. Tufano (2009). 'Assessing the Costs and Benefits of Brokers in the Mutual Fund Industry.' *The Review of Financial Studies* 22(10): 4129–56.

Bickenbach, F., E. Bode, D. Dohse, A. Hanley, and R. Schweickert (2009). 'Adjustment after the Crisis: Will the Financial Sector Shrink?' Kiel Policy Brief No. 12. Kiel, Germany: Kiel Institute for the World Economy.

Bodenhorn, H. (2000). *A History of Banking in Antebellum America: Financial Markets and Economic Development in an Era of Nation Building.* New York, NY: Cambridge University Press.

Bolton, P., T. Santos, and J. Scheinkman (2016). 'Cream Skimming in Financial Markets,' *The Journal of Finance,* 71(2): 709–36.

Brei, M. and L. Gambacorta (2016). 'Are Bank Capital Ratios Pro-Cyclical? New Evidence and Perspectives. *Economic Policy,* 31(86): 357–403.

Cecchetti, S. (2015). 'The Jury is In.' in D. D. Evanoff, A. G. Haldane and G. G. Kaufman, eds., *World Scientific Studies in Economics Volume 48.* Singapore: World Scientific, pp. 407–24.

Cecchetti, S. and E. Kharroubi (2012). 'Reassessing the Impact of Finance on Growth.' BIS Working Paper No. 381. Basel, Switzerland: Bank for International Settlements.

Cecchetti, S. and K. Schoenholtz (2014). 'Higher Capital Requirements Didn't Slow the Economy.' December 15: https://www.moneyandbanking.com/commentary/2014/12/15/higher-capital-requirements-didnt-slow-the-economy (accessed March 3, 2019).

Cecchetti, S. and K. Schoenholtz (2016). 'Leverage and Risk.' May 2. https://www.moneyandbanking.com/commentary/2016/5/2/leverage-and-risk (accessed March 3, 2019).

Cetorelli, N., J. McAndrews, and J. Traina (2014). 'Evolution in Bank Complexity.' *FRBNY Economic Policy Review* 20(2), December: 85–106.

Chalmers, J. and J. Reuter (2012). 'Is Conflicted Investment Advice Better Than No Advice?' NBER Working Paper No. 18158. Cambridge, MA: National Bureau of Economic Research.

Chamley, C., L. J. Kotlikoff, and H. Polemarchakis (2012). 'Limited-Purpose Banking–Moving from "Trust Me" to "Show Me" Banking.' *American Economic Review,* 102(3): 113–19.

Darolles, S. (2016). 'The Rise of FinTechs and their Regulation.' *Financial Stability Review,* (20): 85–92.

Dell'Ariccia, G., D. Igan, L. Laeven, and H. Tong (2016). 'Credit Booms and Macro-financial Stability.' *Economic Policy,* 31(86): 299–355.

DeYoung, Robert, Douglas D. Evanoff, and Philip Molyneux. 2009. "Mergers and Acquisitions of Financial Institutions: A Review of the Post-2000 Literature," Journal of Financial Services Research, vol. 36, no.2, pp. 87–110.

Dhar, V. (2016). 'When to Trust Robots with Decisions, and When Not To.' *Harvard Business Review.* May 17. https://hbr.org/2016/05/when-to-trust-robots-with-decisions-and-when-not-to (accessed March 3, 2019).

Diamond, D. W. and P. H. Dybvig (1983). 'Bank Runs, Deposit Insurance, and Liquidity.' *Journal of Political Economy,* 91: 401–19.

Diamond, D. W. and R. G. Rajan (2001). 'Liquidity Risk, Liquidity Creation and Financial Fragility: A Theory of Banking.' *Journal of Political Economy,* 109: 287–327.

Drechsler, I., P. Schnabl, and A. Savov (2017). 'The Deposits Channel of Monetary Policy.' *The Quarterly Journal of Economics*, 132(4), 1819–76.

EBA (2015). *2015 EU-Wide Transparency Exercise.* London, UK: European Banking Authority. https://www.eba.europa.eu/risk-analysis-and-data/eu-wide-transparency-exercise/2015 (accessed March 3, 2019).

Egan, M., G. Matvos, and A. Seru (2016). 'The Market for Financial Adviser Misconduct.' NBER Working Paper No. 22050. Cambridge, MA: National Bureau of Economic Research.

Favara, G. (2009). An Empirical Reassessment of the Relationship between Finance and Growth. IMF Working Paper No. 03/123. Washington, DC: International Monetary Fund. https://papers.ssrn.com/sol3/papers.cfm?abstract_id=879199 (accessed March 3, 2019).

Foà, G., L. Gambacorta, L. Guiso, and P. E. Mistrulli (2015). The Supply Side of Household Finance. BIS Working Paper No. 531. Basel, Switzerland: Bank for International Settlements.

Gennaioli, N., A. Shleifer, and R. W. Vishny (2014). 'Money Doctors.' *Journal of Finance*, 70(1): 91–114.

Glode, V., R. C. Green, and R. Lowery (2010). 'Financial Expertise as an Arms Race.' *Journal of Finance*, 67(5): 1723–59.

Greenwood, R. and D. Scharfstein (2013). 'The Growth of Modern Finance.' *Journal of Economic Perspectives*, 27(2): 3–28.

Hirshleifer, J. (1971). 'The Private and Social Value of Information and the Reward to Inventive Activity.' *The American Economic Review*, 61(4): 561–74.

Ingves, S. (2015). *Update on the Work of the Basel Committee.* Speech at the IIF Annual Meeting, LIMA. October 10. https://www.bis.org/speeches/sp151010.htm (accessed March 3, 2019).

Kashyap, A., R. Rajan, and J. Stein (2002). 'Banks as Liquidity Providers: An Explanation for the Coexistence of Lending and Deposit-Taking.' *Journal of Finance*, 57: 33–73.

Kelly, B., H. Lustig, and S. V. Nieuwerburgh (2016). 'Too-Systemic-to-Fail: What Option Markets Imply about Sector-Wide Government Guarantees.' *American Economic Review*, 106(6): 1278–1319.

Kovner, A., J. Vickery, and L. Zhou (2014). 'Do Big Banks have Lower Operating Costs?' *FRBNY Economic Policy Review*, 20(2): 1–27.

Kumar, S. (2016). Relaunching Innovation: Lessons from Silicon Valley.' *Banking Perspective* 4(1), 19–23.

Levine, R. (2005). 'Finance and Growth: Theory and Evidence.' in P. Aghion and S. N. Durlauf, eds., *Handbook of Economic Growth, Volume 1A,* Amsterdam, NL: Elsevier, pp. 865–934.

Levine, R. (2014). 'In Defense of Wall Street: The Social Productivity of the Financial System.' in W. H. Buiter ed., *The Role of Central Banks in Financial Stability: How Has It Changed?* Singapore: World Scientific Publishing Co., pp. 257–79.

Lucas, R. E. J. (2000). 'Inflation and Welfare.' *Econometrica*, 68(2): 247–74.

Mayer, C. and K. Pence (2008). 'Subprime Mortgages: What, Where, and to Whom?' NBER Working Paper No. 14083. Cambridge, MA: National Bureau of Economic Research.

Moore, K. B. and M. G. Palumbo (2010, June). *The Finances of American Households in the Past Three Recessions: Evidence from the Survey of Consumer Finances.* Staff Paper Federal Reserve Board. Washington, DC: Federal Reserve.

Moore, R. R. and Thomas F. Siems (1998). *Bank mergers: creating value or destroying competition?* Financial Industry Issues. Federal Reserve Bank of Dallas.

Mullainathan, S., M. Noeth, and A. Schoar (2012). 'The Market for Financial Advice: An Audit Study.' NBER Working Paper No. 17929. Cambridge, MA: National Bureau of Economic Research.

O'Mahony, M. and M. P. Timmer (2009). 'Output, Input and Productivity Measures at the Industry Level: The Eu Klems Database.' *The Economic Journal*, 119(538): F374–F403.

Pagnotta, E. and T. Philippon (2018). 'Competing on Speed,' *Econometrica: Journal of the Econometric Society*, 86(3): 1067–1115.

Pennacchi, G. (2012). 'Narrow Banking.' *Annual Review of Financial Economics*, 4(1): 141–59.

Philippon, T. (2012). 'Equilibrium Financial Intermediation.' NYU Working Paper. New York, NY: New York University.

Philippon, T. (2015). 'Has the US Finance Industry become Less Efficient? On the Theory and Measurement of Financial Intermediation.' *The American Economic Review*, 105(4): 1408–38.

Philippon, T. and A. Reshef (2012). 'Wages and Human Capital in the US Financial Industry: 1909-2006.' *Quarterly Journal of Economics*, 127(4): 1551–1609.

Rajan, R. G. and L. Zingales (2003). *Saving Capitalism from the Capitalists*. New York, NY: Crown Publishing Group.

Rysman, M. and S. Schuh (2016). 'New Innovations in Payments,' *Innovation Policy and the Economy*, 17(2017): 27–48.

Samuelson, P. (1947). *Foundations of Economic Analysis*. Cambridge, MA: Harvard University Press.

Santos, J. (2014). 'Evidence from the Bond Market on Banks' 'Too-Big-to-Fail' Subsidy.' *FRBNY Economic Policy Review* 20(2), December: 29–39.

Schularick, M. and A. M. Taylor (2012). 'Credit Booms Gone Bust: Monetary Policy, Leverage Cycles and Financial Crises, 1870–2008.' *American Economic Review*, April: 1029–61.

Shin, H. S. (2012). 'Global Banking Glut and Loan Risk Premium. *IMF Economic Review*, 60(2): 155–92.

Summers, B. (1975). Loan Commitments to Business in United States Banking History. *Federal Reserve Bank of Richmond Economic Review* September Issue, 15–23.

Tobin, J. (1958). 'Liquidity Preference as Behavior Towards Risk.' *The Review of Economic Studies* 25(2), 65–86.

Wallace, N. (1996). 'Narrow Banking Meets the Diamond-Dybvig Model.' *Federal Reserve Bank of Minneapolis Quarterly Review*, 1(3): 3–13.

Yermack, D. (2015). 'Corporate Governance and Blockchains.' NBER Working Paper 21802.

Zingales, L. (2015). 'Does Finance Benefit Society?' *Journal of Finance*, 70(4): 1327–63.

# Index

account aggregation 142–3
accumulation phase 131, 135–7, 139,
    141, 143–4, 150–1 (*see also*
    decumulation strategy)
Acemoglu, D 108–9
Acorns 70, 179, 185–6
Admati, A R 200–1
advisory relationship 42–4 (*see also*
    digital financial advice; fiduciary
    duties)
Agarwal, S 14
age profiles 1 (*see also* older adults)
    Baby Boom generation 61–2, 129,
      133–4
    Gen-X 69, 133–4
    long-lived households 209
    Millennial generation 61–2, 67–70,
      133–4, 158–9
    overlapping generations 210
Agnew, J R 129–30, 155–6
Akolar, B 8
algorithm governance 52
algorithms 2, 14, 38–9, 52–3,
    159–60, 176
    documentation strategy 153
Alhabash, S 108
Allison, K E 69–70
Aly, Y 4–5, 7
Alzheimer's disease 75, 77–8
Ameriks, J 129–30, 180
Anagol, S 25
annuity 4, 6–7, 150–2, 156, 158
Aon Hewitt 158, 167, 180–1
Appelbaum, P S 77–80
Art, M M 64–6
asset allocation 14–15, 22–3, 39, 44,
    178–9, 182–4
asset placement 39, 50–1
assets under management (AUM)
    163–4

AT Kearney 38
Austin, J T r 154–5
automated financial services *see* digital
    investment advice
availability heuristic 154
Axelrod, S 13
Axtell, B 4–5, 7, 110, 117

Baby Boom generation 61–2, 129, 133–4
Baecker, R 104–6
Baker, T 5, 8, 150, 159–60, 162–3,
    166, 207
Baker, T 150–1, 160
banking industry
    capital requirements 200–3
    cost efficiency and size 202–3
    G-SIFIs 203
    leverage controversy 200–3, 205–6
Barber, B M 53–4
Barr, M S 163
Barrett, J 118
Bednar, J 68–9
Bazot, G 190–1, 193
Behavioral economics and finance
    biased perceptions/preferences
      155, 162
    decision rule effects 154–6, 160–1
    cognitive decline 133, 140, 142–3
    decision rules 154–6, 160–1
    decumulation strategies 129–32, 165
    evaluation 153–5, 160–1
      context and considerations 135–7
      mental representation 153–5,
        160–1
      maximizing utility 153
    mental models 105–6, 108–9, 114–19
    pitfalls 151–2
    'rational' economic behavior 5
    regret 155
    retirement withdrawal sequence 152–3